'Survivors' Stories'

'An Enlightening Journey through the differing lives of Child Abuse Survivors'

Volume One

Stories 1 - 6

'Survivors' Stories'

by

Morven Fyfe

'An Enlightening Journey through the differing lives of Child Abuse Survivors'

Foreword by Peter Saunders, FRSA
founder of the National Association
for People Abused in Childhood

Volume One
Stories 1 - 6

Publisher's Note

This publication is designed to provide useful and insightful information based on the author's life experience in relation to the subject matter covered. It is sold with the understanding that neither the author nor the publisher is engaged in providing psychological, financial, legal, or other professional services. If expert advice, assistance or counselling is needed, the services of a competent professional should be sought. The author and publisher disclaim any responsibility for any liability, loss, or risk, personal or otherwise, which is incurred as a consequence, directly or indirectly, of the use and application of any of the contents of this book.

If this book is employed for the educational purposes of teenagers, it must be used with the respectful guidance of a qualified teacher or responsible parent, who has the child's good self esteem, personal safety and best interests at heart.

The author welcomes correspondence from readers
and can be contacted at survivors-stories@hotmail.co.uk
For information about permission to reproduce selections
from this book, contact survivors-stories@hotmail.co.uk

Updates about the Survivors' Stories project will be available
via the website survivors-stories.co.uk

'Survivors' Stories' First Edition 2007
Copyright © 2007 by Morven Fyfe
All rights reserved

Cover design by Colin Logan and Morven Fyfe. Those who freely donated their services as models for the front cover of this edition have no connection whatsoever with either the subject matter or content of this book.

A catalogue record is available for this book from the British Library.

International Standard Book Number

978-0-9556197-0-0

Postal address only: 11th Commandment Publishing, 8 Gaping Lane, England SG5 2JQ, UK

~~~~~‡~~~~~ Dedication ~~~~~‡~~~~~

This book, and every book in this series

is dedicated to each and every

child abuse survivor

in the world today

It is also dedicated to

each and every

child abuse survivor

who ever lived

Acknowledgments

There are so many influential voices to mention here that I can't include them all, I therefore thank the many I am not able to list. Even though the following people's stories are not amongst these pages, certain survivors became my greatest teachers throughout this project.

William H C Congdon AB, STB (Billy especially) whose erudite support and companionship was the best any lone writer could have wished for.

I thank Sarah Kelly for her incredible support over these four years, who despite her typical protests that she did nothing, devotes much of her life to helping others. I thank Liz Davies BA DipSW ILT (Senior Lecturer for Children and Families Social Work at London Metropolitan University) whose editorial help and professional perspectives were irreplaceable.

Another brilliant woman is the versatile Austrian artist Katja Duftner MA., whose exhibitions upon child abuse themes are immediately understood, in any language. Our discussions in Munich about child abuse in Germany, the rest of Europe and the world were very significant.

I thank Liviu and his family for their patience and dependable support, and our son for the sweet lesson of his childhood. I thank Cecil Sieber, a young mother whose companionship, faith in me and greater religious faith both encouraged and supported me, and still does.

Websites have become a valuable oasis, and places of healing where survivors can explore and express their revelations freer from consideration of response, body language, voice tone and all other complexities of inter-personal reaction that can constrain us all. There were not many websites that I used personally, but I thank all the participants from oneinfour.org, I thank the Irish Industrial School survivors, especially 'Angry' for his ground breaking honesty and fearless inspiration. Also I thank Colin Logan for his support, and acknowledge his untiring drive to modernise the statute laws and bring about justice for survivors.

I thank the National Association for People Abused in Childhood and all its supporters.

I thank each and every person who made contact with me whether they were abuse survivors or not, and I hope that our dialogue will develop further, well into the future.

Towards the end with the practicalities, Paul Eisen and Meriel Siddard helped here and there with their editorial clarity and confidence respectively. I am also grateful to Helen Harris for her last minute proof reading.

These votes of thanks are incomplete without including my father, the late William David Fyfe, who maintained a dignified silence about his childhood, but made sure his own children suffered less. Although my mother, the late Katherine McLennan Fyfe believed in all forms of corporal punishment and was brought up to shy away from sexual matters, she nevertheless provided me with some of the best mothering and support any child could have had.

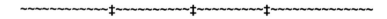

Table of Contents

Foreword by Peter Saunders, founder of Napac, the National Association for People Abused in Childhood

Section		Page
1	How to use 'Survivors' Stories'	v
2	Who is This Book For?	1
3	Introduction	13
4	Why should I need to know?	19
5	Barriers	21
6	How to Talk About Abuse	31
7	'Questionnaire'	48
8	Précis for Stories 1– 6	62

The Stories

One	Michael	65
Two	Vicky	93
Three	Jim	119
Four	Lillian	135
Five	John	161
Six	Karen	195

Section		Page
9	'The Source of Our Silence'	229

The Establishment played along with Freud's denial of child abuse for generations, and sold us a silence we did not cause. At last, we are set free to think and speak for ourselves.

10	Conclusion	253

Every section is relevant to the other sections, and you can read them in any order you choose.

How to Use 'Survivors' Stories'

We're living in unprecedented times, when child abuse and surviving it is finally being addressed. Our culture is changing, and whilst it is, things can feel rather confusing. Most material on this subject seems to make it exclusive, boring, problematic or overly intellectual, but by reading about people's lives, you are enabled to tackle child abuse and talk about it as never before. At last, you can get to grips with something we all, in our heart of hearts, care deeply about. At the heart of this book series are the separate biographies which were written along with child abuse survivors. Throughout, there are some optional questions, and a short essay at the end called '**Reflections**', to stimulate further thought and discussion.

Section One is this page, '**How to Use 'Survivors' Stories'**'.

Section Two '**Who is This Book For?**' lists under twelve headings the roles and professions who would find this book particularly useful, and why.

The '**Introduction**' in **Section Three** describes how this book was written as a project, and the author's background and approach. Further on, it addresses the shared social background that still contributes to our awkwardness on the subject. It describes the frustrations of professionals who try to prevent abuse. It describes the stumbling blocks that stop everyone from speaking out about it. It speaks of labels, their advantages and restrictions, and the rationale behind the language chosen herein.

Section Four '**Why should I need to know?**' addresses statistics, and explores how we'd rather have professionals solve our problems than explore the possible flaws in our own human relationships, that, knowingly or otherwise, allow abuse to go on.

'**Barriers**' in **Section Five** helps us see what prevents us recognising abuse and dealing with it in our daily lives.

In **Section Six**, '**How to Talk about Abuse**' points out conversations that can be helpful or harmful, and gives you building blocks that enable you to be constructive, and express yourself with less worry and more self-assurance.

In **Section Seven**, the '**Questionnaire**' exposes the structural content behind each story, in question form. How you might use the Questionnaire yourself as a personal resource is described in the Introduction.

In **Section Eight** '**Six Precis for Six Stories**', you can find out what's in each story, and make an informed choice about which story you'd like to read next.

Section Nine, '**The Source of Our Silence**' illustrates how the knowledge of abuse was both controlled and concealed by those working in the fields of Psychoanalysis, Psychiatry and even Medicine. Henceforth, we can give ourselves full permission to practice listening to survivors. We can respond to them, and express ourselves in kind.

Section Ten, the '**Conclusion**' draws the threads of this project together, and sets us on our way.

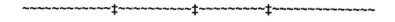

Foreword

In 2001 when Morven discovered the National Association for People Abused in Childhood via the NSPCC, she swiftly wrote in to us at the NAPAC office and began sending in pieces of her writing. Some of her pieces later became newsletter articles. Her first article, 'Time for a Change' (see HYPERLINK http://www.napac.org.uk/) still seems to express something on behalf of all survivors, even now. Once the piece was up and running on the Napac website, people from all walks of life began to contact Morven directly to share their story with her. I distanced myself from the project, and got intermittent, occasional reports … whilst having no real idea or control over what sort of book would result! The one thing that remained constant until completion, was Morven's unshifting conviction that stories were the only means whereby any individual could truly understand what it's like to be a child abuse survivor, and here we are today with 'Survivors' Stories'.

Thankfully, there are differing ranges of helpful books now in publication for and about survivors, some of which have been reprinted several times over the last ten years. More recently, there are books that cover many aspects of suffering and healing, becoming increasingly directed towards various separate survivor groups. There's an ever improving library of books for qualified professionals who work with survivors; for younger survivors of child abuse who are still in childhood or adolescence now; there are books for survivors with learning difficulties and disabilities, books for those who wish to take their abuser to court, and books for co-survivors who seek to better understand a survivor friend or partner, and their perspectives in life. Also, there are nearly 600 specialist services and organisations throughout the UK and Northern Ireland, working away quietly with survivors whilst most of the public doesn't even know they're there. All of these things are useful, but the outcome is that survivors often find themselves in some sort of exclusive group, yet they don't wish to be 'odd' … they simply wish to be recognised and better understood.

This book opens the door to a far wider readership. Communicating about child abuse has been taboo for too long, and if we want to make a difference in people's lives now and in the future, it's by revealing what is hidden within our common behavioural past, and talking about it. The big conversation seems to have started already, and we're in the midst of a climate change that's rippling outwards, reaching for a new level of understanding in nearly all our family and social relationships. That's why this book offers itself to a more open forum, to help a wider public that's often on the receiving end of so many confusing, mixed messages about what child abuse and surviving it is really all about.

By reading a few of the stories that are presented here, you can see how survivors can come from a wide range of parenting backgrounds, from differing social classes and differing social and religious groups. You can see how even the most caring parent, or carer can so easily shut a suffering child off from any possibility of getting help, without even knowing they've done it. You have the resource to explore and consider more fully why up to one in eight adults today still suffer depression and go on suffering manifold because of a situation they found themselves in so many years ago, when they were too young to do anything about it. It becomes far more apparent how someone you've actually known for years could easily be a survivor of child abuse and as such, you can be better informed, and more ready to talk and listen, should ever the need arise.

There are insights and treasures to be found in all of the stories, stories that reveal to us what a child's needs actually are. We meet what was hidden from us before, and whilst it may present us with what seems to be a cripplingly heavy social burden, by reading on we're lightening the burden of our own ignorance. Through that, we can become stronger and far more ready to face both child and adult survivor suffering, and profit from the knowledge and experience that will prevent us from causing such suffering again.

Peter Saunders

Peter Saunders FRSA
Founder and Chief Executive
National Association for People Abused in Childhood

Who is this book for?

1. **Survivors of child abuse**

2. **Overloaded social workers**

3. **All parents**

4. **Foster Carers of abused children**

5. **Doctors, nurses, and mental health professionals**

6. **Dentists**

7. **Teachers and staff in schools**

8. **Police officers and the legal profession as a whole**

9. **Counsellors, therapists, body oriented therapists and healing therapists who work in the field of alternative and complementary medicine**

10. **Those who work within various religious groups, and represent them**

11. **Journalists, writers, media and TV production teams**

12. **All proactive adults who wish to protect children from abuse**

1.   This book is for Survivors of Child Abuse

A survivor of child abuse can only live one life, but they can better understand the context of that life when they find out what other survivors went through. By knowing the variety of acts of abuse and the circumstances where they take place, feelings of isolation and powerlessness ease. Abuse in other sections of society that were perhaps outside their experience as children, become more fully acknowledged. Survivors then see their position in the greater social environment, develop their own opinions and express themselves with more assurance.

As survivors investigate what happened to them. they may find it useful to turn to Section 7 which contains the same Questionnaire that was used to gather material for each story. It was created for survivors who lived in years of silence, but who were in no doubt they had in fact been abused. Part One covers home, school, surroundings, parents, siblings and carers, positive bonding, discipline and punishment. Part Two covers secret abuse suffered in private, and trying to tell someone. Part Three covers adult life and relationships today, and Part Four covers getting help from psychiatry, therapy and healing. The questionnaire was employed as a writing tool, yet can be used in other ways, not least as a conversational guide. Whether you are a survivor or not, you can meet yourself on these pages by thinking about your childhood and possibly recording it in some way. As you contemplate upon the stories in these pages, you can bring your own right into the overall picture.

Section 6, 'How to Talk About Abuse' is intended to help survivors think about what is involved in bringing their pasts out into the open in a safe way. It's also very much there to help loved ones of survivors, and those who want to talk to them, but are unsure about how to do it. From a survivor's and co-survivor's perspective, the self-help angle is principally to expand and develop your thinking. After that, if you choose, you can express yourself in discussions in order to explore and enlarge upon what you have learnt about yourself in the greater context of other survivor's lives.

2.   This book is for overloaded social workers

A social worker is often deprived of the valuable time they need to make positive relationships with the people they're there to help. That's why they can sometimes appear to be cold, frighteningly objective professionals. Much social work literature about child abuse reads like cleverly coded newspeak, and only those with a social work training can understand it. This book is for learning on the simple human level alone, as a useful addition to the available material. In terms of time spent, reading through these stories is like giving a professional three year's hands on experience in a week, but with nothing hidden. Your exposure to adults and adolescents damaged by abuse is diversified, and you'll learn from them without actually having to meet them. As you read, you use your empathy as a learning tool, and self-style new conversational approaches with the people you are there to help. Through having identified with them so thoroughly, you'll understand that different survivors can have very different and varied perspectives about many things, even though they all belong in one 'group'.

3.   This book is for all Parents

As a mother, father, child carer or child minder you will start to get much clearer insights about the power of the circle of relationships that surround a child, but possibly more clearly than ever, from the child's point of view. Gradually, you can accept and make peace with the possibility that at some point in the first eighteen years of your child's life, someone who is a trusted friend or relative, could abuse that child. This book is a first step, and through further reading and discussion, you can improve your role as carer and protector. After first of all reading the story straight through, you can refer to the Question Option that runs through each story if you wish later on, to enable deeper thought and discussion about the child's needs and vulnerabilities. These questions are listed at the end of each story.

4.   This book is for Foster Carers of abused children

Foster carers are unsung heroes who often need insight, help and encouragement with the task of parenting an abused child. In some parts of the UK, it's great how support from social services and other organisations is improving towards foster carers. However, it's not uncommon for a child's placement with a family to fail, whereby that child prefers re-settling in a new foster home, rather than building a bridge of trust with their first foster carers. Abuse is so devastating, that abused children live a 'split' sort of life, making short superficial attachments the preferred option.

As a foster carer, it's hard to perceive where the child's hurt is, if your empathy muscle hasn't quite had the opportunity to develop as fully and specifically as it could. The multi-faceted experience of hurt that's hidden from you can become accessible when the child intuits that you can really listen, identify with the child's perceptions as being totally valid, and stand right beside them in their child's world. This is not all there is to it, but it's a crucial foundation for a strong, constructive bond that has more chance of weathering the storms well into the future.

5. This book is for doctors, nurses, and mental health professionals

A doctor, nurse or mental health professional can feel quite perplexed if a patient in their care is suffering trauma from a past situation of abuse. What can you do, when you operate within a highly respectable profession that's still heir to the conviction that child abuse is extremely rare, or could well be a series of lies and delusions fabricated by the mentally unstable? If your gut feeling states the contrary and you have some respect for the growing body of more recent research, life can be very confusing.

Abused children and survivors need to know they are not the principle source of their own problems. They need to identify the external source of injustice that harmed them, so that they can begin to free themselves from the source of their mental, physical and emotional pain. Section 9 'Source of our Silence', addresses how western cultures were deceived by Sigmund Freud's body of work, and as a result many individuals suffered in a climate of denial continually reinforced and upheld by the entire medical establishment. Prescribed medication and institutions for the mentally ill took a big role in locking away the truth, and story number Six in this volume, and story number Seven of 'Survivors' Stories' Volume 2 clearly demonstrate how modern medical practice has still not freed itself from its past.

It's still practically unheard of for a family doctor to look for a history of child abuse within a patient's medical records. Only recently have nurses and doctors begun to receive training in what to look and listen for from a child victim, yet they can easily be an abused child's first contact. If one member of a medical team suspects a child patient is being abused, another member's ignorance about the manipulative ways abusers behave buys into the abuser's cover-ups, and protective action can easily be thwarted.

Professionals are starting to listen to what their patients tell them, but tenuously from new and different perspectives. We're grateful for a doctor's well-earned mastery over complex sciences few can achieve, but general practitioners in the front line are not required to talk to victims and survivors. Many don't know what to listen for, and how to pose the appropriate questions. As a medical professional, you can employ these stories to immerse yourself in the perspectives of those with first hand experience of abuse. Old perceptions can be sorted through and sharpened, and superseded by newer and more pragmatic courses of action. A ten minute consultation is hardly enough, but by reading these stories, you can hear all the stuff that abuse survivors haven't yet had time to tell you.

GPs are already negotiating themselves into a more solid stance from which to be of help, and sometimes respond to self-help initiatives and counselling links for survivors with their local communities and local government networks. Useful networks can be found via Napac, the National Association for People Abused in Childhood. (see HYPERLINK http://www.napac.org.uk/)

6.   This book is for dentists

Dentists can share the role of protecting children, because whereas an abuser can avoid prosecution by not taking their child to the doctor, they can't always avoid taking them to the dentist. I have spoken to dentists who had child patients go through their surgeries with obvious physical signs of abuse, but they were not confident that any whistle blowing would make any difference. Neither were they knowledgeable, or even professionally obliged to link up to other professionals who could put protective measures into action. These stories can give dentists the perspectives they need, whereby at last they could see the importance of their role in getting help for an abused child. Potentially, the profession could develop solid procedures that enact down to earth, practical directives linking up with other agencies involved in protecting children in their community.

Because of their childhoods, adult survivors have also expressed an intensified vulnerability in the dentist's chair. Many dentists and other professionals who work with touch are advised to increase their awareness of abuse, so that they can handle that sensitivity more respectfully, and more effectively.

7.   This book is for teachers and staff in schools

A child forms bonds with the adults in their second most important community, which is their school. A child's days in school communities could span up to fifteen years, and if you are an adult working in one of those places, you form a very important part of children's lives. When a teacher stands and looks at their class, a child is just one part of a much larger working group. When the child looks back at their teacher, they are looking at by far the most important person in the room. Even through struggling phases of defiance, children are inescapably linked into ever changing positive and negative bonds that can originate from pupil, teacher, or both. All the same, teachers do their best to be constructive, and find themselves in an especially powerful position of trust.

When teachers don't know how abuse can happen to a child, they are unable to keep a door open whereby a child could approach them for help. They are also unable to respond appropriately to the thoughts and actions of proactive adults around them in the school community. They might feel intimidated if their workload is burdened further with even more demands to read upsetting theories from child abuse literature, wherein they can't really see or understand their role in relation to it. Increasingly, they have to spot, assess, and respond to many special needs, and they've had to reorganise their teaching day substantially in recent years.

As a teacher, you may not feel able to add 'abuse spotting' to your agenda, but you don't need anywhere near the expertise you think in order to be the first point of help. Today, the greatest proportion of child abuse referrals to police child protection units come from schools, and teachers sometimes even act as witnesses in court cases. At the present time in the UK, there are plans to have an on site social worker in schools for pupils experiencing problems. That person can provide some sort of practical follow up for the children, but these workers will not have anywhere near the potential advantage of trust that you have, as a child's teacher.

Looking out from the eyes of a child, it is frightening how their teacher fits in to a greater group of staff that acts so unpredictably within the power structure. If teachers don't understand what sort of authoritarian power structures fail children, it's impossible to create any other impression. Basic personal safety is a human need, and in the old classic school culture the primary ethos of respecting only adult authority as the sole authority over safety has been blind, one-sided, and overly forceful. A child's sense of place was either hindered by overly restrictive boundaries, or to too few whereby the child hardly knew here s/he stood. Now the pendulum is swinging towards discipline, and mutual respect between pupil and teacher. In a better-informed environment, it has a far greater chance of staying there. Where the school ethos is cohesive enough and bold enough to state how important a child's safety and well-being actually is, that's when children begin to feel safe.

In recent years schools started putting anti-bullying campaigns in to action, and it showed how children can respond positively to ideas about justice and fair play. Everyone was surprised, yet uplifted by the upsurge of positive proactive response from the children themselves. Equally, schools can adopt other campaigns under other banners. Like educating children about how to recognise abuse and be safe, in a context of communication about what good and harmful relationships are all about. Teenagers can be helped in how to handle bad relationships, and get better informed about healthy and unhealthy sexual relationships. In the same way that bullying is challenged, children can actively help each other stamp out various forms of abuse. In year six in my local primary school, eleven year olds are currently collecting old money, foreign coins and old mobile phones to raise money for Childline in the UK. Every child was been exposed to the project in a sensitive and caring way. Further on in secondary schools, adolescents can be better informed about how some adults they know could have been affected by abuse. In some schools children are taught what destructive and constructive elements in relationship are, and the importance of improving them. They are being helped on the way to more positive relationships at a far earlier stage than was ever possible before.

Teachers say it's the homes children come from that dictate their conduct and success at school. In turn, many parents mistrust teachers, probably because of the incompetent teaching and condescending treatment they may have had at school years ago. Ping-pong arguments that bounce blame back between home and school seem to get us nowhere, yet complaining teachers really do have a point. It **is** the homes children come from that dictate their conduct and success at school, and schools can become an extremely dynamic influence to effect change. A child's need for appropriate discipline, support and protection can vary enormously during the varied phases of their development, and increasingly there are books, organisations and charities out there to help and guide parents through the more impossible stages. Perhaps in time, schools can become community venues that provide the right tools to endorse positive change in the home. With this community support, parents can meet other parents, develop clearer discipline directives together, and gain in self esteem about their existing parenting skills, and their improving ones.

Culture within schools can drop the condescending attitudes of the past and embody a healthier respect for a child's natural instincts and intelligence. To this end, these stories form an excellent resource. They are a thorough foundation of understanding about what could be happening to an unknown number of children in any class, and how that child could be affected for life.

8.   This book is for police officers and all legal professionals

Police officers, probation officers, solicitors, Judges and those who work in solicitor's offices and the Courts all have some professional involvement with survivors of child abuse at some point. Law enforcement in matters of rape and domestic abuse have improved, especially in terms of professional skill and sensitivity towards victims throughout arduous legal processes. As professionals increasingly come up against abhorrent acts that used to be so well hidden, compassion becomes a very real requirement on both sides. Gaps between professional and personal development were identified in recent years, when several solicitors working with survivors from the Industrial School scandals in Ireland experienced traumatic stress, some to the extent of a nervous breakdown. These solicitors were not prepared for the work that came their way, but things have changed. A.C.A.L., the Association for Child Abuse Lawyers acknowledges a need for support, and fortnightly counselling sessions and other forms of support are now the norm for those whose work involves these particularly upsetting sides of human behaviour. This material is intended to help professionals prepare, and acknowledge the crucial importance of working from within a team who all share a knowledgeable support base that is aware of human needs, as well as professional goals. Nevertheless, it seems it's those who have the last word in the legal process who are also the last to acknowledge the lifelong consequences of abuse upon a child, namely the Judiciary.

Judges operate from lofty perspectives that save them from full, personal integration of a more human understanding of the realities of child abuse. In the way the law is interpreted to the letter, children are arguably less important than animals. For example, just as 'Survivors' Stories' is going to press in June 2007, Judge Julian Hall is in the headlines for saving a paedophile from a long term jail sentence because his 10 year old rape victim dressed 'provocatively'. The media also remind us of a previous case where he instructed another paedophile he convicted to give his seven year old child victim money for a bicycle, because it might cheer her up. A repeat offender, this paedophile received only a suspended sentence from Judge Hall. This judge's work denotes something both typical and extraordinary about how the law is interpreted and enacted in the UK every day.

The public do not feel the Judiciary are thorough enough in protecting children from child abusers, and certainly their sentencing perpetrates the view that children don't matter. Police agree it is the Judiciary who seem to lack the perception of the seriousness of these crimes, and they are at times appalled by the ignorance Judges display. Child pornography for example, at its least involved is about the commissioning, and the buying and selling of child abuse images within a secret criminal community. The cost of remaining a member either runs up to many thousands of pounds, or the production of more pornography whereby 'fresh' new images brings even more status than money. The more extreme the abuse, the more accepted the perpetrator is. This means creating yet more crime scenes, where children are filmed and photographed just as the abuse is actually going on. Judges rarely demonstrate any understanding of the many and varied separate criminal acts of abuse involved, without which child pornography just couldn't be made. It is hoped that through exposure to these accounts, Judges can de-programme themselves from the old public school mindset, that a child 'unlucky' enough to suffer abuse is little more than unfortunate 'minor'. It is hoped that this collection of accounts will give both parliamentarians and our more lofty law enforcers the pilgrimage back through childhood they sorely need to take.

9.   This book is for therapists

The material available to counsellors and therapists is ever on the increase, and as a child abuse survivor who works as a bodywork therapist, it has been my life's experience sorting it out. A collection of separate stories is not the sort of thing that's normally provided as educational material within the therapy and counselling world. However, many counselors and therapists think these stories should form a necessary part of it. This material isn't presented as a comfortable, solvable part of a greater body of knowledge. It is for you, as you unearth and examine these situations, to bring your skills and experience to what might be for you, entirely new perceptions of a primordial problem. You can catalyse a fresh new approach from where you can re-think your role in society, and what the aims, objectives, perspectives and limitations of your work are really all about.

Therapists adopt their own views towards a client at any given time, and these views are based upon previous case histories, dogmas, theories, personal experience, and the spiritual and human ideals embodied in their training. One counsellor I met was also a university lecturer in women's studies. She had very strong views about the way women as mothers are seen as icons, or deities. For her, child abuse survivors stood out as having particularly unreasonable amounts of anger. She gave me one example, whereby she was stunned by the seemingly limitless power of one survivor's anger towards their mother, for not protecting her from her husband, the survivor's stepfather. As a counsellor, she felt this was because of the way society cultivates a supernatural image of motherhood, and could not see much further into the survivor's rage. Her role was to help the survivor work through her anger and come to terms with the fact that her mother's ignorance was understandable. Many therapists aim to free their client from sanctioning righteous anger and blame upon anyone in a parental role, but there's a great deal more to it than that.

The therapist concerned had very little to say about how this mother is still perfectly happy to continue her relationship with her husband today, in the full knowledge and belief of her daughter's abuse. The mother expects her daughter to live beside all the betrayal she endured, remain a member of the family, and forgive everything. We might find all this startlingly surprising, but then we would, wouldn't we? How far do we extend our tolerance to listen to the truth about these things, and to what extent do we give ourselves the permission to enquire? Our culture tidied child abuse away very effectively, and women as parents have been unable to hear, assimilate and integrate the truth about what adults have secretly done to children for generations, and still do. This mother is unable to recognise or identify with her daughter's pain, she lives in a greater social structure that is happy to accommodate an abuser in what looks like a perfectly acceptable family. 'Life as it should be', is for this survivor to keep everything locked up in her childhood, yet as a woman of childbearing age, this survivor's whole idea of 'future' and 'family' are poisoned forever. Within the entire community of adults who now know about this situation, any thoughts about whether this stepfather could still be abusing or not are continually lulled into a deep, undisturbed sleep.

Is a survivor's experience supposed to be taken seriously, or is that too offensive, self–indulgent and trivial a question? Just like Billy Connolly, Heather Mills McCartney, John Peel, Mick Hucknall and Ozzy Osbourne, plenty of survivors struggle with the burden of being unable to change abusive patterns in society, and this struggle is rarely perceived for what it truly is. A survivor cannot comprehend the depth of immunity that surrounds them. There is too little concern or expression of distress about what repeatedly happens to helpless children, and it's nobody's job to confront the behaviour patterns that perpetrate these cyclical patterns of harm.

Therapy provides an honesty that cannot be expressed in the real world. There are many survivors who will tell you about the healing merit in client centred approaches, that clear away burdensome, negative emotions that had no other outlet. Many survivors end their isolation by becoming therapists themselves. They will certainly feel freer and more liberated at times, but could well finish up living in a cocooned world.

Where criminal, statutory, case law and punishment are ill considered and very rarely even brought into question, there's a lack of reference to what damaging relationships are all about in the real world. If a therapist can see no further than changing their client's 'negative' habits of clinging to the past, however well intentioned, a therapist inevitably becomes yet another abuser. These 'therapeutic' attitudes are still very strong because this area of mental and spiritual health is still burdened by concepts of the responsibility of the individual ego (referred to in Section 9). This is adhered to as the most basic, 'responsible' way to become a singular, wholly liberated individual who must learn to live positively and productively in the here and now. But if a survivor's healing, as an individual never affects any change into the abusive situation that damaged them, how could that ever be enough? Their rage isn't selfish, immature and unreasonable. They are perfectly aware that they are a tiny part of far larger patterns of hidden abuse that are habitually and conveniently ignored.

The opposite scenario is also on the increase, whereby a therapist will insist upon notifying the police as soon as a survivor discloses who their abuser was. This is some improvement, but is terrifying for the survivor. When the survivor loses control of the situation, they simply get abused all over again. There are issues of the survivor's safety to be considered, and the kind of life they are likely to have in relation to all the people they knew as a child. It is up to the skill of the therapist to steer the survivor through each and every possible course of action, and every possible consequence before any action is taken.

Body Oriented Therapists

These therapists do massage, bodywork and many other therapies that involve touch and physical contact. Through an awareness that somewhere between one in three to one in four clients may well be child abuse survivors, it is easy to understand the need to develop better counselling skills around the matter of physical contact itself.

By exploring as many survivor's perspectives as possible, you can improve your rapport with your client immensely. This is because survivors rapidly intuit when their perspectives are being understood, and very empowering work can commence when their perspectives are embraced. The opposite is true when survivors intuit their perspectives are not being understood, and losing a client in this way begets a sense of two-way confusion and failure. Apart from having a growing emotional and intellectual understanding that's unafraid, sensitive and honest in its exploration, therapists need to be rigorously practical. They need to create an atmosphere of safety, and be able to talk about inter-personal physical and professional boundaries in a respectful way, that they are sure their client understands. They need to be aware of flashbacks, and triggering points that connect not just with previous childhood memories, but connect into the relevance of ongoing life situations as an adult as well. All this has to be done in far more detail than with other clients.

Body oriented therapies are wide and varied, and therapists must address the limitations of their work realistically with their clients. They need to be knowledgeable and clear about what they don't have to offer, as well as what they do.

10. This book is for those who work within various Religious Groups, and represent them

If any disillusionment with traditional forms of religion is being felt across society, abuse survivors have more reason than most to feel disillusioned. Yet religion still has a positive healing role for some survivors and their families. A few of the twelve survivors in these two volumes of stories do have actively religious lives that vary from one to the other, and they speak openly of their relationship with God. For example in Story twelve Volume 2, Lizzie talks from the heart about her healing journey as sourced from God, and her church.

To abuse a child within any faith is very damning for that faith in itself. It's more than a betrayal of human trust, it's the destruction of a lifelong ability to trust in religion, and possibly in God.

Ironically it's the desire to avoid the damage that public shaming could bring, which makes most religious groups run away from these matters. At a later stage, they can find themselves in the full glare of the media, unavoidably engaged in successions of capricious, volatile conflict, whilst they deny the very thing they originally tried to avoid.

9

The Times recently uncovered figures published under the Freedom of Information Act by the Home Office, which clearly show that one in two sex offenders now serving time in prison declare some sort of faith, whereas one in three of the rest of the prison population do so. Buddhism, Anglicanism, Free Church Christianity and Judaism are some of the faiths listed.

The Catholic Church has received the most constant media exposure so far. For over thirty years prior to the millennium, a mounting number of abuse claims were steadily growing all around the world. Pope John Paul the second fought these claims consistently in his efforts to resist the damage to his Church. The majority of his followers supported him, and failed to report criminal acts to the local police. Canon law (internal church law) was often given priority over secular criminal law. The Catholic Clergy engaged themselves in efforts to pressure the victims, their families and independent witnesses into not reporting the incidents to civil authorities. There were resignations of some Catholic Church leaders after they were accused of "perverting the course of justice", which is in itself a criminal act.

In the UK, the Nolan Commission finally reached its conclusion with 82 recommended procedures in 'A Programme for Action'(2001) to manage abusing priests, but there were still difficulties in getting Church personnel to actually follow these procedures. Personnel were having trouble believing that such respected, well educated, sensitive and 'civilised' people who were so at home in their communities actually did these things to children. It's not just that there was no understanding of what sort of suffering child abuse really causes victims, there was no consistent approval for that understanding to exist. Wherever there were priests with empathy and understanding towards survivors, they remained isolated, because any communication between them and the Church was not welcomed. Through being unable to discuss child abuse realistically, and communicate effectively about it, the Church has derived a tarnished reputation worldwide, and a significantly diminished congregation throughout Europe.

Other religious leaders and representatives can take something from this example, and see that in these changing times, there is no excuse for any religious authority to make the same mistakes again. If you are too easily shocked, you cannot keep a listening door open to the people in your care, and you cannot protect their children. Culturally, the six child abuse stories in this book just happen to be against a backdrop of Christian, Jewish and Spiritualist upbringings. I have also worked with Mormon, Jehovah's Witness and Muslim survivors, but children born into every known faith in the world are also abused. Religious organisations need to be seen to face up to these problems head on, and have procedures in place ready to manage abusive behaviour and its effects if and when it arises. Religious leaders can use this book to help them develop the practice of empathic discussion as a learning tool amongst themselves, and communicate outside their own circles about these matters more effectively.

11. This book is for journalists, writers, media and TV production teams

Professionals like these often work under pressure, and find it hard to second-guess a survivor's perspectives. One producer once contacted me because he was looking for a survivor who was still in touch with their abuser. This survivor had to have forgiven their abuser, and both parties would have to be happy to go on air and talk about it. I wondered how I could make this producer see that they were looking for a needle in a haystack, and even if they found it, this particular pair wouldn't represent anywhere near the majority of cases.

Survivors are always glad to see something about these issues in the press, but they often tell me about their disappointment with the short sighted perceptions journalists have. The press are interested in what abuse took place, but most often only if it's actual sexual rape. When the survivor was a child, only very rarely would they have suffered just one singular form of abuse. There's a real lack of background portrayal about the variety of abuses and in what contexts they could have happened over a period of time. Survivors are often portrayed in a manic way, as either outstanding people who despite the odds, overcame enormous obstacles and achieved miraculous success and fulfillment, or they're eternally lost in a suicidal depression. When working under pressure, journalists are only going to discover little of what a survivor's experience is really about. Lack of knowledge can be very inhibiting, and it can make them feel uncomfortable about interacting and formulating questions. But by taking the time out to read these stories, they can develop a much better rapport. They can improve the press, radio and TV coverage that's out there for everyone, making the work they do more representative and useful for society as a whole.

12. This book is for all proactive adults who wish to protect children from abuse

Countless people I speak to are amazed that doctors, dentists, school nurses and the many others who children run into from day to day, would not *NOTICE* an abused child. They wholeheartedly believe that if any child was being abused, *somebody else* would know. Most of the adults who see children every day have no idea how to notice an abused child, and 'Survivors' Stories' helps you to build up your perceptions. A proactive adult is anyone who has a relationship with a child, who sees themselves as that child's protector. They can have any role; they could be a big brother, big sister, aunt, uncle, parent, husband, wife, cousin or dependable family friend. They can also be working in any profession that brings them into contact with a child. They encourage discussion and aim to help the family make child safety and protection an acceptable facet within that child's entire circle of relationships. Through reading these stories, you can recognise how much society needs more proactive protective adults, and enjoy being more confident about the importance of your role as one.

No one need be daunted by
the size and scope of this book!
Any part may be read on its own,
or as a part of the whole thing.

Introduction

Whenever someone is unexpectedly called on to say something about child abuse, there's usually a moment or two's hesitation about how to respond. Nobody wishes to be insensitive or uncaring, yet that's how we often feel when we broach the subject. Maya Angelou and Oprah Winfrey were amongst the first celebrities courageous enough to speak out about their abuse. In the UK, the expanding list presently includes Billy Connolly, Heather Mills McCartney, John Peel, Mick Hucknall and Ozzy Osbourne. But why do celebrities risk the tarnish on their image? Well, celebrity is the magical antidote to the trepidation that normally restrains most people's attention on the subject, so campaigners are grateful when celebrities speak out because they pave the way for others to do the same.

Talking about this as an actual life experience encourages a sharper watchfulness over children. Matters stop getting sucked into our dulled social conscience, where we often imagine the worlds of justice, psychology and social work set the balance straight. Celebrity or not, each and every child abuse survivor has something to share that can help teach society about what really happens to children, and how adult lives are affected. Survivors have kept a great deal secret for a long time, and very few of us really know how to understand them or know what to say, but now it's time to engage in a more constructive conversation.

Welcome

If you arrived at this book to meet child abuse survivors on the page, you've come to the right place. Nevertheless if you only picked this book up by accident, you are warmly welcomed on this journey through childhood and adolescence.

In my efforts to get this published, I was quite struck by how separate social groups always make child abuse and adult survivor issues somebody else's concern. Book companies in particular couldn't identify any clear market, and principally suggested a rather narrow market for adult survivors. To date, there is no section in our bookshops entitled, 'Child Liberation and Survivor Issues'. If there were, 'Survivors' Stories' would be there, sitting right next to several hundred other books that in my view, are currently hidden. 'Survivors' Stories' could be housed in several sections that could include social work, self–help, counselling, therapy, mental and physical health, sex education and parenting, with no one category being more significant than any other.

Author's Background

As a survivor of child abuse myself, I knew I kept mainstream society at a certain distance, but it took some time before I really understood why. After my studies and experiences in humanistic psychology in my early twenties, and the bodywork training I did in the USA, I embarked upon a career as a one to one bodywork therapist. In the eighties most of my friends and colleagues were psychotherapists and counsellors at a time when there were no university-accredited courses in the UK. I worked from a healing centre with an open minded MD, who was there to advise all practitioners, ranging from nutritionists and acupuncturists to hypnotherapists and spiritual healers, offering a holistic and open-hearted approach. I worked from a motherly dynamic using touch, the catalyst whereby the client's 'energy blocks' could be explored. Integration between body and mind, and the experience of 'coming home' to the innate wisdom within the body led the way through various levels of self-discovery. Those years of working through layer after layer of understanding in such an intimate way, taught me a great deal.

Within my 'aware' alternative community, what I suffered in my teens had never been secret, but nor had it ever been labelled as abuse. It was well aired, but then put away in a box marked 'sorted'. I was lucky to have come from a loving family, but I also believed it was a dysfunctional family within a sexually confused, repressive, power driven culture. To me wholeness, integrity, self-responsibility and living in the present were my spiritual goals, and I had worked through any lingering anger or bitterness about my past. My abuser disappeared from the family entirely when he got married, but I was unable to see how my relationships with the rest of my family, especially my main carer and life giver (my mother) had been eroded over the years. I had no real foundation of honest relationship with these people, because I'd been required to hide. I doubted myself so much that I had shrunk; indeed I didn't exist as a whole, but rather as a composite sort of mask of whatever I thought my family could accept.

I feel for the many out there whose lives are similarly veiled, especially as there's so much we can all learn from them. Survivors know they live a split sort of existence. Now it's time to move their experiences more fully into central stage. Society can re-balance as it responds, whereby patterns of behaviour have the opportunity for change.

Human Experience

There are countless objective views about these problems, but I come from the voice of human experience. After all, it's our own human experience that we bring to those who profess to offer any sort of help or representation, and it's our individual and collective human experience that we have to live with in the end, whether we seek help or not. When we look into patterns of behaviour around abuse, we find patterns that are nothing more than hangovers from the traditions of the past. Opening up this subject in fresh new ways can give everyone far more clarity and self-determination, and that's the purpose of this book series.

Volumes of Stories?

From reading one story, you might think you'll understand the basic stuff of surviving child abuse, but the whole issue is far greater than any one story. Most people don't know what abuse is, and child abuse has such wide discrepancies of understanding that we fight shy and trip up so easily when we try to express ourselves about it. We haven't been shown how to understand it, and it just can't be grasped and fully understood via statistics and objective information. It can only be understood sufficiently when it is looked at subjectively, with empathy, and in context. It may even be ironic that this material comes to you in the form of a book, because this material is not here simply to amass information. It is here to assist you on a journey of human experience.

As you go further, although you'll be 'listening' to an adult, you'll be holding on to their hand as a child. As you see through their eyes, you'll sense their experiences in context with their circumstances, surroundings, and relationships.

The Project

The sixty or more who were interviewed for this project were enthusiastic about being a part of a piece of work that would engender more understanding. Twelve stories were selected, making up a fairly characteristic slice from our social environment in terms of what role the abusers had in each case, and in terms of what the child concerned experienced. These accounts are truly the backbone of the 'Survivors' Stories' series, and they can teach us all a great deal.

All contributors to Survivors' Stories were born and brought up in various parts of the U.K. Nevertheless, similar testimonies can easily be found within and beyond all national boundaries right across the world. Child abuse is perpetrated wherever there is ignorance about the reality of it and the ways it can be prevented. To those who already have a ground knowledge, these stories will seem like a selection of both the typical and the exceptional. They don't profess to be a statistical representation of the whole; but were especially chosen to serve you on the broadest possible educational journey.

I edited contributor's writing styles as lightly as possible from draft to draft, but only to eliminate repetition. In the end, reading the stories is rather like listening to someone pouring their heart out to a close friend over coffee, well into the early hours of the morning. Some experiences can be found that seem universal in every story, but any survivor of child abuse could be just as shocked upon reading some of these stories as anyone else whose childhood was different. Wherever the circumstances and acts of abuse had never once occurred to you as even being possible, the story will have the power to shock. Nonetheless, each and every story is completely true.

Each of the contributors put everything into words in as much depth as possible. They have immeasurable gratitude towards you, because each and every child who has ever suffered without good reason, will now stand a better chance of becoming a more worthy part of modern thought and expression. By reading their accounts, you are possibly becoming part of a gentle change within the heart of our social consciousness.

Listening

In this first decade of the twenty-first century, comedians are happy to pepper their repertoire with the odd paedophile joke, and as offensive humour goes, this is hardly the first to leap over the invisible line. In the UK, increasingly you can find child abuse and its effects in TV productions like the BBC's EastEnders, and in serialised dramas like Talkback Thames' The Bill. Hollywood has been weaving child abuse themes into their story lines since the 1990's, and the amounts of material in the press and the media are on the increase. Even so, it's a completely different matter when your sister, your son, or your oldest school friend suddenly tells you that they were sexually or otherwise abused. When you discover the perpetrator was someone you both knew and trusted throughout shared childhood years, everything changes. The closer the relationship, the greater the shock.

Listening still feels unnatural for most of us because the truth of abuse has been siphoned off almost exclusively towards social workers, police and criminal justice systems, mental health and psychological expertise. It has been kept from us for generations, it's no wonder that listening can sometimes have a strange, paralysing effect. In fact, the active listening to accounts of child abuse is purely a matter of practice. With each and every survivor of abuse I have ever spoken to, their caring towards me as their listener has moved me deeply. They wanted to protect me from the shock of the worst hurts they experienced, and there were often periods when they tested the ground, to see if they could go further. There's a structured form of advice about talking and listening in **Section Six (page 31)**, entitled '**How to Talk About Abuse**', which aims to help you through any doubts that you might have. Essentially, listening to either a child or an adult is about bypassing the temptation to make judgments and assessments. You hold an open space from where you can listen more. To that end, reading these stories can help immensely as an exercise in expansion of concept and thought.

Project Guidelines

Although a few participants have now become friends, each contributor started from scratch and none of them knew me personally before the project began. Each one shared their story confidentially, and none of the participants ever worked together or shared any aspects of the project with one another in groups of any kind. After we went through the questionnaire, more questions seemed to want to be asked that were relevant to the answers already at hand. In some cases we went beyond twenty drafts, with an average number of twelve. Each contributor discarded or added whatever words and sentences they liked. Some had much more to say than others, but in each case their story has been as well portrayed as the survivor could allow. In every case, the final draft was sent back to me in hard copy, with each and every page signed by the contributor as an honest account of their lives.

Some said that there was something freeing about not working with a therapist, and simply working together as an equal with another survivor on a writing project. Most revealed more in these written words than they had ever done in therapy, within what felt to them like a wider forum. The absence of the counsellor–client type dynamic helped, plus my understanding and openness as another survivor. The words of the latest draft, staring back at us from the written page served as the biggest stimulus for further questions, recollections and insights.

Labels – An Explanation

Labels can irritate or liberate, as we all have different future choices and varied insights of the past. Nevertheless, labels are a device that define people, and shunt them into groups so that we can all talk about the situations we want to improve. I hate pigeonholing people, and admit that at times the text may seem insensitive because of course people are people, and they live, grow, change and develop in their own unique ways.

'Survivor' means an adult who experienced an abusive childhood. This is used as an alternative to the old term 'victim' of child abuse. Some survivors feel 'victim'

16

describes them better because it's an accurate description of them throughout various periods of their lives. Some others disagree, and some hate both terms and prefer to have no label, and be called 'a person who was abused as a child'. Just like other categories of people, survivors are a vast variety of people who have quite individualistic views about everything.

'Co–survivors' are people whose lives get affected, even though the abuse didn't happen directly to them. They are in some sort of relationship with a survivor, and through their empathic (or other) involvement, their lives can change considerably. For example, I realise I could be described not only as a survivor, but also as a co–survivor.

When survivors become divided into sub–groups and categories, shortsighted assumptions about what sort of child abuse is more valid or less valid can create defenses and cause separation. When that happens, the awareness of the child's situation living and growing up in a child's world, along with the universal needs and vulnerabilities that all children have, easily get lost. Labels can serve us, but they sometimes deceive us by appearing to sort things out when they can't. Our concern about them can absorb too much of our time, imposing limits whilst we're right in the middle of multi faceted dynamics of possibility and change.

Furthermore, many 'non–survivors' are genuinely interested in child abuse and survivor problems. They have different levels of experience, perception and understanding to offer us all. I apologise in advance for any annoyance that I may cause if I make 'non–survivors' appear wilfully indifferent or ignorant, as many are only too willing to offer their valuable time and attention to these issues. Other labels you'll find further on may also cause annoyance, but the ever–changing debate about which label is correct for who will always be there. Preferences change, and there will always be far more of us in number than there are labels that can perfectly describe us.

Pilgrimage

Reading 'Survivor's Stories' could be compared to setting out on a pilgrimage through a strange new dimension of our shared lives, and it takes courage to do that. Many have read these stories and grieved, and subsequently went through many a sad and sometimes angry day, as they re–balanced their lives around a truer and more compassionate understanding of the relationships going on around them. Perhaps in order to touch upon the personal merits of travelling this journey, I should share with you what I unexpectedly discovered upon mine.

Before I embarked upon this project, now and then I felt intimidated by gay people because I was confused by their perspective of 'straight' society. Today, I couldn't imagine life without my gay friends, and I'm so much the richer. This didn't come from the ground–breaking ideas of Andrea Dworkin and the Women's Press, or studying human biology, or social, or legal history but via an entirely unexpected route.

Through feeling my way into the suffering world of each and every abused child, I could see what violation is, and what the destructive nature of deeply emotional and sexually abusive behaviour upon any child actually destroys, in itself. As I grieved for what was lost, I understood what was important, and everything just fell into place. My present conclusion is that you can't begin to understand sexuality at all, until you see why labelling people at this level is just so unimportant. When you go through the components of abuse upon a child, and witness how they destroy the child's natural, god given integrity, and sexual integrity, you understand how fragile and unique the entity of human sexuality is within each and every one of us. People can and do change sexual orientation throughout their lives, and they either celebrate their splendour and their human foibles within adult sexual relationships, or they don't. Now, I see myself as neither a 'heterosexual' nor a 'homosexual', but just a 'sexual'. It makes life much simpler!

For those who are uncomfortable with an open mind and prefer to preserve all life just as it is, these stories may not have a lot to offer. Those who have explored their childhood often carry a broader concept of what it is to be a person, but they may not have studied other childhoods in such an open, non-analytical way. It's easy to feel cheated and deprived by what we didn't get, yet as we discover other kids who lived through forms of destruction and deprivation we never previously conceived of, the reality of what we actually did receive gets a far clearer perspective. That's one of many riches that await your discovery. A voyage with an honest companion can change your life, and although these stories may feel upsetting at times, they bring a strength that can act through our lives in a positive way.

Dart to and fro in this book as you wish, and seek out the part that speaks to you most of all.

Why should I need to know?

Professional Attention is Not Enough

We've always tackled child abuse via various kinds of social work, police and criminal justice systems, mental health and psychological expertise. Systems professionals have to work within push them to perform to targets on time. Services get run with a mechanistic managerial approach aimed at a high turnover of cases. There's little time to simply listen, and develop better ongoing relationships with the children and the family units these professionals are there to help. We would be a lot worse off if these services weren't there, but they alone can never really counter the day to day ignorance that causes child abuse.

Statistics

If statistics are not intentionally offered up as a kind of solution, most of us certainly receive them that way. If we equate for a moment, dishing out statistics to feeding the hungry, it's about as effective as handing a large bag of raw potatoes to a starving family, when there's nothing in their house to cook them with. When we talk about it, it's like passing a red hot potato around the campfire; everyone either drops it or throws it to someone else, and all we achieve are several burnt fingers! As the potato falls out of our hands, we're trivialising our own responses, and delegating matters to experts. But as the seconds tick by, these experts are not actually engaged with the many who need their attention, and for the most part, their corrective presence is in fact little more than a fantasy in our social consciousness. The statistics certainly do prove one thing … only a small proportion of the children who need attention, are actually getting it.

The most conservative statistic states that one child in eight will suffer life long consequences from their abuse, but it seems somehow impossible to take in. For every ten families, somewhere between two and three will suffer life long stresses and separations for the same reason. We grab this information like a drunk clutching on to a lamppost on their way home, with newspapers and media news spinning around us in a blurred, unintelligible reality. But we can easily revert to our own schooldays, and count the heads we used to see around us. In your class of thirty, three or four children (perhaps a close friend), will have suffered abuse. If we hold that focus, we see that these other kids were no different from us.

There is no absolute definitive ratio, but various studies reveal anything between one in four to one in nine suffering children or survivors. Here is a sample of seventy children travelling in a London double decker bus …

"Every full double-decker school bus at the end of the day is likely to be taking home around 7 seriously unhappy children. Most of the lower deck [capacity of 32] would at some time during their childhood have been going home to serious worries. Approximately 10 children may be going home to a 'double-shift' of cleaning, laundry, shopping and preparing meals, and 2 or 3 will be in fear of violence between their parents while they are out, or of what might happen that evening."

(Cawson et al. (2000) <u>Child maltreatment in the United Kingdom: a study of the prevalence of child abuse and neglect</u>. London: NSPCC. p.93).

To those who are not statisticians, the difference between relative and absolute statistical comparison is quite beyond our grasp. Most studies I've found separate physical abuse and sexual abuse from emotional abuse, which is a rather disconcerting separation. Apparently emotional abuse can exist independently with neither physical violence nor sexual abuse, but most survivors will say that life–long emotional scarring is an inevitable bi–product of all other forms of abuse.

Leaving Conflicting Knowledge Behind

Even though our understanding of brain and neural development during childhood has greatly increased, both objective and subjective views of child abuse still seem unclear. Given the substandard view that we have of ourselves in relation to the experts, things may even have worsened since psychoanalysis and psychology began. But we could be a lot less confused about what the truth is than we actually suppose, and if we simply trust our own instincts, we can begin to liberate ourselves from the silence we inherited.

It's in the moments we're still so unsure about what might help or hinder, hurt or offend that we accommodate the climate of denial. We can lean on expertise when we need it, but expecting experts to actively lead us only means we will repeat the past and blame the experts for our lack of progress later on. Each and every one of us holds an important key towards a better future, as long as we have the courage to look, learn and act further.

Barriers

Even when abuse is going on, because it's so upsetting we tend to rationalize what we see, hear, and feel out of existence. This next section is about what stops us from acknowledging it, and facing up to it for what it is. Under the sub-headings that follow, we explore the possible causes and barriers.

Silence

In order to explore this heritage of silence we still carry, we need to understand how children have been perceived. Taller ones tend to look down on children, assuming they are less significant, their smaller size signifying their lesser importance. Historically, western, Jewish and Christian approaches went further, and dictated children could never be trusted and needed severe command. Corporal punishment was greatly revered for its sharp moral righteousness in getting on with the task of driving the 'demons' out of children. Whatever mental torture or physical pain necessary between adult and child in the alchemy towards betterment, it would be administered without a second thought. Juvenile minds were believed to be inherently manipulative, deceitful and defiant, yet the pain children had to endure could well have induced this reaction, in itself. In happier households where the children didn't suffer, those families were nevertheless compelled to respect virulent taskmasters, for example in schools. Those taskmasters commanded the highest social respect, and in their absence, it was thought civilisation would be enslaved to the demands of spoilt, inconsiderate savages.

In the absence of a welfare state, family meant life went on. Family wasn't just inter-dependent physical survival within the greater community; it was social respectability, and ordinarily the shaper of the requisite reputation for professional status. From the religious culture of the fifth commandment,

"Honour thy father and thy mother: that thy days may be long upon the land which the LORD thy God giveth thee"

... meant it was a sin to disobey whatever a parent commanded, and children were, (many still are) viewed as being their parent's life-long possessions. Any private disclosure of either parent brutality or sexual abuse would be cripplingly reprehensible for the confessor in itself. It would be seen as weak, selfish, manipulative and malicious, and would cause outrage in the home. Public disclosure would seriously damage the family name for generations, which would have consequences for extended family as well. It didn't matter that the brutality, molestation or rape of a child was against the law, any involvement with the law at all meant unbearable shame, bar none.

The previous two paragraphs may conjure up a Dickensian world, but many elements of this are still as true today as they ever were. Certainly, this behaviour may not be acted out as blatantly in public view as it once was, or as often, but the way parental behaviour passes down through the generations is quite tangible. For example in the astounded way parents feel when they suddenly catch themselves behaving towards their children exactly as their parents did towards them.

21

Looking more deeply at core attitudes of thought towards babies, toddlers, primary school pupils, secondary pupils, adolescents and teenagers, we can see how society's children may be loved, but when any abuse comes to light, they find themselves surrounded by exactly the same old 'Dickensian' mind set. When an abused child grows up and turns into an adult, this mind-set hardly changes one whit. As you go through the stories, you'll find that people are bonded into behavioural blueprints that replicate themselves into many of our most modern abuse situations.

That sort of thing doesn't happen here

Our forefathers shut child abuse out of their minds, but the time has come when we can no longer do that. It's true there are pockets of aware people in society, but we're still tethered within an environment of overwhelming denial. For example, nearly half of the contributors to this book are going to show neither their family nor their close friends their stories; and the others have told only a chosen few. All but one participant has used pseudonyms, and the sorts of constrictions survivors live within will uncover themselves to you as you progress through the stories themselves.

Some still think denial is a good thing. The facts indicate that by far the greatest proportion of abused children have always cared for their families by keeping silent. I've had letters from survivors thanking me, but also stating proudly that they will not tell another single soul about their abuse. "Doing that wouldn't help anyone" they said. They encourage me to help, but to tell those I help to keep quiet. They wish their lives to be a vote of thanks, confidence and gratitude to carers who did their utmost for them in an imperfect world; anything else breaks the bonds. After all, as children, they certainly wanted their abuse to stop, but they didn't want to lose their whole world. They'll throw their innate sense for justice, integrity, and equality away, maintaining a self-sacrifice in a secret world that few can ever contemplate or imagine.

Shame, and the Most Precious Part of Being Human

Sixties psychology and other influences left us with notions telling us our sexual repressions came from religious ideas about virginity, Victorian modesty, and who knows where else. Then science gave us the pill, and we hung up our hang-ups as more cavalier, light-hearted attitudes towards sex came into play. For those who wish to be sexually liberated, you could 'cure' your inhibitions by taking a photograph of your genitalia and slapping it up on a giant billboard for all to see, but would that take away your shame and embarrassment forever? Hardly. You protected yourself in advance by the very fact that you engineered it. But if somebody tricked you, secretly took the same picture and put it in a porn mag right next to a photograph of the respectably clad you, with name clearly displayed, something else happens. You are shocked, robbed, taunted and severely hurt; the most painful aspect of which is the experience of shame. This entirely natural response can be traced to all kinds of circumstances. In its pure form, shame is nothing to do with sexual inhibition at all, it's to do with the most fragile part of being human.

Aspects of shame are explored more fully in the stories that follow, showing how abusers perpetrate their abuse within this, the most vulnerable aspect of a child's responsiveness. How can we generate more respect and awareness for what human vulnerability is, in both children and adults? We all know violation hurts, but can we cultivate more communication as a society about what is precious about our needs and vulnerabilities? Abusive situations emerge wherever there are secrets and communication breakdowns, and we haven't fully addressed ideas about creating better relationships within families and communities as a serious objective.

We share our feelings by listening to modern music lyrics, or through literature, theatre, music and film. We talk about what we watch on TV, yet how can we flex our 'relationship muscle' and expand the boundaries of expression in which we live? By refusing to feel feelings of shame and embarrassment, we abandon the precious parts of being human that badly need our respect and cultivation. To be incapable of addressing the intricate problems of child abuse in open dialogue is to be incapable of tackling all that is valuable and precious about being a child, and also about being a human being.

Self-Censorship

It is wrong to picture adults with children and underage adolescents sexually, and we know such images are in any case, criminal. Such prohibition may be good, but is it good that we feel so compelled to slam our fingers down on the mute button as soon as our minds wander in that direction? Newspaper headlines tell us how child abusers get released from prison early or avoid it all their lives. We shuffle matters over to the psychiatrists, the police, the probation officers, the Church and the social workers, yet this recurring havoc is like a chronically painful memory we do our best to escape. To approach this is to feel helpless, or even foolish for broaching the subject, so we often seal our thinking off, as well as any attempt to express ourselves about it.

We can ease our own suffering by attacking the subject with more self-assurance. As we learn just how the traditions and social practices from the past constricted us, we'll also see that it wasn't we who created these restrictions, at all. When we know why it is important to be able to talk, we'll be a lot less worried about causing offence.

When Good Bonds are Red Herrings

Anyone might feel some trauma when listening to a survivor tell their story, but it's often those who were not abused who feel especially uncomfortable. Whilst seeking out the truth about an abusive family, they associate the abusive uncle, or mother (or whoever had the abusive role) with their own relatives. It can often be anxiety about being disloyal towards their own family that makes them afraid to even contemplate abuse issues. Many go on lightening speed searches in their heads, questioning what were for them, mostly wholesome bonds within dependable relationships. By visualising ugly photofit faces upon their dearest kith and kin, instantaneously they feel attacked, and frightened of these new, almost sinister feelings. Unguided, badly directed listening like this happens because they have no other reference points, and that's not really their fault. Many simply reject possibilities of child abuse out of hand because naturally, they simply can't take the information in in this way, and as you would expect, they reject it.

Society likes to think there are only two sorts of family; healthy families, and atrocious families of the kind that turn up in child abuse and neglect scandals in the newspapers. But families have a large range of lifestyles and attitudes in between those two extremes. Putting income and social status aside, the actual quality of life for children living in the same street will vary. Life for the child in number fourteen can vary enormously from the child living right next door, which again can be quite different for the children further up the road in number seventy-eight.

Inadequate knowledge offends people so much, that they may avoid examining abuse within any families at all, forever. This typical response of disgust and rejection has been a massive proportion of our low tolerance for conversation, and our social denial en mass. To really understand child abuse, we don't need to disengage from our feelings, but we do need to consciously step out of our own backgrounds and actively enter into a completely different house, through a completely different front door, with an open mind.

Peer group barriers

In the same vein, we often arrive at false understandings, both individually and collectively, because we plaster our own life experience on top of a survivor's. How can we stop checking our own bank of experience for a sense of validity, and develop truer perceptions? Whenever one individual complains from the ranks of their generation about excessive punishment, the response is often

'We all got punished in exactly the same way!'

A whole generation will act towards the complainant like a jealous sibling who resents the 'special' attention their brother or sister is getting. Whoever 'tells tales' about a parent's or a school teacher's bullying and brutality is often seen as pitiful. They think, fancy being an adult, and still being unable to understand the context of their parent's or teacher's 'justifiable' frustrations? To fit in, you shut up and got on with it, or else you'd forfeit your equality and right of place with your piers.

This social pier pressure has stopped survivors from speaking up for aeons, and as a result destructive behaviour towards children has continued, unchecked. It's the stuff of fantasy that survivors gain a lot from tea and sympathy, when in fact they detest that response and have far more to lose, than to gain. The hell they went through is finished, nevertheless they may choose to hide the injustice of their beginnings no longer. Their disclosures are not shared in order to be an 'interest case', but to live their present lives with more honesty and henceforth improve the lot for children now.

It's blatantly untrue that all children get abused and punished in the same way, and the sooner we face up to this, the better.

Gospel of Forgiveness

Even the word, 'forgiveness' sounds like a healing balm that erases acts of perpetration away as if they had never happened. Someone who seems to lack forgiveness can appear scary and barbaric, especially if we let our minds drift towards extremes of vigilantism. It's pointlessly illogical, self destructive and bad for your general health to go on feeling angry. It's better to engage in constructive acts here and now, instead of dwelling in the past. This unerring aim of forgiveness as some sort of pinnacle of human achievement has been here since the bare beginnings of the Roman Catholic Church, yet the same sentiment may today be most prevalent of all within contemporary spirituality.

All survivors I met who confronted their abuser with what had been done to them in a civilised fashion achieved quite a major release, no matter the outcome. When the inner tortured child as victim at last finds a worthy representative in the adult survivor, the inner child's suffering gains a healthier context within the adult survivor as s/he gets on with the daily business of living. The guilt and shame at last is shed, and put back upon the abuser's shoulders.

To keep the abuse separate from the perpetrator's life is to pretend nothing happened. This isn't a living active forgiveness, but a detached forgetfulness. It is the aspiration towards this sort of forgetfulness as being more mature, or 'spiritual' that keeps the true knowledge of what happens to children so distant from our collective awareness. Forgiveness shouldn't be a medication, to anaesthetise the survivor into a 'higher' form of awareness. Survivors know how abusers don't change, but abuse repeatedly, with very little going on in their external world to prevent them.

When we think of what happens to children, the sort of forgiveness we aspire to obviously lacks basic common sense, and for our part, it's somewhat of a cop out to put the focus on the victim's improvement. We avoid the truth of what goes on in an abuser's mind, and how easy it is for them not to change, especially as hardly even two percent ever get convicted. Perhaps it is we who are afraid to face abusers, yet we would confront abusive behaviour more often if we thought more deeply about what happens when we don't. Forgiveness can only become a force for good when it's unafraid to search the source of destructive behaviours that created the misery in the first place.

Happy Families

As children, we learn very quickly about cultural ideals of what a happy healthy family is. Whole communities find them reassuring, and enjoy expressing their respect for them; after all children by their very nature have a need to belong to a secure group. Dysfunctional families have no trouble getting the abused child(ren) in their group to project the 'right' sort of image, and these ideals we project on families blind us from realising that families are like chalk and cheese. These stories break down the myths and enlighten us about what it's really like to be born into a completely different family, and to grow up within it.

Protective Instincts Freeze Parental Interest

Although the advent of parenthood is an initiation into a new life, the role doesn't necessarily make you an all-knowing person who can do no wrong! Still, the long tradition of blind trust and unconditional respect towards parents hasn't changed much from what it was hundreds of years ago.

As a parent myself, I know how receiving criticism, or even gentle advice about how I'm raising my child can be incredibly challenging to take in. Even disagreements about sleeping and feeding regimes for the baby can feel like monstrous bones of contention, as powerful protective instincts rise up like monsters of the deep! Most parents can't see how they could ever benefit from the attention of a prying onlooker. Parenthood is exhausting enough, never mind coping with outside criticism. Recent television series, like Channel 4's 'Supernanny' (also released in the US) and other TV productions on a similar theme have shown us there is another way. Parents can adopt more effective behavioural techniques towards their kids, without neglecting their own personal needs.

As parents, our very real love and protective instincts often tempt us to end up in family groups that are defensive, tight knit and isolated. Parents can feel so vulnerable and insecure, that they unconsciously worry that outside interest may mean their children will be forcibly removed. They have primal fears about false accusations, and therefore stoke up very resolute attitudes based upon their rather scary perceptions of the world around them. I've seen people in parental roles attack even before they've had an opportunity for defence, for example by asserting that smacking is an excellent disciplinary method. Even then, their most virulent protests don't truly stem from that concern, but rather the huge annoyance that their parental authority might be distrusted, in itself. The payoff for this 'I'll protect and deal with my family and you protect and deal with yours' attitude, means other families that abuse their children to a far greater extreme are given masses of unconditional trust and respect. If more parents could only see how their insistence upon being the all-powerful ultimate authority within their family unit affects the countless children who live beyond their front doors, less children would be abused; many lives improved, and many saved.

Beyond a parent's obvious obligations, they can also gain massively by being more open about their difficulties and successes. Parents erect unconscious defences whereby they can publicly criticise their own child, but not talk about anybody else's. Further interest is rarely welcomed, but through our growing knowledge, maybe more support can be shared. As parents, we're often just at the point of breakthrough when we're at our most tormented by our kid's impossible demands, yet succeeding through the challenges our children bring us is an incredibly major element of our long term fulfilment. Perhaps the strongest motivational force of all is our exposure to the truth about abused children's lives. Through that, a more realistic perception of a child's true needs and vulnerabilities takes shape. As taboos and social barriers soften, a less rigid but more responsive, lighter and brighter form of authority and protection can naturally evolve.

Professionals Avoid Causing Offence

Professionals are the ones who are placed to hear more first disclosures of abuse than most, but it's a very difficult job. Parents and carers are compelled to be involved, but no matter their rank in society, parents can be very hostile, and block outside attempts to help the child with aggression or avoidance responses. Parents exert a degree of involuntary control over social workers, police, psychiatrists, psychologists, health care workers, teachers and policy makers. There's even a term, 'professional dangerousness' which describes the negative dynamics between professionals and parents that prevent the child's interests being understood as paramount. Professionals need to be fully informed about how child abuse dynamics work within a family group. That way, they can better prepare the work for the family concerned, and they don't fall into the trap of professional dangerousness.

Such is the climate of social ignorance though, that no matter how tactfully professionals address parents and child carers, strong primal protective instincts (in their positions as parents towards their own children especially) ensure that no further useful communication between the two camps can ensue. Is it worth risking the unnecessary upset and greater misunderstanding that might result from informing society as a whole about the realities and consequences of child abuse? Educating the masses is not really a psychiatrist's, a psychologist's, or a policeman's, or a social worker's job. It's only when the greater public better understand abusive behaviour and a child's need for protection that we'll all feel the influences of positive change.

Unconditional Love and Belonging

If you didn't suffer abuse that had any adverse effect upon you, you are very unlikely to instantly believe someone else in your family who did. Apart from the fact that abusers usually deny it, it's often easier for everyone else to reject these shocking ideas. Those with little knowledge of abuse will resist any de-valuing of the normality, safety and happiness of their original group. The 'love' mentioned in the heading above is not expressed as a surge of emotion or sentimentality, but expressed by actions of rejection or silence towards the abuse survivor. This rejection can be either instantaneous, or slow and progressive as the group's ongoing loyalty towards the abuser gets re-affirmed.

The source of this is unconditional love and loyalty. It seems just as true for an adult partner in relationship with an abuser who abuses one or more of their children, as it is for an unaffected sibling who grows up alongside their abused sister or brother. Most people in abusive roles appear to function normally. If you are not the abuse victim, and any member of the family group is accused of being an abuser, that can be very hard to bear. Just as you have a role like daughter, brother, aunt, husband, wife, grandchild, cousin or dependable family friend, likewise can an abuser. No matter how you are treated through infancy, your childhood perspective of love, and bonded links towards your main carer(s) is unconditional. This is true for all children, whether they become abuse targets or not. As we grow up, we're constantly fine-tuning our own unique place in the scheme of things and we cannot go back and re-live those years with different people.

Many families expect all its members to lead dutiful, considerate lives whereby the most dominant member's ideals must be fulfilled. It's just not customary to check out genuine feelings and true levels of individual happiness. Sometimes, keeping the family 'strong' by denying that any betrayal of trust could ever happen is the only available source of strength. There's a resistance to explore what abusive behaviour might be like in a completely different family. Fear of contamination halts any possible learning about how a whole variety of other families live. When the need to belong to a perfect family group overrides the need to listen to one or more of its suffering members, whole families can easily split up, and go through various periods of turmoil. Because of our ignorance, many abusers lead undetected lives. It is extremely uncommon for any abuser to either admit their crimes, or express any wish to make amends. It will take time for us to accept that this sort of behaviour can be a lot closer to home than we think.

What if it's all Lies?

We're so afraid to take the horror of abuse in that we obsess instead about what the survivor has to gain by lying. Many guard themselves against those who starve for attention, who may create malicious rumours to feed their manipulative obsessions. Why would anybody talk about such an ugly thing? Admittedly, it's natural to find all this too exhausting to pursue, but many stop right there. We don't explore patterns of abusive behaviour in anywhere as equal a measure as we doubt the words we're hearing. Is telling really such a cakewalk? What does a survivor really have to gain by telling?

What if we believe survivors? We fear the world and his wife will 'join in' making up stories. We'll become a weak society, floating around in a sea of compensation claims. But if you run scared before you listen, you're not likely to learn that there is life after exploring and accepting the reality of abuse. People do survive that knowledge, and children's and people's lives progress in a far safer way than they ever did before.

Opening Up the Doors

The good stuff that goes on in families is often just as well concealed as the bad, but perhaps it's a blessing that we are living in the age of reality TV. Through programmes like 'Wife Swap', the camera has adopted an encouraging role. Everyone knows someone with video technology, so most of us have seen ourselves on a 'TV' screen at home. As a society, we've opened our doors and seen ourselves from a new angle, and we can simply be taught what children's needs are by other families. We can open our eyes to the incredibly different journeys different childhoods actually are.

Social Taboo

Our ongoing education through the media has meant we can be quite frank and talk directly about all sorts of things in our private and public lives. Even so, the free love and sexual liberation going on in the sixties didn't prepare us for the advent of HIV and aids in the eighties. As soon as we knew sexual activity could kill, we broke through much of the stubborn pretentiousness that had restricted our conversation before. Parents don't encourage promiscuity and underage sex between adolescents, but many make sure their kids know where they can find a supply of condoms. They'd opt for health and life over and above morals, any day, and at least they haven't avoided the issue. Perhaps parents in particular are especially relieved that so much of what was once taboo, is now compulsory conversation.

You can't be prosecuted for taking part in most forms of adult sex in the UK where consenting partners are sixteen or over. Marriage is no longer the standard that allows sexual liberty. Today, families have changed whereby almost every other child has parents who no longer live together, and it's nice that we can enjoy the humour of, say, nailing up a placard with the words (of the French revolution) 'Liberty! Equality! Fraternity!' onto our bedroom doors. One component of European law filtered across to the UK workplace in the year 2000 when despite their resistance, the government was forced by the European Court of human rights to withdraw its ban on homosexuality in the military, enabling the British Navy to shed centuries of repression. In their partnership with the Armed Forces Lesbian and Gay Association, together with other gay expertise, Admirals, generals and air marshals are far more clued up about what the lives of gay men and women truly are. Old taboos got broken as both conventional and gay oriented representatives from all ranks stamped out old redundant policies and brought in the new. Personnel admit how disorientating it is looking back before these changes took place; they wonder what on earth all the struggle and fuss was about!

Taboos haunt society like ghosts, but our fears of losing a sense of respect for others and ourselves become groundless when matters are considerately and carefully addressed.

Respect

We now have more respect than ever for people with disabilities, people with diseases, chronic health issues and rare, previously misunderstood syndromes. With autism spectrum disorder, one in every one hundred and sixty may be affected. We could compare our quite substantial response to that, to how we address the one in eight who survive abuse. People are born with neurological differences, and it is right to make their lives as useful and fulfilling as possible, but abused children endure problematical environments they don't create. Without exception, they will suffer a diminished or damaged life as an adult. Clearly, we're interested in all those who were previously misunderstood, but with child abuse, we tend to adhere to the comfort of convention. We imagine the alternative is to rip private lives apart and cause irreversible upset that will fly back in our faces. There are many ordinary people around us who still carry suffering from the years through which we all pass. They have a great deal to teach us.

These days, children's environments are less oppressive, and the removal of corporal punishment in schools has prompted a massive revolution. Teachers are now mavericks of innovation, with new skills to command children's respect and maintain class control. Thousands of parents and child carers have shed the control that was exerted through violence and emotional abuse, and found a different way. But concerning how children often quietly suffer without our knowledge, we still have a lot to learn.

It comes back to the old thing of core attitude, in that those attitudes have sealed off sides of our children's lives that up to recent times, we haven't had any opportunity to see. Ironically, it's the ideals we picture upon the children we see around us that prevent us from seeing them as they really are. We forget to look out from within their child's world, and we forget that childhood is a universal vulnerability.

Psychoanalytical Convention versus Human Experience

Sociologists have been telling us for years how nobody is excluded from the fallout from child abuse, and collectively, most professionals expect the psychological proportion of the solution to be a substantial part of the answer. The use of psychology has widened considerably, and has been a positive influence upon many aspects of life and living. But through talking to abuse survivors, I've found psychology may not have helped ordinary people to talk about child abuse at all; in fact, it placed a highly influential chill over the entire process. This expertise has been used to damp down, contain and suppress what it is survivors have to say to society as a whole. Psychologists, mental health practitioners, and even those from the growing field of alternative healing arts claim to know the answers. But when the learning process of feeling, perception and thought increases awareness and therefore the prevention of abuse – abused children and the adults they become will no longer be an obscure, unquantifiable burden within our families and wider groups. Until ordinary people feel empowered enough to communicate about these issues, 'experts' may continue to form the greatest barrier of all.

How to Talk About Abuse

We haven't been exposed to much valuable conversation about child abuse, so of course we're not used to talking about it. It's difficult to even get started, knowing you can hurt and offend other people without meaning to. It takes time to learn how. Therefore, by just working these communication structures into your thinking, you may find ways to avoid suffering and causing offense.

Inside and Outside

Everyone should feel able to talk about abuse; after all, just being a human being should be reason enough. However, because of the way our culture has developed there are two different worlds. There is the inside world full of people whose lives have been hurt by abuse to the core, and the outside world of people, most of whom are unaware about how and why abuse actually occurs, and why so many are affected.

Some may call the 'outside' world conventional society, but it's any part of society where child abuse hides. It can take the form of one person, or groups of people in any shape or form who share certain understandings and beliefs. Those beliefs will result in child abuse being ignored, inadequately addressed, feared, and misunderstood.

The inside world of abuse is made up of countless secrets. Aspects of these secrets have peeped out in our culture in more recent years, but within the intimate realm of the family, or group of origin, these secrets lie dormant for years. Not necessarily being about sexual abuse, they can equally be to do with shameful aspects of emotionally manipulative victimisation, neglect and violence. These hidden experiences compound themselves into an extremely dynamic force over time, and stay within, packed together in a mire of raw, crude feeling. The wall that hides these feelings is largely of the survivor's making. It stands strung together with nerves, and it's threaded through with sensibility and fear, all orchestrated into an living wall of protection. This self made wall will involuntarily protect the survivor from themselves and their pasts. Likewise, it works intuitively on the outer world of indivduals, to protect them from these secrets as well.

When a survivor talks about their abuse they put themselves into a very vulnerable situation. Equally, people in the outside world can feel threatened when they are told about the 'dubious' suffering of a child they've suddenly become informed about so long after the event(s). A solid foundation of mutual respect and safety is the main component of constructive conversation, as well as an awareness of the important aspects as set out below. Those 'inside' and 'outside' worlds get referred to again under the headings that follow.

As opportunities open up for dialogue between these two worlds, we need to be patient. We need to give ourselves time to process the knowledge before us, as our understanding grows.

Who is Talking to Whom?

First thing's first. This book gives you a picture of survivor's lives, it is not primarily to give advice about talking to someone who has been in an abusive role, or how to

31

confront him or her. Safety issues are paramount, so it is never good sense to confront abusers if they have a history of violence, or severely emotionally abusive or manipulative behaviour. That subject is briefly brought up again further on in this part, under 'Denial', but from reading the stories, survivors and their friends can learn from other's experiences. They can consider confrontation issues and how they might go about approaching their abuser, if they wish.

Authority from the Inside

For a survivor on the 'inside', there are certain conditions that need to be respected before you communicate at all. You need to have the final word about what your experiences were in childhood, together with whatever you think or feel now as an adult. It's equally possible to maintain this authority whilst going through periods of self-questioning and self-doubt. Even when you are with someone who is helping you explore your past and perhaps at times challenging you, they have to respect your authority in having the final word.

Survivors can be drawn into periods of unnecessary pain even when alone, when they devalue and reject their own experiences out of hand. They may have allowed someone else's story to somehow either shrink their own suffering or enlarge it further. As your field of understanding expands, it's natural for there to be a period of re-adjustment whilst a new awareness (perhaps from another survivor's story) is being taken on or absorbed. It's quite possible to lose sight of yourself entirely, but this adjustment period whilst you've been exploring whole new ranges of events, concepts, contexts, thoughts and feelings is quite natural. Be wary of critical 'battles' about the severity of suffering between childhoods, even when one of them is your own.

Listening on the Outside

Some people believe only 'experts' should be allowed to listen to this sort of thing, yet many experts disagree and actually think most adults are capable enough. There is probably no better preparation for listening than reading the stories amongst these pages.

Whether you are another survivor on the 'inside', or someone new to it on the 'outside', it's good to reassure the survivor that you will not disclose their story to anybody else without their permission. You can offer this assurance at regular intervals, as you will need to make sure how comfortable the survivor is about various people knowing, and that can change. You'll need to be ready to adjust to those changes over time.

If you both know a third party who also knows, the survivor must give permission should you want to speak to them. The one exception is when you have sound reason to believe that the abuser is still actively abusing children. For the sake of protecting those children, you should waste no time in going to the authorities. As a citizen, you've been informed about a criminal act, and ultimately, even if they don't give you permission, you have a duty to safeguard children and must report it. Of course seek permission and try to provide a 'bridge' between the survivor and the professional who will act to protect the children. Should that scenario develop, both you and the survivor will need to seek support and understanding when the time comes.

With listening, we can lift the barrier between childhood and adulthood away, as 'testing the ground' is exactly how children often 'disclose'. Some professionals in the field call it 'drip feeding', when the child starts giving them clues, testing them out as listening adults to see whether they can hear them or not. The child assesses their response to see whether they are damaging their listener too much, and if they dare go further. If a child tells someone they love or like, then they are frightened to lose that person by scaring them away. The child will only continue if they feel safe, as will an adult too.

***Listen, ask questions, and offer acknowledgement by echoing back what was said. Open, and non leading questions are best. 'Tell me ..."Describe to me ..."Explain to me... facilitate the telling of the account. Once the open questions have led to a free narrative account, you can then ask non leading questions such as

"You told me he used a car ... what was it like...?' "You said it was clean, but with an odd sort of smell ... what did it smell like?

If you sense that those questions are too invasive, take a step back by saying something like,

"Do you want to take a break from this, or talk about other aspects ... like the places you went ... and the other things you did? We can leave this for another time if you'd like. How does that sound?"'

For all kinds of reasons it's sometimes very hard for a survivor to talk, but they may still want to. Another technique is to give a survivor or a child a cassette recorder and they speak to it in private. When you meet again, you will be able to acknowledge what you understood from the tape, and help the survivor speak further if they wish. When, Where, How and What questions add to information already given, and add to the clarity of the account. A question, asked with an open mind for any answer at all, is always far better than a conclusive judgement. The questionnaire on page **48** can be used as a resource to cover areas of life experience the survivor wants to discuss.

Diagnosis

Everybody is on a learning curve in these realms, and many are touched by abuse either as co–survivors (ie. those who are in any sort of relationship with a survivor) or more indirectly. It is therefore invasive and destructive to express some sort of 'diagnosis' or practice amateur psychoanalysis on a survivor.

***Quick note for Child Protection Purposes*

A proactive protective adult can usually establish quite quickly whether abuse might be happening to a child. They are there to provide a calm, caring but non–frightening response to the child. Knowing their limitations as a non–professional, they will not have sufficient skill to establish exactly what abuse occurred. They therefore write down whatever the child told them as soon as possible, and keep it in case it is required as evidence. Next, they guide the child towards a specialised child protection social work and/or police unit. Both child and proactive protector can get support via Childline (the NSPCC) in the UK. The proactive protector can maintain moral support should that child need to go through legal processes, and then again continue to watch over the child after those processes are over.

The best communicators know the most powerful and enlightening skill of all is simply listening. Follow the speaker by asking relevant questions, and offer a word or phrase of acknowledgment based on empathetic response. There are at least ten different ways to ask one question, and there again, every question has to have its own context. Actively listening to a reply builds upon the mutual knowledge that is already there. Closely echoed acknowledgments with a question here and there, are better than conclusive judgments.

What Language to Use when you talk about Child Sexual Abuse

We are not describing the intimate sexual acts of some private adult relationship; but talking about a criminal event that happened to a child, and there is a world of difference between the two. Other cultures in Europe reveal far more in the press and media about how children are sexually abused in a quite a matter of fact way. The public acknowledge it one to another in an empathetic way, much as we might acknowledge the details and consequences of a mugging or a murder case.

To talk about child sex, most of us feel that we have to skirt around what we really want to say, mainly to accommodate the listener and not to offend. This results in such ambiguity, that the listener has no more permission to hear the truth than the speaker has to speak it. There is no need to force ourselves to speak in this sort of detail if we don't want to, but there are aspects to our own liberty that should at least offer us the choice. Different situations call upon the truth to be said to varying degrees. A police officer will gradually go into a lot of detail over a period of several hours and possibly days, and a first disclosure can be extremely hard work. Many survivors keep these more intimate details away from their families, especially if home was the 'scene of the crime'. That conscious choice has to be respected.

If we choose to go further, we can prepare the listener by warning them that we are going to talk frankly about how a child was hurt sexually, and ask their permission to speak openly. When that permission is granted, you can then negotiate what sort of language you want to use. When professionals like social workers, police, therapists and health care workers interview children, they say,

'You can use any words you want to in this room, even words not allowed at home and school.' This principle works equally well with adults too, so long as speaker and listener both agree.

With either children or adults, they may not disclose something because they think the words are 'rude' or unacceptable. Terms can be clarified. Eg. If a child speaks of their 'minnie' the child has to clarify what that means, and thereafter the listener continues to speak with the child using the child's own word. When the listener uses the same language, perhaps by respectfully repeating part of what they just heard, they automatically empower the speaker to use that language. Universally, we all know what 'bad language' is. As long as we know what the words actually mean, either the anatomical or the slang words that describe our bodies are equally good. They can be cross-referenced and clarified just as they are in any court of law.

We are living in a new era where society is teaching itself to speak out about these matters. These criminal acts that invaded our childhoods were harmful, but if they are not clearly stated, we will continue to handicap ourselves with self–imposed foggy ambiguities that in the end, will serve no one. With the 'Survivors' Stories' project, when participants saw the rationale behind going into intimate detail, they simply did so. Throughout that phase of writing there were shifting phases of numbness, anger and grief, but there was no sense of losing anything of our humanity. The question is 'Do our bodies belong to us, or to those who secretly abuse children?' Talking and writing about what happens to children takes some bravery, and it's a courageous way for survivors to take back their own bodies, the territory that should rightfully and unashamedly belong to them.

We're Unique

Growing up is all about living through a mixture of good and bad experiences that may have lasted for minutes or days, or gone on repeating for years. Events per se may 'agree' with similar events in another childhood, but each person has proportions and combinations of experience within certain surroundings and circumstances. Everyone experiences everything in their own way, so ultimately each experience has to be totally unique. Each member from within the same family will have individual and unique memories of the same event. One detailed account that applies to every member of any group simply cannot exist. It cannot be emphasised strongly enough how separately we need to hold and respect each childhood, in order understand it.

The Comparison Trap

When communicating with other people you may feel like 'counting' levels of suffering from one childhood to another, as if you were quantifying the time spent suffering, as well as the nature and degree of whatever that suffering was. Within courts of law, cases are given differential weighting in order to arrive at a sum of money for compensation, or come to a decision about sentencing. In terms of money paid out between differing civil cases, and the number of years in prison or the complete lack of them, even these judgments don't exist within an equal and consistent judicial result overall. The justice system performs a certain role, and operates in a different situation from our collective interpersonal understanding of abuse and its effects. As you find out more, you'll see how abuse testimonies can exist side by side and still enlighten us, without measuring one amount of suffering against another.

Any form of child abuse at whichever end of the spectrum is damaging. Abuse associated with violence that involves betrayal of trust from a relative or primary care giver, or extends over time is generally defined as more severe in impact. Put bluntly, one form of abuse should never trivialise any other, because *any form of abuse is harmful.*

Comparing 'severities' often parades itself as an expression of deep concern and interest, where people want to display an earnest desire to learn and understand. You can't sort out a selection of childhoods by putting them into their right 'boxes', and I sometimes intuit that this need to categorise serves to prevent people from feeling. Doing that doesn't change people's lives, and it only beguiles us with a false impression of getting some sort of control. Nevertheless I have seen many a survivor get sucked in to conversations that attempt all this, and all that results is an unconscious erosion of respect towards each survivor as an individual.

Admittedly it's very confusing how on the one hand it is good to compare, and on the other it isn't. You are allowed to compare the circumstances and events from one story to another in any way you want except one thing; you must not compare or quantify the survivor's subjective pain and suffering. When 'patches' of someone's childhood are hung up alongside someone else's 'patch', feelings can become trivialised. At the same time, comparing childhoods by discussing their content is an invaluable educational tool and it does help you get perspective. But it's not only the childhood that needs exploration, because a survivor's childhood provides the circumstances for their adult years.

For example one woman endured horrendous suffering as a child from multiple abusers, that her mother knew nothing about. As an adult, things were disclosed to the mother gradually over a phase of several years. They both came to terms with it together and now enjoy a good relationship. Another woman endured what appears to be far less suffering as a child, but when she told her family, she was cut off and branded a liar. This survivor is no longer welcome in the house she grew up in, and she told me how much it pains her because her children miss their granny and their other relatives so much. She doesn't know what on earth she should tell her children when they are older. From this example, perhaps you can see how hard it is to know how much subjective pain is endured.

Sexual Orientation

People sometimes jump to odd conclusions about a survivor's sexual development and orientation. That again is for the survivor to decide upon. It's true that it may be useful to hear other survivor's experiences and beliefs about how their sexuality developed, but any discussion about bi-sexual, and homosexual versus heterosexual development and where the deciding factor came in, is little more than a chicken and egg discussion. Some survivors are asexual and prefer to have no sexual relationships at all, or long periods without relationship. Whatever their past, people have a right to celebrate whatever their adult sexual choices are without external judgments and conclusions. It's their own private matter. Keep the context safe; it is for he or she who is exploring his or her own story to have the final answers; to make their own conclusions and have their conclusions respected.

FROM THE INSIDE

If you are a survivor, parts of this text may not fit in with your background and circumstances. All the same, I hope you may find some benefit in the basic insights laid out below.

Abandonment

For a survivor, the one feeling that acts as the foundation upon which all other feelings rest, is abandonment. It's like a mundane backdrop that's been central to their whole life. It's not difficult to see why, as when they were growing up their abuser(s) were playing a charade of denial; that the abuse wasn't happening, or that it was, and had to be a secret no matter what, or lastly, that everyone knew, but nobody cared. In most cases, all the adults known to the child are involved in a charade. When the victim grows up their truth still has no place, but at last this social convention is beginning to ease. Just as listeners are practicing to listen, survivors are practicing to talk.

Telling

Most survivors reach a stage when their understanding of what happened to them becomes magnified, and they feel compelled to let it out. There is a cyclical process that periodically returns throughout their lifetime, whereby new insights pop up in between various stretches of time. These surface with the fuller understanding that only comes with maturity, in adulthood.

Survivors' thoughts and feelings gravitate towards the very people who demonstrated care and support towards them as children. For most that means family, but for others it means foster carers, or the staff who worked in children's homes and the authorities that employed them. For the rest it's the staff in detention centres and boot camp type establishments for teenagers run by the Home Office and the government. It is whoever had the power to care for them and protect them that will cross their minds most of all.

If the same crimes had happened to them as an adult, their communities would be outraged, and respond with care and concern. But when these same crimes happen during childhood because of a perpetrator within their family circle, their community, or within the institution that surrounded them they are often neither believed nor supported. For the survivor, this signifies an immense betrayal.

Confidentiality equals External Control

Other feelings of betrayal can happen in unexpected ways. From Jim's Story number 3, after a couple of drinks in a pub, Jim told a close friend for the first time. This friend passed the story around, which put pressure on Jim to tell his family well before he felt ready.

Some survivors are sick of the social silence about child abuse, as it keeps it firmly on the 'inside', and they hate the whole idea of confidentiality. I respect that view, but even if confidentiality doesn't feel like an issue now, it can well become an issue later. Generally, it is never wise to talk about matters from your own childhood or hand around something you've written willy nilly, unless the respondent understands how harmful it could be to talk about your story to someone else without your prior knowledge and permission.

If you ever decide to write or record your story, however cavalier or controlled you may feel about it, is it okay if your kids or anybody else at all finds a tape, a computer file or papers about your story and reads or listens to it? You need to think about every possible consequence of not keeping all that private. You may need to think about good hiding places that change, or keeping your info under lock and key. With emails or documents on computer, you might need to think about printing them out and deleting them from the system. You might need to change your computer password regularly, maybe even daily.

Working with your truth by putting it down on paper really helps, because it's like 'telling', yet you are in control of the paper until you feel ready to share what's on it. This goes for other media as well.

Secondary Abuse and Surviving It

Many survivors hold the most important people from their childhood in a sort of 'fantasy scenario'; they stand, waiting in line whilst time stands still. The moment each one hears the truth there is a gunshot, and one after the other they fall to the ground. When the victim tells, it is they who are blamed for a devastation they did not actually cause. Most commonly, everyone looks back to the victim as the source of upset, as if it was them who was 'holding the gun' when they became injured with the truth. Once disclosed, there is no going back.

That's what sustaining secondary abuse is all about, and many a survivor has taken the job of telling squarely upon their own shoulders, and through no fault of their own suffered enormous loss because of the backlash they got. Inevitably, once the family know, that original group can never ever be quite the same again.

Family groups go into shock, and then start to feel angry and confused for being denied a future of solid, straightforward relationship. They feel the previous lives they once shared slipping away out of control. Many react in a flash without even knowing what they are feeling, or why. Each one in the group is challenged because of the shared history of trust with the abuser. It is very difficult for any family circle to see how even accepting the truth can ever be a part of any future.

Reactions – the reason you need Support

Firstly, family members experience either immediate or delayed shock. They feel shamed and isolated, as it's unlikely they know any other families who have been through any scenario like this one. Instantaneous rage and anger often flare up, and members get consumed by blame and disagreement. Even when responses appear relatively mild, family members often form into two or three separate alliances. The abuser usually denies it, therefore some side with the abuser, and some with the survivor.

When the violation of one or more children is revealed, that child's group cannot avoid sharing exactly the same feelings of shame and violation. To avoid that pain, it's quite common to become numb, adopt a facade of 'strength' and dish out a wide spectrum of control strategies, ranging from giving advice to the survivor, to blaming the survivor for upsetting the equilibrium of the family. The survivor often leaves the situation laden down with a whole rucksack full of 'shoulds', which spring from the belief that when the survivor learns to handle their past differently, the situation will get better for everyone else.

The idea that each member of the original group needs to question what it was in their thinking, their actions, their attitudes and their feelings that caused the care and protection around the child victim to fail is still a very new one for most families. If the whole family decide to deal with the situation alone without outside support, many members of the group could be in for an entire lifetime of estrangement and separation. Years down the line, they can still be entrenched in the positions they first took seconds after they were told. Healing from this violation is never an overnight process. It takes months and years to process the abuse, or the alleged abuse, and for trust to be slowly rebuilt. To get a new, and healthier perspective upon the family's shared lives once again, it will take time and patience.

Denial

In most cases, the person in the abusive role denies the abuse. So how does that affect the survivor's right of place within their original group? In one case I heard of, the survivor wrote to the abuser before telling any family member about their abuse. Many counsellors and therapists encourage letters to abusers in order to explore survivor's feelings, but this was completely different.

In this confidential letter, the abuser was offered the opportunity to tell the family about what had happened, and to make amends. They were asked to seek out some rehabilitation and specialised therapy for themselves. They were also asked to contribute towards the survivor's healing, by paying for counselling, therapy and life coaching, plus asked to pay for family therapy when the time finally came to tell the whole group.

Why would a survivor do such a thing when obviously, they should just go to the police? In many cases, the Crown Prosecution Service will not prosecute because of the Limitation Act, or insufficient evidence. Each survivor is different, and this one wanted to protect themselves from the trauma of going to court. So they wrote to their local Multi Agency Public Protection Panel – MAPPP (you can get their contact details via your local library). This panel is chaired by a Detective Chief Inspector, and is responsible for protecting the community from child sex abusers and people with a known history of violence. They also wrote to the child protection team in social services.

Admittedly, this survivor is unusual, but what shone out from their unique idea, was their sense of self respect and self awareness. But they didn't get to that stage alone. It had taken them months of talking through what they might do within their own support system before they felt clear and courageous enough about what to do, when to do it and why.

They waited for a reply from that letter, and it never came. What followed were two weeks of telephone conversations from the abuser about it not being 'the right time'. The survivor simply had to tell their family in the end because they wanted to ensure their nephews and nieces were safe. The abuser then disappeared from the family and said he would never come back. At that stage, the survivor finally went to the police. After three months, the police decided to take no action.

On an emotional level for this survivor, this was a struggle at almost every stage. Their requests for payments towards counselling and so on were never met, but as the children became safer within the family unit, that was all that mattered. Every case is unique, and at no stage did anybody know what would happen next. Each and every situation turns out in its own way, as a result of each and every single person's reactions.

Positive Image

Society holds very few images or visions of families who face up to having an abusive member, overcome it, grow and change through the experience and become happy again, but these families do exist. Members who accept that abuse has happened become co-survivors, and these co-survivors often need support too. Support is available and out there, but not many have the courage to explore it.

When I asked survivors to read these guidelines for feedback before publication, they told me to write more supportive words for the 'outsiders', in that they need to take care of themselves too. If you are a survivor and your listener knew you when you were a child, you may reach a stage when you can share thought and consideration towards the people that you both knew and loved, and still know today.

Who and Why

For many a survivor, it's a necessary kind of healing to tell, mostly for reasons personal to themselves. Everyone knows the safest person to tell is a counsellor or therapist because of their rules of professional conduct and confidentiality. Hopefully that counsellor will be able to explore the 'why' of telling the most significant people, long before a survivor actually chooses to tell. But often a counsellor may not know how to prepare them for the wide range of reactions and eventual outcomes which could ensue.

Quite apart from the natural wish to unburden yourself, why choose Uncle Raymond? Why choose mum instead of dad or vice versa? Why choose brother Paul? Why best friend Karen? Why *that person* in particular? As a result of your disclosure, do you have an expectation of warmth, with increased mutual insight, and closer ongoing support? Each person will have a greater or lesser emotional charge from within each unique relationship. The consequences of telling are life long, and vast. Telling can easily attract more abuse and condemnation, which happens especially with families and groups of origin. If respondents split off into separate groups, you are likely to have very little control over these groups and how they develop their thinking in your absence. Also, whether your respondent is an individual or an institution (like a school, a club or a foster home) the difference is minimal when it comes down to the true nature of response.

How honest can you be with yourself about what your needs and expectations are? This alone may take a few weeks of reflection, and it is very difficult to examine your expectations on your own. Your telling may bring about a more guarded, more superficial relationship with your respondent, with mutual insight suddenly erased, and your respondent withdrawing any previous support. To know how your respondent will respond, you will have to know them a great deal better than they already know themselves.

People you knew you over your childhood years are particularly difficult to tell. Child abuse upsets different people in different ways, and any initial support you may or may not get back after your disclosure can change and vary. This happens even within the deepest bonds. For example, if your respondent expresses interest in child abuse issues in TV or a magazine, that doesn't mean they will be interested in your life experience of it. They may find all that way too personal, because of what you mean or represent to them in the first place. They might be so shocked, that you will lose them and not be able to continue talking to them (or they with you) for quite some time. Any family member who had no idea about this before may be so devastated by the news that they can hardly deal with it themselves, never mind think about your needs. Many resist the whole idea because of their attachments with the abuser and abuser's other alliances.

Your Comfort

With the sharing of your story comes your responsibility for your own comfort. If the atmosphere changes and things get tense; just stop talking. It's true that talking about this isn't easy anyway, but listen to your body and your internal signals. If you feel there's a wall between you and your respondent, allow yourself to take notice. Give yourself permission to say that you don't feel comfortable if you feel over–vulnerable and unsure.

"I had wanted to bring something up, but I've changed my mind."

"Never mind, I think I'll just drop it; I'll leave it for another time."

Most people would express some warmth or acknowledgment to that in some way, so if they don't, remember you are the one who is in control. When you meet again you can remind them what you were talking about before, and gage their response again. If they seem disinterested and keep changing the subject, you can 'score them off your list'. You can find ways to take care of you, so that you can withdraw and wait, or be choosier about whom you share your story with.

If some sort of battle ensues, with a competitive atmosphere whereby your respondent is fighting for more importance than you, that's just not conducive to the vulnerable position you are in. When their needs are greater than yours without any balanced give and take, you are just not going to be heard.

Be Prepared with Support

Most survivors have such strong patterns of self reliance, resilience and independence, that they might mistake their strength for isolation. They don't know how strong and independent they really are compared to other people, and often prefer to do things by themselves. As a survivor, you are not likely to be able to offer any sustainable support towards those you have to tell, unless you've already found some yourself.

If you are a survivor who hesitates to look for support, what does the concept actually mean to you? If you have decided to tell your family or your original group, *why on earth should you do this on your own?* You are strongly advised to explore as many avenues of support that you can before you go ahead. Getting support isn't necessarily about being in a desperate state with suicidal feelings, or feeling unbearable loneliness. It's about sharing and widening your experience with someone for a short time, then returning back to yourself enabled to go on in an easier, more enlightened way. Should you decide to start telling your friends and family a more truthful account of your childhood, it's practical to cultivate say, three, four or more sources of support to fall back on if you feel things are starting to go wrong.

41

Communicating about abuse gets easier with practice, whether you are on the inner world, or the outer. There are people and organisations you can contact, set up especially to provide a place where survivors can just be themselves. In the UK, Napac runs an information database that you can access v.ia the Internet on http://www.napac.org.uk/. Currently, their helpline number is **0800 085 3330**.

There are different ways of telling, and they all need to be considered in detail. Ideally, it is good if there is a support person for both the survivor and their families or loved ones, and support can take many different forms. Some forms of support feel more natural; some will be completely foreign and almost uncomfortable at first. One survivor who recently got support told me it was like walking from 'A' to 'B' in a pair of size three shoes, but then when they got to 'B', 'B' knew somebody else they could really relate to. For example many people may never have discussed anything like this with their local doctor, and doctors vary considerably in their knowledge and response, but one doctor who knows very little may know someone else, or some organisation that can respond with far more knowledge. Some people who almost never write letters may get help with writing to their family ... but even then ... why must any letter come *solely* from the survivor?

As you grow through the support you receive, in your own unique way you will become more fully present inside your own 'skin'. It is you who makes the choice about which people you are willing to explore this new sort of relationship with. In putting your abuse experiences into words and sentences for the first time, you might like to try being in touch with support on the Internet and there are many various Internet sites you can use under a pseudonym. If you want to try professional help, there are sources but you will need to give yourself a few months to find professionals who are either survivors themselves, or are counsellors or therapists with professional supervision. These professionals would have to have extensive experience with abuse survivors or significant experience within their own personal lives. You do not have to be directly involved in therapy or counselling; however if you already are or just starting, it is good to show this book to your therapist or counsellor, and talk its relevance over with them.

Confusion

With or without support, the number of years you spent with your respondent whilst you were growing up is no measure of how able they are to hear you.

When you do tell your story, at that stage they may feel so numb with shock that it may be impossible for your respondent to even be aware of whether they are even interested or not. It may have never once occurred to them before, and they may go into a very blank state. They can also become quite upset, or convey that child abuse issues in your life are distasteful to them. The significance of whoever it is that is listening can denote vast differences (sometimes expressed, sometimes astoundingly silent and incomprehensible) between one person's reaction and another's. Those reactions may put you under a strain and an obligation to do or say something more, whereby you can find yourself on very rocky ground, and landed in a communication process you aren't prepared or ready to get engaged in.

Looking out from the survivor's world, other people's reactions can make them feel a great deal. For example, a survivor is quite often firstly listened to, and then the next time they bring the subject up their respondent gets 'amnesia', and behaves like they are hearing everything for the first time. This subtle form of denial is not uncommon, and there are many more forms of denial than that.

Naturally this can prompt anger, perhaps frustration that it is you who's is in the wrong again, that it is you who always has to make the effort to make everything okay again, when you've been doing that anyway all your life. Ironically, the things that actually happened to you as a child were anything but okay. The outside world can be sometimes appear to be incapable of understanding why your words might even be important, but that doesn't by any means translate that you are unimportant. What you have to say is far too big for them to conceptualise and take in.

From your world on the inside, you're in the middle of such a painful process that you can lose sight of what it is you are even trying to do. What you're doing is picking abusive events up, gathering them altogether and bringing them back to their source. It is not very likely that you will get much thanks for doing so, and that's why a wide variety of support is so important.

Put simply, support is putting yourself in a different situation, where you do not have to hide. What would this look like for you? It could include one or two friends, a survivor's Internet chat room, whatever pastoral care or preferred spiritual healing you have the courage to pursue, a survivor's group of some sort, a few books, and some telephone helplines. All these sources will offer different forms of support with varying opinions and thoughts. For a multi-dimensional problem, you will need multi-dimensional support from those who have a simple open willingness to support you, each in their own way.

Right and Wrong

At some stage, a simple moral belief that your respondent should know that something wrong happened when you were a child can't always remain buried. It becomes a matter of setting the balance straight, to redress your innate sense of simple moral justice. But the very reason you need to be careful and prepared with whoever you share your story with, is you could be opening yourself up for further abuse.

You could be on the way to a phase of disappointment, and it's quite possible you may never really get the sense of how any injustice from the past is even being taken in. Indeed you might feel taken aback when despite other positive aspects of sharing within this relationship, with the abuse there's little more than an inexplicable void. Perhaps a difficult phase awaits, when happier, more positive aspects of your shared past will become temporarily banished or distorted in your memory. Even when you've carefully thought about it, at the point of speaking there are no instant answers. The consequences of your disclosure might end in a chaotic muddle, and certainly won't look pretty.

Nevertheless, when you feel stronger at a later stage you can go back and express your sadness in having had to share something so appalling. Make the point that abusers who victimise one or two members from one family actually abuse every member of that family. Make it clear that it wasn't you who originally started the hurt or even caused it, but that it's an injury that needs to be sourced, recognized and acknowledged. The consequences of telling are not simple, and processing whatever happens afterwards can take weeks, months or years.

Preparing the Ground Behind You

Sometimes it takes the greatest amount of courage to see that your respondent just isn't interested, and telling undoubtedly fails. No matter how significant they were throughout your past, or how significant they are now, you'll have to accept that this is one issue that cannot be shared. Often the only thing you can do is step backwards and just let the matter go. Hoping that things will change can be a bit of a fool's errand, but there is still something you can do.

You can put the onus on them to contact you. Give them the option to either bring up the subject or not, and tell them you will be willing to talk about it whenever they are ready. It doesn't mean that you've failed, you can still fall back on the support you've already created, and prepare more ground in front of you by linking up with other people who are more open to these issues.

FROM THE OUTSIDE

Hold the Thread

For survivors, there's often a sense of relief shortly after releasing the truth. But survivors' feelings of abandonment tend to escalate, especially shortly after their first disclosure. For them, it actually feels like they don't have any skin. It gets worse if after a week or a few days, their confidante appears to abandon the subject. They often feel self remorse, like they should have known to keep it quiet, and they feel oppressed by the bad atmosphere all around them. It's therefore good to say something like ...

'You know, I do still sometimes think about what you told me the other week. I really do feel for you.'

'I haven't forgotten what you told me about what happened when you were a kid, but I just don't always know whether you want to talk about it or not.'

'I know what you told me about is really important to you. It is to me too, and there's probably a lot I still don't know. Maybe over time, we'll both find it easier to talk about it.'

Recognise it's an ongoing process, and you don't have to fix anything or solve any problems at all, you can simply somehow express your respect for the individual you're listening to. The discussion may develop over what could be a series of talks over a period of time; and just as the survivor needs to think about their needs, you also need to think about yours.

Listener's Care

You can express your feelings, and say whenever it's too much if you need to take a pause, or you need time to absorb what's being said. You may need a few days to increase your knowledge elsewhere (for example via books, other people, help lines or the Internet) in readiness to talk further. If you find yourselves fixed in a steely silence, you can speak about the silence, ask questions to see if there's a willingness to continue. You can simply hold the thread, and trust that there may well be a later date when it will be easier to go on. In the days that follow, if you do find yourself thinking about the survivor and their past, you can tell the survivor simply that. You can share your feelings, like shock, or anger, or confusion, or compassion, indeed whatever is true for you. Apart from the abuse and its affects, there are many other aspects about the survivor's life where you can keep going with your particular thread of friendship, interest and moral support.

Shared Impact - Shared Telling

Support people and aware co-survivors deeply understand that when an abuser abuses a victim, they hurt the entire circle of potential protectors and carers who were watching over the child whilst s/he was growing up. Those with long bonds of relationship with the child are also victims. They were fooled, and any trust, and any relationship they had with the abuser is shattered. Support people recognise how like a death this is. It's the death of trust, the death of a whole range of positive human progress and relationship – all gone in an instant. It's like the family photograph album got ripped apart, and in the aftermath the concepts of happiness and security within this circle can't be put back like before. When the time is right later on, it will have to be built up in a different, and new way.

Therefore, someone trusted by both the family and the survivor can take on the role of support messenger. I know some survivors who at an early stage of disclosure brought a supportive friend or representative along for a short family visit. If everyone present has given their permission in advance, it's possible for a non family member, like someone from some supportive organisation or other to be there at the first disclosure, or soon afterwards. Just being present as a gesture of respect and acknowledgment towards each person and their feelings, can be invaluable. Anyone with knowledge of abuse and how it affects families can make a difference. There are a growing number of charities in the UK which may have volunteers willing to find a helping role in these situations. When professionals already involved in pastoral care, social work, in community centres, and those connected to schools and places of further education become better informed about how these disclosures affect families, they could increasingly fulfill this need and perform a more active and supportive role.

Difficult Feelings

To varying degrees, survivors need to live through periods of anger and grief before they can come to terms with their inner and outer worlds. At times they feel outraged for the misuse of power that continually victimised them in childhood. In their more intimate relationships, their friends or partners can easily become the catalyst for these feelings. Times may get chaotic, whereby as listener you feel like a sort of punch bag. It is perfectly okay to call a halt to this, 'step outside' and try to see the situation more objectively. After some clear and careful thought, you can declare where your own boundary lies. It is not okay for the dynamics of abuse to be reenacted, and you can assert your own ideas about the importance of your safety and comfort when you are together. Within the give and take of relationship, a safe place for each of you as an individual has got to be one condition for happiness.

Many are brought up to think grief is a luxury that must be denied, but there may also be times when a survivor needs to reach out to someone close and express how their god given innocence was used and betrayed. An abused child cannot cry as a child for what they lost, as it's only a person's adult understanding that can recognise the whole truth of so many aspects of loss.

For those able and ready let go, grief can be a profound teacher. Enabling this natural release to happen can enrich an existing foundation of intimacy, and the periods of shared grief could ripple on for periods of weeks or months, as your relationship strengthens and develops. There may be phases where anger and grief merge, and dissolve into one another, but just maintaining a simple respectful openness to witness such intimate truth can really help to heal a survivor's life. Through 'holding' someone, and sometimes holding them literally in your arms, you can heal levels of self–esteem in a far deeper place than could ever otherwise have been reached.

Groups

Whenever groups set themselves up especially for the purpose of supporting each other by using the questionnaire in this book to write or record their stories, they'll gain a great deal from the process. Like the comments mentioned above under 'Difficult Feelings', it's important to remember abuse is an abuse of power; hence it's important not to bring any bad group dynamics (from the backgrounds group members originated from) into the group processes. An active willingness to nurture, and do whatever it takes to maintain a deep sense of personal safety is extremely important. Each and every person will need to declare how safe and secure s/he feels firstly as an individual, and secondly in relation to the group at regular intervals.

Confidentiality will be imperative, and a group member who slips up just once may well find out how just one small disclosure can transform itself into a malicious rumour going on outside the group. Either one member or the entire group can end up feeling victimised, as suddenly gossip pulls them into a situation they can't control.

Refining ways of listening that enable telling will be the main pathway upon the group's learning curve as a whole. The courage and sensitivity of the other group members around you will help to guide and gage your own sense of pace, as you begin to vocalise the things you really need to express.

If you choose to do a writing project within a group or with a partner, throughout the time you are developing your story, allow yourself plenty of time and space. Sometimes when new things come up it's better to keep them to yourself for a few days rather than divulge everything at once. Again, putting it down on paper is like 'telling', yet you are in control of the paper until you feel ready to share. Talking to tapes and playing them back can be helpful too, but you may not feel ready to play your tape to a whole group! Choosing a partner to work with within the group often works well.

Sometimes keeping things to yourself isn't important, but sometimes it is. If you're not sure whether it is or it isn't, just assume that it is, and you'll feel that much better and more secure throughout the process of writing, recording, and perhaps sharing your story.

Apology

Just like everyone, many survivors are so busy getting on with their lives that they rarely focus on the deeper level, of how their true right of place in the world simply vanished. Most adjusted to this life a very long time ago. When they were children almost everyone living in their external world failed to protect them, and later on as adults they are rarely understood. For a survivor to be greeted with silence is understandable, but we must move through this pause in our understanding because there is far more that has to be said.

Whoever you are in relationship to a survivor, it is good to state some sort of apology using any words of your choice. People don't always instantly understand why I say that, but the mere fact that a survivor is exposing this part of their lives for you to hear, means that you form a very privileged and important part of their external world. Of course, you personally may have had nothing to do with their abuse, but no matter how they appear to behave or communicate, for sure, they are touching upon their pain.

Comments like,

'I'm sorry to hear that that could happen to a vulnerable child.'

'That was wrong, that should never have happened to you.'

'I only wish I could have known, I would have done something.'

'It's outrageous that these things happen to children, it really upsets me to hear that this happened to you.'

... all come from the heart, and offer a far more down to earth type of healing than months of therapy ever could.

Getting it Right

Humans are rarely one hundred percent perfect at communication, so not to worry, the accidental transgression of ground rules that ban judgment, comparison and 'therapisation' of one another are almost bound to occur. Wherever it does happen, a simple apology and gesture of standing back is the most fitting thing to do.

When they feel ready, survivors need to talk about their abuse and bring it into the open, and they don't always remember to get ground rules right either ... even between themselves. Between survivors on the 'inside', it's not uncommon for one to find it hard to understand another's situation, at least at first. Even so, when it comes to having the opportunity to break the cycle of abuse and abandonment, survivors are grateful whoever they are speaking to. Both speakers and listeners will learn from their mistakes along the road and with practice, a very special bond of healing will gradually materialise.

For all kinds of groups of people willing to go the distance, inner and outer worlds begin to overlap as truer insights begin to erode previous divisions. As our capacities to listen, learn and express ourselves gradually widen, we meet new friends on this journey and find the power to strengthen old friendships further. We are establishing a foundation upon which a stronger, more authentic realm of human relationship can rest.

As you flip through these pages, you may instinctively find relevant aspects in your own life and relationships.

The Questionnaire

This is the questionnaire that was written to broaden and define the testimonies of survivors who contributed to these volumes. Its purpose was never to gather statistical information, and in some places it may even seem biased or leading in its influence upon survivors' accounts. However, its very purpose is to enable a survivor to tell their story in a society that rarely allows them that privilege. It was created as a tool, to stimulate a survivor's awareness of how abuse played its part in their lives.

Writing Your Story

Should you decide to write your story, this questionnaire is a starting point to get going. You can record your story on tape, write it down with pen and paper, type it onto your computer screen, make films or video clips, indeed do all or any combination of these things. Not all the questions will 'fit' your unique personal history, so if you feel a question is unnecessary and there's no need to answer it, go on to the next. If you find you've already given an answer to a question in another way, then skip that question too. If you find there's no question that asks you about a point that you feel is important, then just make your own point, express it and say whatever it is that you want to say. The questionnaire is your servant, not your master.

Please take as much time as you need to reflect on the questions where necessary. If you can imagine the path of your life as a circular spiral winding outwards from the centre; deep and powerful memories tend to overlap and merge at certain areas of the bigger pattern. We can't be with all our memories all the time because we have to get on with our lives. Quite a lot of the information you will need for your story will seem quite superficial, yet even small superficial details from the past spark a connection to the bigger, more important memories.

The questionnaire is in four parts:

PART ONE is to do with the kind of surroundings you grew up in right from the time that you were a tiny baby. It's about what it was like for you at home, at school, going out to clubs, doing sports while you were growing up. It's mostly about the behaviour that happened towards you at home in front of the other people there, and in more public places, like your school or anywhere else at all that you went to outside your home.

PART TWO is about the secret abuse you suffered in private, behind a closed door. This may also be abuse that often happened in front of your family group, but never in public. It's about the stuff you were very afraid to tell anybody else about.

PART THREE is about your adult life today. It has few questions, and is something that you can create and add to as much as you like.

PART FOUR (if relevant to you) is about your experiences in getting help from the world of psychiatry, therapy and healing; and how you feel about getting professional help today.

Some say that testimonies of abuse are often very similar. That may be so, but only in a general way. Your feelings, your circumstances, your responses and your decisions and the combination of all these things and more over time, really are totally unique.

PART ONE

The Grown-Ups Around You, and Your Home

1   How many people lived in the building that you grew up in? Can you describe them eg. parents/brothers/sisters/relatives/friends of the family.

- Please give them names (you can choose to make it their real names or not, whichever makes it easier for you to talk about them) and ages, so that your age and the age gaps between people are clear.

2   Who were the people you would describe as your major carers, who would protect you and usually covered your simple physical needs for a place to eat, keep warm, live safely and sleep?
- (eg Mum, Dad, older sibling or relative – who?)

3   When your were growing up, did you move house a lot, or did you spend many years in the same house? How many different addresses did you have in the end?

- If you did move, how old were you each time when you had to adjust to a new environment/group of new people?

4   How big was the house/were the houses you lived in? How many rooms were there?

Control, Discipline, Punishment
(in an ordinary environment, whether inside or outside the home)

Think back to when you were quite small (when you spent most of your time tilting your head back, looking right up at all the adults, just so that you could see their faces), think back to how different the world looked to you when you were only 3, 4, 5, 6, 7 years old … to your earliest memories …

5   How did the adults (or older siblings) *in your home* control your *social* behaviour, when it needed control?

- By social behaviour, I mean from the earliest age controlling you by punishing you when *you did not do* as they wished eg.

- how early or how late you went to bed, not spilling your food, your table manners, making sure you didn't run off in a public place, making sure you didn't run off into traffic, making sure you kept quiet, stopping you from fighting or arguing with a brother or sister, making you help out with some domestic work in the house, making you tidy up your room, speeding you up when you were too slow – eg getting washed, getting ready in time to go out, etc

How much and how often did you get hit you when you were growing up?

6   Did the punishment change much throughout the many years of your childhood?   How many different kinds of disciplinary punishment did you endure from the ages of :

0 – 2 ?

3 – 5 ?

6 – 8 ?

10 – 13 ?

14 – 16 ?

17 – 20 ?

Exactly how was this punishment (whatever it was) described to you by the very adults who punished you? What were their exact words?

- Who was particularly good at dishing out statements and comments about your *appearance* that was essentially

- patronising
- sarcastic
- humiliating
- bullying
- insulting

- In general, what kind of things did the adults in authority say to you to maintain control? What were their exact words?

- Who hit you most often?

- Remember, this is just *social behaviour*. What did you do for your own defence? How did you behave so that the punishment would stop?

- What other kinds of punishment did you suffer?

- Which punishment(s) were you most of all afraid of?

Good Bonding in Relationships

(These are random questions that aim to stimulate, you don't have to answer exactly, but do reflect upon how much well intended genuine loving contact you recieved at different ages and stages, using the age list below)

7   At home, wherever you ate and slept every day …. your earliest memories

- Can you remember how much kissing and cuddling you received at home throughout the day throughout these ages, taking one age group at a time

How did you feel when you got a kiss and a cuddle?

For example, did you get a goodnight kiss? Did you get a cuddle if you fell down or had an accident?

0 – 2 ?

3 – 5 ?

6 – 8 ?

10 – 13 ?   getting any hugs now?

14 – 16 ?   does anybody say 'good morning' to you? or are you just getting ignored?

17 – 20 ?

- Which adult did you feel closest to, that you could trust most?

- Which brother or sister did you feel closest to, that you could trust most?

- If this varied, between what ages did you trust those people, and at what ages did the trust stop, and why?

8   Outside the home, was there anybody else, another adult relative or friend that you felt close to, that you could trust?

9   How many school friends did you have? Which ones were the closest? How often did you see them outside school?

10 Did your friends suffer the same punishments as you did, or were your punishments more extreme than theirs?

11 Did you talk with your friends about the naughty things that you did, and what the punishment was that you got for it?

Your School

12 Can you remember your first day at school? How old were you at your first day at school, and how did you feel? How did that first day at school go?

13 Weeks and months later, which teacher(s) did you like most at your primary school, and which did you hate most?

14 Using the questions under the previous heading, **Control, Discipline, Punishment,** can you describe how the teachers and the other adults controlled your social behaviour and made sure that you did your schoolwork?

   • Just think back to how you felt, sitting at your school desk. Did you get punished for doing something? What? What else are you afraid of doing? If you do it, what will happen?

   • Which adults/older people did you *not* feel afraid of?

   • Was there any older person that you most admired, so much so that you might do almost anything for them?

The Grown-Ups at School

15 Please read through the questions again under that heading, **Control, Discipline and Punishment**. Please answer all the questions again, but make it about the school, and not the home.

    Amongst the *adults* in the School,

    Again, who are you most afraid of?

16 Did the teachers and other adults at the school relate to your parents?

53

- what was important about that relationship with your parents and other people who took care of you at home?

- How much did your parents/carers care about what happened at school, and what the teachers said about you?

The Grown-Ups in other Institutions

16   What other institutions did you spend a lot of time in/were important to you as a child? (eg. Church, other groups, whether privately or publicly run, Scouts, Clubs for sports, art etc)

17   Did the teachers and other adults at the institution relate to your parents?

- how often did the leaders of those groups speak to your parents/carers?

- what was important about that relationship with your parents and carers at home?
- How much did your parents/carers care about what went on at club, or institution?

- How much did your parents/carers care about how you felt about what happened there?

Money, Possessions and Resources

18   Would you describe your background as poor?   rich?

- What profession did the breadwinner have?

- Do you think they were happy at work?

- Did your parents manage the money they had for family things

    like holidays?
    music/piano lessons?
    any other kinds of special lessons? eg horse riding
    or sports of any kind?
    special presents, eg. a bicycle, a special toy?

- Were your parents/carers fair in the way they spent money between you, your brothers and sisters?

- Did they show favouritism, or administer punishment(s) by not buying something they had previously promised?

- Were they consistent and fair with giving you whatever they could afford to give you?

- Did your parents or carers squander money?

- Were they open with you about money, or was all that a big secret they thought you would never understand?

- How straight and honest were they with you about money and the sharing of possessions?

- Were they straight and honest consistently or just sometimes? What was your earliest memory of that, and what other memories do you have?

PART TWO

The SECRET Abuse (More serious physical, verbal and/or sexual abuse ALWAYS carried out behind closed doors or unnoticed when in public places)

19 Apart from the kinds of abuse that many children either experience or see other children experiencing, was there other abuse that happened privately, that you absolutely had to keep secret?

- Which adult(s) abused you in private?

to

More than one abuser? Please list them separately and apply these questions each individual list. State who they were (whether a single abuser or a group) and how long the abuse lasted.

- To the best of your recollection, how old were you when the abuse began?

- If it was an older child or teenager, whether alone or in a group, who were they?

- What role did they have amongst all the other grown-ups that were in your world at that time?

- How did you feel about them?

    i.   What did you enjoy about being with them in the beginning, if anything?

    ii.   Were you afraid of them?

    iii.   Did you admire them?

20   Think back very hard, to your earliest recollection.
What was it that they actually *told* you, in their own words when the abuse *began?*

- What did you say back to them?
- When they told you things so that they could control you
- and make you do what they wanted, how did you reply?
- What else was said in the actual conversation that you had?
- What did they say, what did you actually say back?
- What other ways did they use to control you?
- Did they humiliate you in a group?
- Did they threaten you? Did they insult you?
- How?
- What insults, threats or situations did you find yourself suffering from?
- Which were the most painful of all?

21   If you suffered regular abuse,

- How often did they see you?
- Did you feel after a while, you always knew what to expect?
- Exactly how distressing was each private encounter with them?
- Was it just as distressing each time, or did it vary from
- encounter to encounter?
- How long did the period of abuse last with the abuser?
- How long did the relationship last with the abuser?

22   **The Secret**

How did you feel about what happened to you when the abuse was going on?

Think back to how you felt as a child. Would you have kept what happened a secret anyway, even if your abuser had not told you to keep it a secret? What are your feelings about this?

What did you tell yourself?

What kind of internal conversations did you have?

What did you understand would happen to you if you told anybody about it?

What were you most afraid of happening?

Were you told what would happen by your abuser if you did not keep a secret? How often did they say anything to you at all about the secret?

23   When the abuse started, were they ever very nice to you? What kind of relationship did you have together in public? Did you ever feel like a favourite? Did your abuser give you attention and/or presents that nobody else gave you? How did they treat you in the beginning, when the abuse started?

Think back to when you had the understanding of a child, what did you expect of your abuser in the beginning?

What kind of conversations did you have together in the beginning?

24   When you were in public and you'd be surrounded by your family, and/or other children your own age looking at your abuser in public, how did you feel?

Think back to the places you used to go to as a child. Where were you when you thought about your abuser? In class, in a club? In Church or another religious place? In bed alone at night?

When you thought about them, what did you feel?

How often did you find yourself thinking about your abuser(s) when you were a child, how much time do you think you spend doing that?

25   Think back. When the abuse was going on, how did you really see yourself in relation to everybody else?

- Looking around you at all the faces around you
- Who was better than you? Who was worse than you?
- How did you feel about yourself, where did you fit in amongst all these people?
- Was there anybody else that you wanted to become?
- What did you imagine would happen if the secret ever got out amongst all the people that you knew then?
- How far did you yourself feel that what the abuser was doing was right or wrong?
- Looking at it in black and white – At the time, did you know that

what they were doing was wrong? Yes or No.
- How old were you when the answer was yes, how old you when the answer was no?

Please note, this next part is NOT about talking to a professional counsellor, psychiatrist or psychotherapist. It's about talking to anybody you knew who was not a therapist.

26   Over the years, was there anybody you wanted to tell about your distress?

- Did you ever tell them, or even just try to tell them?
- Who did you tell, or try to tell?
- Exactly what happened, and when?

27   If you told them, when was this (how old were you). Where were you when you told them?

- How did they (your confidante) express themselves towards you when they heard you saying your words?
- Were they very guarded in their response?
- Were they open with you?
- Did you remember to tell them everything?

28   How did they respond?

29   Were you able to tell them the whole story, or just part of it?

- If you did not feel able to tell them everything, what bits did you miss out?
- How did that affect your relationship with them from then
- onwards?
- How did you feel about them afterwards, considering the response that they gave you?
- Did their response surprise you?
- Scare you?
- Shock you?

30   Were you afraid that they would then go on to tell anybody else?

31   Did they tell anybody else?

- How did you feel about that (whether they told anybody else or not?)

32   If they told someone else, how did that affect you in your standing amongst the people that you still had to continue relating to on a regular basis?

33   Essentially what did the person that you told about this (your confidante) actually do after they heard you speak?

34   Did they sympathise, were they hostile? Did they completely ignore you? Did they accuse you of something? What did they accuse you of? Did they no l onger trust you? Did they tell you to never to talk about it again? Did they tell you to go and tell someone else about it? Never to tell someone else about it? Did they get instant amnesia and tell you the conversation never happened?

35   Did their opinion of you change?

- How did it change?

36   Did their attitude and expectations towards you change?

- How did these things change?

37   Essentially how did you feel after having told them about your story of abuse?
- on the same day
- one week afterwards
- a month afterwards
- a year afterwards and so on

PART THREE

Becoming an Adult (from age 14 or so onwards)

38   As you were growing up and adolescence was underway, did you find that you started

- Drinking alcohol?
- Dieting too much, getting obsessed with food,
- Bingeing and purging
- Taking any kind of drugs?
- When did it start?
- How long did it go on for?
- Did you do this alone or with other kids/people your own age?
- How did you feel in yourself?

39   If you found you did start abusing your body in some way, is that still going on now, to some extent?
Are you abusing your life in some other way? If so, in what way?

40   How did you feel about having a sexual relationship of your own when you actually reached your legal age of consent (ie 16, 18 or 21)?

41   How did you feel about yourself as an adult who could be sexually active if they wanted to be, at the ages of

      16 – 18
      19 – 22
      23 – 28
      29 – 35
      36 – 45
      45 – 55
      56 – 65
      66 – and so on.

Were you sexually active?
Happily so, or not?
(please say as little or as much as you like)

42   Your Adult Relationships

Do you feel that you give and get what you want from your adult relationships right now? Share whatever comes in to your mind.

Lover
spouse
friends
family, older relatives, younger relatives
children
colleagues at work
bosses or employers
clubs
professional bodies and institutions
any other institutions
religious groups and institutions

PART FOUR

Therapy and Healing

This section is about any form of professional help you received from anybody who set themselves up as the person who could help you cope with distress and unease about living. Professional helpers work from a wide range of disciplines. This person could be a paid professional like a Doctor or psychiatrist who administered drugs, a clinical psychologist, a hypnotherapist, psychotherapist, a body therapist who also worked in a psychotherapeutic role, or even a student or volunteer who worked in a therapeutic role.

Over the years, whether as a child or an adult, did you receive any form of counselling, psychotherapy, therapeutic healing or psychiatric help?

43   How did you come to know about the therapist?

44   When did it begin, and was there any particular reason it began then?

45   What did you know about your therapist at the outset?

46   Did you establish any goals?

47   How long did it last, and how much did it cost you financially?

48   Please describe your process and your experiences throughout the course of the therapy (everything you say, in whatever form at all, is valid).

The first session (what were your first impressions?)

After four weeks, how were things progressing?

- two months
- three months
- six months

49   What are the things that being in therapy has taught you, that you might not otherwise have known?

50   Did your therapy extend into group work? How was that?

51   Did you make any friends as a result of engaging in groups? How have these relationships worked out?

52   Are there professional therapists out there who you feel you can fall
      back on when you need to?

Any comments you feel are uppermost in your mind about the therapeutic community
and your experiences of it, are very welcome.

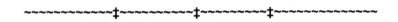

Précis for Stories 1 – 6

Story One Page 65

In Michael's family, strict physical punishment was inflicted on all the children with the cane, the slipper, or a wooden spoon. The cane was administered in the evening after father had been informed about the offence. It was done with the intention of being 'fair', yet when Michael got asked, "Did you commit the offence?" Saying no would create more trouble, so thence the punishment.... whack, whack! He was rarely praised by his parents or offered their companionship, suffering emotional neglect to the point where his elder sister became his main carer. Her husband groomed Michael from the time he was eight and abused him sexually, together with persistent verbal and emotional abuse. This brother in law was a prominent figure in Michael's local school. Some of the teachers there were decent people but a number of the other teachers abused him emotionally, verbally, and physically and some others sexually. His secondary education especially was hell, yet he went to college years later and trained to become a schoolteacher himself. He now works as a department head in a college of further education. A divorcee on good terms with his ex wife, son and daughter, he recently married a second time and now has another two daughters.

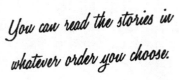

You can read the stories in whatever order you choose.

Story Two Page 93

Vicky Jennings had a happy childhood in a well to do, secure and loving family. Whilst growing up she always sought to develop her talents and use them not only to her own best advantage, but to other people's as well. Today she's an extrovert with a vocal sense of humour and she enjoys her work as a partner in a business consultancy. On closer inspection, her childhood wasn't entirely happy after all, as whilst she was growing up she couldn't get away from the boy who was the son of one of her parent's closest friends. When this boy was fourteen and Vicky was eight, he started to abuse her sexually, and this went on until she was eleven, when she made it stop. When she turned sixteen and her abuser was around twenty–two, Vicky wrote a balanced and fair letter to him, fully detailing what abuse he had done. All Vicky was yearning for was simply an apology and some kind of closure, because the memories of what she had gone through as a child were still very much with her, and were tearing her up. Later on at university when she was twenty, Vicky met her husband, and now eight years on they maintain a mutually supportive marriage, each sharing a fulfilling mixture of friendships as well.

Story Three   Page 119

Jim grew up in Plaistow in east London, and for years he used to drive all over London working as a taxi driver, but he recently started work as an ambulance driver because he wants to work as part of a team. He's going to get further skills in the caring sector and as he isn't one to sit around, there's no question that he'll be further up the ladder this time next year. A few years ago when suicide was almost constantly on his mind, he found out how rape crisis centres also help adults who were sexually abused as children, from the local library. At this, his lowest time, he had no choice but to tackle the problem of his own child abuse, and he started to attend the crisis centre. His abuser was his sister's father, who abused him at night whilst his mother was out working shifts at a hospital, and also an older boy abused him for a brief period when he was nine. After two years of counselling and some group work, he's come to terms at last with his abuse. He's also recognised patterns of suffering abuse all over again in his adult relationships, and he's tackling those patterns, raising his standards and choosing his friends more carefully now. Now that he's thirty-six, Jim wants to get married and have a family of his own. When he's not working, he joins in with fund raising projects for various children's charities throughout London.

Story Four   Page 135

Lillian suffered physical and verbal abuse since early childhood and was molested continually by her father from about the age of four. Her mother blamed her for her father's behaviour and emotionally rejected her, but bonded with her younger brother instead. Her father openly admits his abuse and thinks that as long as he talks about it, the family can get over it and everything will be all right. Her family expect her to forgive them for abusing her and resent what they perceive as her desire to 'divorce' the family. She was always very successful academically; this aptitude has proved to be a vital source of income and freedom, but during childhood it completely obscured the abuse that Lillian was suffering, so neither teachers nor anyone else saw that she was in trouble. Lillian now works as an editor for a publishing firm. She is bi-sexual, has never been in a long-term relationship, has very rarely had any sexual contact in adulthood, and suffers from self-harming from time to time. She still enjoys fulfilling long-term friendships however, and has a very interesting career.

Story Five   Page 161

John Nygate is a fifty-three year old Oxford graduate from a Jewish background who for years suffered unknowingly from undiagnosed depression and two non-dangerous personality disorders. He has spent most of his life unemployed or underemployed, and at times during his twenties he lived in squats or was homeless.

He tried desperately to get a career, fulfil his parents' desires and keep up with his peers, but he could not seem to do this. He was the victim of horrendous emotional abuse mostly orchestrated by his father. He felt so starved of loving behaviour from his family that as a child, he asked other children's parents if he could go and live with them. At school he was continually terrified of being humiliated or caned, and in his early twenties he had anorexia nervosa. Even though he never experienced sexual abuse, he has never been able to trust anybody enough to enjoy a sexual relationship. He has never received any decent help from the NHS or the state, but at thirty-four he found some spiritual solace when he discovered an Indian guru whose philosophies he found helpful. Over the years he has skilfully applied his mind to various projects but hasn't been able to hold down a job on a permanent basis. In the last ten years he has become a self-taught child abuse expert and campaigner. He sometimes protests in public places, raising awareness and handing out leaflets. Currently he receives no form of state benefit and lives at home with his eighty-four year old mother.

Story Six   Page 195

Twenty-five year old Karen is now a wife and mother, and once when she was on a routine antenatal check up, she found herself looking at her hospital records, where she read strong evidence of the severe abuse she had suffered as a child. As a little girl, she was informed that she was the result of one of her mother's affairs, which made her into the catalyst for abuse from her entire family, mainly due to her 'father's' influence. With her mother suffering from depression and alcoholism, her younger sister with diabetes and her older brother with behavioural problems, she was regarded as the 'cinderella' of the family, and to this day she still steps in to help the family out. As a kid, there was a lot of alcohol about and her father raped her regularly, as did his friends at various times and places. When she was eleven, one of her father's friends took her to a pig farm and slaughtered a pig in front of her, telling her she would be next if she ever told anybody about her abuse. Having a successful marriage and being a good parent are the most important things in her life, and as part of a community of young parents and children today, she finds it impossible to conceive of how anybody could treat a child the way that she was treated. She has had counselling for the last few years, and although she's not fervently religious, she's quite involved within her local Church community. She is now studying the German language and IT, and keeps working towards her own healing whilst doing whatever she can to support others.

Story One

These stories are all based on true life events, and I have related and arranged the facts and the information just as it was told to me.

To protect people's privacy, I have disguised the identities of the survivor and the other people in their story by changing details such as names and places. The actual number of family members and others from their group, their sexes and their geographical locations have been changed in order to protect everyone's privacy. The sexes of the perpetrator and the victim were not changed, and none of the other changes significantly alter the circumstances whereby abuse occurred. All those whose names have been changed, are innocent.

Michael

Michael recently married Sue, who, like Michael, is also an abuse survivor. They've spent some great times together and are looking forward to a promising future as a couple, but the past hasn't been easy. They supported each other in turning their adult lives around radically, despite their difficult childhoods. Sue is a senior social worker with two grown-up children of her own. Michael says he would have been lost without Sue's support, because she knew more about recovering from child abuse than him. She had undergone years of good therapy (her story is well documented in Jean Renvoize's book '*Innocence Destroyed*' [Routledge 1992/3]), and by the time they met, she'd developed a lot of strength and clarity. Michael supported Sue through a highly stressful court battle with her ex-husband (who had been abusing their daughter but still wanted visitation rights), a battle Sue eventually won. Those dark days became the catalyst of Michael's and Sue's support for the cause, and in improving children's lives today.

Michael has had all sorts of jobs; early on in his youth he worked at the post office as a clerk and did voluntary work overseas. In his mid-twenties, he decided to go through college and qualify as a teacher. Now, he holds a position as department head in a College of Further Education. Michael's father died when he was thirty-eight', when all his memories of childhood abuse flooded up to the surface. Michael then started making contact with survivors, and through regular meetings, his knowledge about the extent of the problem grew. For years, he had thought he was 'the only one', yet deep inside he feels he's been observing the sort of damage abuse does to people, for most of his life.

I grew up in a three-bedroomed semi in a very pleasant, quiet part of Richmond, Surrey. We never moved house in my childhood, and I was born up the road in the local hospital. Houses are expensive there now, but it was nothing special then, just an upper-working-class lower-middle class kind of area. There were my Mum, Dad and five brothers and sisters. Dad was an accountant with British Gas. We weren't poor, but had a decent house in a nice area.

I came along when my eldest brother Eric was already fifteen. He left school the week after I was born, got married when I was about seven, and went out of my life in 1964. Most of my brothers and sisters left home when I was still very young, so while I was growing up I didn't see a lot of them. I have no recollection of living with the eldest

67

sister Noreen, or Eric. Noreen is fourteen years older and when I was only three, she went to live in a convent for the next ten years. Her escape from our house was going to that convent, and when she came out she married and had kids of her own. Today, she's the sister with the most authoritarian influence on the family. The last sister Eleanor is thirteen years older than me. Then there's a six- or seven-year gap between Eleanor and Simon, and Simon is six years older than me. I came along as the fifth and last child in 1959, the baby – or 'the mistake', as I was often referred to. I guess that's something that, in a subconscious way, never helped me in life, being told I was a mistake, albeit jokingly, by the elder siblings.

By the time I was seven or eight, all the older brothers and sisters had gone except for Simon. Noreen was still in the convent and would be for a few more years. Simon was my only real friend at home and I got into play fights with him. Looking back, I could see why he wasn't that concerned because when I was just born, he was six, and when I was six, he was twelve, and he wasn't much interested in his little brat of a kid brother. I don't remember Simon being a bully, although he told me recently that he thought, in retrospect, he used to be unkind to me, but it didn't affect me. I just remember wanting so much to play with him, and was probably quite a nuisance at times. Today, he is a very sad character who got into 'long hair and drugs' at an early age, and now he's hooked on alcohol – badly. If he doesn't pull himself out of it he's not going to live to a great age. He cannot function without alcohol, and is totally consumed with his own needs, to the detriment of all around him. I feel for his children, who grew up 'without a dad'.

Dad was very work-oriented: he did his duty, didn't have a great deal to do with us, didn't go out much other than to Church, was very interested in lots of Church stuff, and kept very strict discipline. I'm told Dad used to organise more activities for the others when they were young, like taking them to museums, but I wasn't taken anywhere like that. I can only remember Dad taking me places once a year on holiday. So I guess Mum was my main carer, but she was pretty tired out. She was forty-four when she had me and I don't think she or Dad were that bothered. I never felt comfortable about expressing myself, and felt sort of suppressed, oppressed and embarrassed generally. It's that absurd realisation that I probably was a mistake.

§ Optional Questions 1 and 2 §

(In the first instance, it's best to read the story through without reference to these questions. The corresponding questions can be found at the end of this chapter.)

Mealtimes were a family occasion around the dining-room table, always starting and ending with prayers. Dad started the day with cereal, an egg and tea. I just used to have cereal and we sometimes had big cooked breakfasts at weekends. Mum wasn't a bad cook. If you put your elbow on the table Dad would 'flick it' off, and you didn't dare think of leaving any food or of leaving the table without permission. Mum never went out to work, although there was a brief period when she was a dinner lady at my school, maybe only for a few weeks. She briefly did some cleaning for an elderly parishioner too. She cooked and kept our house pretty spotless.

This sounds awful, but I remember thinking how 'old' my Mum was, when I was in the infants' at primary school. Once I got used to the idea that she never came to pick me up from the infants' playground, I was kind of glad because the other mums seemed so much younger and happier, and pleased to see their kids; anyway, I used to come home by myself. We had no telephone or car. Dad resisted getting a television for ages, and when we finally did get one, it had to be in a bedroom, not in the living room as in other houses. We got it just before the men landed on the moon in 1969'? I remember being allowed to sit up and listen to the moon landing (which, of course, never actually happened, did it!) I was nine then.

§ Optional Questions 3 and 4 §

Eleanor turned out to be my major carer, and this continued after she got married and moved in to a house with her husband just around the corner when I was eight. She married the man who started to abuse me. I remain convinced that part of the reason Kevin married my sister was to get to me, as Eleanor was the adult I felt the closest to. She was the one who used to make a fuss of me and I can never remember her hitting me. The day Eleanor moved into her new house, I came around and she made me boiled eggs or something for tea. I always remember it because it was just so novel, so exciting, that I had a sister who was living somewhere else. Instead of coming straight home from school to Mum and Dad, I would often go straight around to her house from school; it was on the way home. I had bonded with her closely while I was growing up, so I sort of left the parental home and went with her.

Kevin

Kevin is sixty-nine now and still fit, able and wanders the streets around Richmond. He isn't married to my sister any more, and has a woman in tow. I guess that's a good cover for someone who likes to molest little boys: having a woman in tow. I used to pray to God that I was his only victim, but I know he also abused one of his sons, who has not spoken to me in the eight years since we each revealed our 'pasts' to each other. I also spoke to a boy who attended the school where Kevin taught, and he said there were 'rumours' about him and 'certain boys'. My opinion is that Kevin is corrupt, because he has displayed tendencies that I can only describe as evil. I actually pity him and know this may sound perverse, but these days I try to pray for him sometimes. I have spent too much of my life thinking about him, and in recent years, I have learned not to: it's unhealthy for me. Since I confronted him three years ago he's not on my mind so much any more, but because he's father to some of my nieces and nephews, and still exerts some power over Eleanor, I am in a situation where he is still very much around. However, since starting to write this account of my life I have remarried, left my mother's home and 'am now living in a place where I am much less likely to bump into him, and this pleases me – a lot.

At times I find it hard to live with the fact that he's never going to face justice in this world. Without my year of therapy, I might not be able to talk about it in the way that I am able to now. But even after all that, I sometimes just fantasise about doing something really unpleasant to him, but 'without ending up in prison – probably smashing him to pieces and cutting his balls off! But I'm a calmer person now, so that isn't going to happen. He's still got his nice house, his comfortable life, he's retired and he's got his money. He and his woman go on holiday two or three times a year, yet when he was married to Eleanor all those years, they and their four children never once went on holiday. I remember Kevin being offered his dad's car, but he refused to learn to drive, saying, 'I enjoy drinking too much...why should I want a car?' He had no thought for his wife and four kids for whom he did nothing. He never changed a nappy or even picked a child up. Over the years, I was more of a father to his children than him. That's sad, and I hardly ever see them now because it's all too much for them.

Early Memories

I do have some fairly vivid memories, but also vast blank areas, which I guess is pretty normal. I remember being held over my potty by my Dad in the living room when I could only have been a toddler, and being bathed in the kitchen sink, the big enamel kind of those days, big enough to stand a three–year–old in. In the photos, I look like a pretty normal, happy, healthy kind of child.

§ Optional Questions 5, 6 and 7 §

I remember feeling very small. There was a lot of love and nice people around me when I was a little boy. Quite vivid memories are sat on my Mum's knee, and being in the bath with her, which would put me in the two to three age bracket. Also, of being cuddled up in bed with Eleanor, who'd come home late perhaps from being with a boyfriend or being out at a dance or something. I'd often be awake and hear her footsteps on the stairs, then she'd sneak into my room and say,
'D'you want to come and get into bed with me?' I don't know if that was appropriate or not, but I was a little boy. I liked cuddling with Eleanor, feeling safe. I used to get a goodnight kiss.

It's a bit funny when I think about the things I did *not* get. At times they said, 'Clean your teeth!' but nobody ever made sure I did. I had a mouthful of rotten teeth by the time I was about twelve, because nobody took much interest. I had to kneel by the bed to pray. Dad used to kneel with me, but later on it was,
'Don't forget to say your prayers', or he'd put his head in and say,
'Have you said your prayers?'
And I'd reply,
'I've said them lying down, Dad' or something...it was weird, bizarre at six to eight years old.

The only time I was away from the family was when I was in hospital overnight for a little hernia operation, at about eight. I have vivid memories of that: something shoved up my backside, some kind of enema or something. One of the nurses was nice; another was a real bitch, a nasty piece of work who clearly didn't like children. She made it clear she didn't like *me*. Those five or six days may seem extraordinary, but, of course, I couldn't complain as it was like that in the bad old days!

Spoilt

My family always told me I was very spoilt, but I don't see it that way, and feel put down in some way. I certainly didn't get material things. All my brothers and sisters have always told me how easy I had it compared to them whilst I was growing up. I'm a parent with two kids of my own and I'd challenge that now. And, until recently, they didn't know what had happened to me in terms of the abuse from Kevin and stuff. Maybe they're saying that I got something special that they were deprived of, or that I took something special from them. Maybe they got less attention after I came along. Maybe they were so deprived of positive parenting themselves, that seeing their parents giving attention to another smaller kid offended them. I don't know. I've wondered what the effect of a baby coming would be when you are a teenager. Recently, I mentioned it to Eleanor and Noreen, and they said they were thrilled to have me. Eleanor, whose life has always revolved totally around her own four children, said I was like an answer to a girl teenager's dream...a 'living doll!'

I remember the day Eleanor took me to her school. Incredibly, Mum let her, and I ended up surrounded by adoring young girls in the convent playground. Eleanor now laughs and remembers how one of the nuns took her to one side and said what a beautiful little brother I was, but that she must not bring me to school. I wonder whether Dad knew about this. There may have been some jealousy, but it was more likely their memories of a wartime/post-wartime childhood. They'd been crammed in a one-room flat with Dad away in the forces, and a frugal lifestyle, whereas by the time I came we were in a brand new house with a big garden, three bedrooms and holidays! I suppose I was lucky in that I seemed to get a holiday every year, but those were rarely 'child-oriented' affairs. It tended to be the Swiss Alps, with lots of church visiting thrown in. I was very much on my own, and loved those holidays. I bought one of my first records in a shop in Lucerne, 'Oh Happy Day' by the Edwin Hawkins Singers (I still have it from 1968), and used to play some of my favourite records of the day in café juke boxes, like 'Honky Tonk Woman' by the Stones, and 'Paranoid' by Black Sabbath (still have that one too!).

§ Optional Questions 8 and 9 §

Discipline

My social behaviour was controlled strictly. Mum would occasionally go for the kitchen spoon, chase me and whack me. Dad and Mum both hit me, and with Dad, punishment was a sort of ritual. Spontaneous whacking, although it hurt, was less scary than the ritual warning, 'Wait till your father gets home!' Those words can still make my blood curdle slightly, but 'God help you when your father gets home!' hit me like a thunderbolt. Dad punished me on many occasions in a very formal, disciplined way. When I'd been naughty, I'd hate it when he came back from work. I'd keep well out of the way and listen to him and my mother muttering downstairs. If Mum told him, I'd be summoned and asked about the crime. Punishment was administered a bit like a court martial and there was no sense in denying it, absolutely no question. Both the cane and slipper were used. I was hit by the cane or put over Dad's knee and spanked, and it hurt.

§ Optional Question 10 §

Basically, you just didn't misbehave; it wasn't on the agenda. You certainly couldn't be cheeky; swearing was absolutely unheard of in our house. You never dared leave the table before asking, and we always said grace together after meals. Come evening, we gathered in the living room around a statue lit with candles and all said the rosary together. Quite strange, looking back now at the things we used to say on our knees every night, and if you know about Catholic stuff, you'll understand that. I don't remember Dad hitting me after I was fourteen or fifteen, but before then I spent a lot of time as a child anticipating physical pain. Weeks rarely went by without getting a bashing from one bastard schoolteacher or another, but at home that was all strictly private.

School Days

I remember my first few days at school when I must have been five. They were pretty traumatic. I remember our first teacher in infants' and I think she was okay; she wasn't a bad person, she did not scare me, and I don't remember her hitting us. I can remember a sandpit in the classroom, and the precise location of the classroom in terms of the school; it was in a kind of prefabricated old wooden hut in the playground. As I got a little older I began to hate school. It was all discipline, and I didn't like most of the teachers. Maybe only a few of the teachers at both primary and secondary school were bad news and quite cruel; even so, it felt like there was a lot of cruelty and physical discipline was very much the order of the day.

I was seven when Kevin came into my life, and in a sense he made more of a fuss of me than my parents. The first time we met, he brought me a really fantastic toy for no particular reason, but looking back there *was* a reason. I even remember thinking he did it to make me like him, even at the time it was happening. It was a strong, shiny blue and red metal Security truck with 'gold' bullion in the back. And it must have cost about seven and six, which was a hell of a lot of money back in those days.

In primary school, I didn't talk much about the teachers there, but some of them stand out. There was a Miss Chivers, whom we used to call 'slobberchops'. Aren't kids horrible? She'd grab you by the shoulders, shake you and shout at you whilst spitting in your face. It was a mixture of both terror (because you knew that she was capable of hitting you very hard) and dying to burst out laughing! She's probably long gone now. She was in her fifties then, and anybody over forty always seems ancient to kids! And there was a Miss McFarlane. She had a nice side to her; she seemed very friendly at first, but by God, she had a temper. She also used to grab you by the shoulders and shake you till your head spun, and she hit you quite hard on the top of your head with a book. There was another, Miss Cousins, who my sister also remembers. She was very, very vicious. She resembled the Queen Mum! When she got into a temper she'd hit you as hard as she could with a ruler, and you'd go home with the marks still on your body. She was really terrifying. She was also in her fifties. There were one or two nice teachers at my primary school, but those three used to put the fear of God into us.

All school punishments tended to be very public...and all the more humiliating. I can't remember many specifics, or being punished for something I didn't do. All the same, I always thought of myself as intrinsically naughty, so I had to accept whatever I was given. I don't even remember taking my 11-plus, which I didn't pass anyway. Throughout primary and also later, I didn't really have friends of my own age. Though I went to school and back, Mum never wanted children coming back to the house. I

72

was very much on my own at home. Mum went 'off' children a long time ago, and still doesn't much care for them. Over the last seventeen years she's rarely asked me about mine (that is, her grandchildren), for example. I have a rather grim memory of Mum and one of my school friends at our house. I was between seven and nine when Arthur, a boy who lived down the road, came to visit. He was very privileged, because although he wasn't a Catholic, he was still allowed to come into the house; Mum and Dad could both be very bigoted. Arthur and I were playing in the living room when we both decided to run upstairs. The loo was right at the top of the stairs, and as we came up, we saw Mum sitting there on the loo with the door wide open. She used to do that a lot, and still does. I can't tell you how embarrassed I was because Arthur was right behind me. I felt very uncomfortable and ashamed about that. Mum had always sat on the loo with the door wide open, and there was no chance of my saying anything to her about it — I wouldn't have dared. I think that more or less told me that bringing people to the house was not a very good idea, and it rarely happened again.

§ Optional Questions 11, 12 and 13 §

Friendship

I had maybe one somewhat close friend. His mum was always full of him and he had two brothers who were younger. I don't know if jealousy is the right word, but I remember thinking, 'This is nice; I really enjoy the atmosphere here'. I'd be offered biscuits and drinks. Most of my friends did get whacked; that was the culture, but I don't think they got the ritual court martial followed by punishment at home like I did. My best friend's mum was more like the kind who would have clipped him on the ear, and not very hard, because she never seemed to have repressed anger or bad stuff around her. We used to do pretty naughty things, but I wasn't used to talking about my home life to anybody. I didn't want to reveal how I felt.

§ Optional Question 14 §

When I went to friends' houses I can remember wishing their mummies were mine, and even their daddies. They seemed to have a lot more interest in their children and used to talk to them nicely and praise them, which was something that I never got from my family, which continues to this day. I felt my lot was my lot though. I never wanted to leave our house and live elsewhere, and I never dreamed about having a different life. I always felt rather powerless, and thought poorly of myself: I think that was our peculiar 'Catholic' upbringing. I wasn't completely ignored, though. I was there, yet in the background. I never felt like the centre of attention, or at least important or valued. My brothers and sisters tend to feel the same way, although Noreen is pretty self-confident. I guess that's because she got out when she was quite young and became independent by marrying a really nice guy when she emerged from her ten years in the convent.

Dad

Dad and I went to confession together every fortnight without fail throughout my childhood. I'd think, 'Why on earth does Dad go to confession?' There wasn't a single sin he was capable of. I experienced much confusion as a child, and I thought it was me who was the great sinner. To me he was a sort of saintly figure, but a very strict one. I was horrified that I was 'stained with original sin'. I never knew what that meant, but it wasn't good news.

When Kevin came in to my life, he subverted my thinking and corroded my relationship with Dad. He used to put my family down, particularly Mum and Dad, which was wicked. He'd talk about Mum as a 'stupid woman' and refer to Dad as a 'coward' for not confronting her stupidity. Then he'd contradict himself by calling Dad a 'saint' for putting up with Mum all those years, and that affected how I saw them. I was truly convinced Mum was 'stupid' and Dad a 'coward'. I was utterly innocent as to how his words were driving a wedge between me and my parents and changing the way I thought about them. But nothing changed in the way I spoke to my own parents, though. The good behaviour they demanded from me didn't involve a hint of anything that might insult or upset them, or bring any other adult's authority into question, no matter who it was.

I never heard Dad say a bad word about anyone. He was very 'pro-Catholic'. When we met someone and they turned out to be RC they immediately became part of the family. Dad always seemed to have a wise answer to my questions, yet, sadly, I never really got close to him until he was dying. When I was nineteen, I was in Rhodesia doing Voluntary Service Overseas and whenever I wrote he'd always respond immediately and send something of interest to me. He was a great letter writer, writing at least once a week and sending me newspaper clippings about cycling, or things about Zimbabwe from the British papers. He seemed to have a better relationship with his kids from a distance.

I didn't have stuff as a kid, although all my friends had push-bikes, go-carts and other street toys. I wore second-hand clothes, and for school I had my brother's old clothes, old rugby and football shirts and so on. I had little to teach me what fairness in the family was, because my brothers and sisters weren't around when I was a kid. Yet there was a kind of fairness that still persists, in that while our mother is living in an old people's home, my sister looks after Mum's estate. Everything is to be divided equally between the four remaining brothers and sisters, just as it should be.

Powerless at School

In the last couple of years, I found out that Mr O'Keefe, the headmaster of my primary school, was an abuser. He's dead now, but he was moved from that school to another because of complaints from parents that he'd had little girls and boys with their pants down and goodness knows what else. I remember him taking my trousers down to spank me. I can't remember others doing that, but Mr O'Keefe certainly liked to spank bare bottoms and I don't know whether it was hand or slipper; I would've been too terrified to care! It feels horrible looking back, because the good old Catholic authority merely moved him on to another school. That's how it goes. The next head teacher was a nice guy and far from abusive, but by then Kevin was already abusing me anyway. In a sense, everything in my life was downhill from then on in lots of ways.

I didn't know until quite recently that my brother Simon had been abused when he was at school. He's never been able to tell me more about this, only how Father

Kennedy used to put his hand up his trousers and 'have a feel'. But Simon also belittles this by saying that some of the other boys were taken to the 'dungeons' (i.e. the cellars) for things that were a lot worse. He doesn't like to talk about it but he's usually so immersed in alcohol it's hard to even hold a meaningful conversation with him. On Mum's 90th birthday party recently he was extremely drunk and could barely walk. After my divorce I lived in our old family home for a few years with just my mother, I being her main carer until she recently went into an old people's home. Going by her habit of making abrasive comments, I guess she feels that I owe her more gratitude than she owes me. I've never responded to her bitterness, but when I think about her there's a feeling of emptiness inside. I still struggle to accept that whatever joy, praise or recognition could have been there between us will probably never happen.

I had been going to a modern secondary school for two years when Kevin advised me to move to the grammar school where he worked, a bit closer to home. Simon had gone there too, and it was the local school where Kevin was head of the Physical Education Department. It was Kevin's idea entirely. He said,

'Oh, I need to get you into Richmond College; it's a lot better than that shit school you're at.'

My family, amazingly, went along with that and I was moved to Richmond at thirteen. I was moved from a school where I had apparently been doing all right. I was average in some subjects and a bit above average in others, but going to Richmond was a big, big mistake. Not only was Kevin head of a department, but many of the grown-ups I knew from my sister's house were Kevin's friends and colleagues there. They used to come round, drink beer and watch the rugby on a Saturday afternoon along with me in my sister's front room, and I was naïve enough at thirteen to think that Kevin's friends would be mine as well.

We'd share beer and watch rugby games together quite regularly, but when I started attending the school where they worked, most of Kevin's friends turned against me in a pretty nasty way. I failed to understand this. Maybe they hated Kevin and took it out on me, or thought I was swollen-headed. Even so, the physical stuff I endured from some of those teachers would make your toes curl up. Our line master was this guy called Robert Cox. He would grab me by the hair or ear and physically drag me down the corridor. He'd slap me across the face really hard, simply because I had looked at him, or because he felt like doing that. There was absolutely no way in the world that I'd done anything to deserve that, but that's what he was like.

Other kids bullied me, and some of them were pretty rough. I once foolishly went up and reported it in an official way, and, of course, it was Cox who dealt with it. He had me standing in his office and commanded,

'Stay there.'

He walked outside to gather the five or six shits who had been kicking me, spitting at me and bullying me any way they could. They all walked back into the office together and lined up in front of me in a group. Then he repeated to them basically what I had told him, and asked them whether what I had said was true or not. Surprise, surprise! They all looked back at him and said,

'No, Sir!' And he looked at me and said,

'Well, there you go.' And I was asked to leave. As I was leaving, the boys were muttering,

'You're *dead* now.'

That's the depth of the depravity of some of the teachers, and that incident is just one of many. There were some good teachers too, but you remember the bad when you've been at the brunt of it. It carried on. I got whacked over the back of the head, and spat at, and more. Then one day I challenged one of the bullies and we had a fight after school in one of the classrooms. One of them was small, but he had a very big mouth so I made sure it was him I picked a fight with! I wasn't stupid. It was the only fight I ever instigated, but after I won it, the bullies tended to leave me alone.

I'll always remember an incident in an afternoon physics class when I was there. We had a teacher, Colonel Wesley (who always insisted on being called 'Colonel'). He used to spend the whole lesson reading the *Daily Telegraph*, while we had to just sit there and read a book. From time to time he would put the paper down and wander up and down the rows of desks, but once, quite out of the blue, his knuckles whacked me on the back of my head. I'll never forget the pain: what a bastard...and I don't think I had done anything other than perhaps daydream for a moment. One comment of his I always remember was, 'When I was your age, I had hundreds of men under me!' We were fifteen! And he used to pick his nose continuously.

There were also two Jesuit priests at Richmond College who had a liking for little boys. When I first met Father Kennedy, he mentioned my brother Simon to me because he remembered him from six years ago. He lived on the school premises, and used to ask me and maybe a friend to come to his room at lunchtime. He seemed elderly then. I can remember going in and being asked to sit down, and then he'd sit and rub his hands up and down our legs as we sat there next to him. Then he'd pat us on our bottom or on our front and give us a Mars bar. I didn't understand this stuff as a child then, and only recently found he'd done the same thing to Simon. I didn't give it much thought at the time; I just remember thinking, 'Hmmm, I've got a Mars bar.' If something like that happened to my kids, I'd want to go kill the bastard.

§ Optional Questions 16, 17 and 18 §

Good Times and Bad

Christmas was great, and I'd get three or four presents (my kids get about forty-three), and relatives might send ten bob or whatever. I didn't get a lot materially. I have some of the photos from the holidays we went on, with the dates and places on the back in my father's handwriting. Before Simon left home, we went to Spain twice when I was very young. The first holiday abroad was to Juan Les Pins when I was two. Then the next couple of years we went to Rosas in Spain. I remember the apartment, the heat, the burning sand, and the lizards crawling along the tall wall at the back of the beach, the smell of Ambre Solaire, and the straw beach bag Dad used to carry. Rosas was a quiet fishing village then. All the child-oriented hols happened up to when I was five and six, later we had holidays in the UK for a couple of years; Babbacombe one year, then Westgate-on-Sea. When I was about 11 and my brothers and sisters had already left home, we started the 'mountains, lakes and churches' years. Holidays from then on meant I was very much on my own, but I don't think it particularly bothered me. I was always grateful that I was on holiday and going somewhere nice. Dad liked places like Switzerland or Austria, and we would look round churches and so on. He made an effort to take us up on mountain trips, but they weren't child-centred holidays.

Dad used to play the piano at home and I always wanted piano lessons, just as I always wanted somebody to take an interest in me and to do things, but none of us got piano lessons. Noreen has the piano now. Although I had a great interest in cycling as a teenager, I didn't get a bike. I was simply there, went to school, came home, did my homework reluctantly, behaved myself and went to Church both Saturday and Sunday with Dad. I had to fight to get my first bike at sixteen, and it was Noreen who bought it in the end, not Mum or Dad. I don't understand how I could have been spoilt. Mum and Dad had only two kids at home to fork out for, as when I was twelve every other brother and sister had gone. I may have been deprived in this way on purpose because of religious principle, or because none of my brothers and sisters had had a bicycle before me. I'm sure they could have afforded new things for me now and then. It might have been their misguided sense of fairness, or it might have been that they just didn't care to think about my needs. I never dared ask for what I wanted too often, speak out of turn or challenge them in any way. It just wasn't done.

Distance

At both schools I was never conscious of my parents taking much interest in what was going on there. In those days kids didn't go to parent–teacher evenings with their parents as they do now. Possibly Dad did go to parent's' evenings, but it wasn't ever discussed with me. I don't think there was a relationship between my parents and any of my schoolteachers (with perhaps the sole exception of their son–in–law Kevin, who was my head of PE from when I was thirteen). In those days and given the discipline in our household, there was no question at all of going back home and saying what had happened at school. I always felt I was to blame in some way for everything anyway, and it just wouldn't have occurred to me to say,
'Oh, a teacher beat me up today, Dad.' I'd have got, 'Well, you must have deserved it'. In terms of corporal punishment or any kind of physical protection, there would have been no question of ever saying anything.

Control

At thirteen I had to start going to the school where Kevin taught; indeed, the most dominant of all the school memories are of Richmond. It's basically fear, and wondering when I was going to get belted next; I couldn't wait to leave the place and left at the first opportunity when I was 16 and a half. I'm not going to say that there are things that I should be grateful for, because there aren't. When I was there Kevin taught me to swim, but he had reasons other than my welfare when he did these things; also, it was his profession and what he was paid for.

I vividly remember the first time he abused me sexually, even though it's nearly years ago now. I had probably been around to my sister's for dinner, sleeping in the darkened bedroom at the back. I remember him coming up to me and crawling on top of me: it's quite hard to talk about. He played with my genitals and I hadn't a clue what he was doing. It was all pain...pain of every kind. There was no hint of pleasure in the slightest. The words he said to this seven or eight-year-old boy were,

'Do you want to come? Do you want to come?'

I'll never forget those words, and they meant nothing to me. Nothing. It was meaningless to me, I didn't know what he was talking about and was in sheer terror. The idea of 'sex' didn't exist for me. I didn't understand and just blanked it out. I don't know whether he was masturbating or not himself, because it was dark. He must have thought I'd have an. The next day, everything was back to normal, as if nothing had happened. My sister was oblivious to the fact that he had slipped out of their bedroom into the spare bedroom to where I was sleeping. Probably, much to his disappointment, he never once managed to make me 'come'. I'd be a liar if I said I could remember threats from Kevin in a literal sense, but I sensed implied ones. The physical abuse never went beyond what I've described, and he abused me sexually that way right from when I was seven until I was about twelve or thirteen. When I think about him doing that to me I want to hurt him – I want someone to pin him down and inflict something nasty on him. I know that doesn't square with praying for him, but I can't forgive him for what he did. I think you would feel the same way as I do. If someone did that to my children, I know I'd want to kill them.

§ *Optional Questions 19 and 20* §

Kevin continued to dominate me psychologically. I was easy meat because no matter how much pain he caused, I somehow found myself looking up to him for his approval. In my sister's house, he was the master, and I had always felt compelled to stay there because Mum's house was empty, and there was never anything going on. Eleanor's first two kids were a lively pair at that time, and there were always new games to play and ways to help out. It was all family and all normal.

I remember that I finally rejected his sexual advances when I was thirteen, which was around the time he introduced me to his porn books. I thought those books were great at the time, and masturbation was fun, but it was something I wanted to keep private. Most of the sexual abuse occurred in my sister's house around the corner a few times a month, although elsewhere Kevin abused me psychologically, by humiliating me in front of the other boys at school.

Of course, I wanted to keep this private sexual abuse from other people, because it was so deeply humiliating. Kevin made sure it was always in private, but by the same token his behaviour in public was often pretty tormenting, as he was often quite a loud, brash figure. A few years before Dad died I was in a pub with him, his 'woman' and some of his kids. We were all rather drunk and I remember Kevin loudly referring to my 'huge chopper'! I don't think anyone else picked up on it or if they did, they ignored it. He'd stalk me in the school showers, creep around and enjoy ogling me. His voice would echo through the entire changing area,

'You won't please the girls with *that*.'

He'd say in my later teens how big my 'chopper' was and how his a lot smaller. I know how perverted or stupid all this sounds, but it all had a bearing on my life. He used to instruct the entire class,

'All you have to do to 'bed' a girl is get her drunk!' From the few longer relationships I had (apart from the one I have now) most of them started out with drinking...followed by 'bed'! What a fucked-up man he is. And he used to tell me Eleanor was the only woman he'd ever had sex with. They didn't marry until he was thirty-ish!

My poor sister was every bit as much of a victim of Kevin as I was in so many ways when I look back at the horrendous way he used to treat her. Eleanor's told me she was oblivious to my abuse, and I do believe that and sincerely hope that its true. When his schoolteacher friends came around we'd all be in the living room as usual in front of the telly watching rugby. I detest the game so much now, having been forced to play it at school and watch it in his living room. Not being one who ever wanted to grope other men's parts, it's something I've had rather a problem with, what with the showers and the general humiliation that followed when Kevin was around.

When he was in the house with his mates, he would think nothing of grabbing Eleanor and putting his hand up her skirt and right up her knickers in front of them all. Was this normal behaviour: what would you expect husbands to do to their wives? What did I know? In no way did I connect this sort of abuse with 'sex' and the word sex was *never* mentioned in our house – never. I hadn't seen anything like that at my parents', but they were so detached, and from an older generation, that they were completely oblivious to what was going on in this part of the family. I remember Simon trying to tell me about what sex was one night in bed. I must have been pretty young and hadn't a clue what he was talking about. I think I was old enough to understand what sex was at the time I started looking through Kevin's porn mags.

A lot of drink went around and some of Kevin's friends' behaviour towards my sister used to mimic his. I once went to the kitchen to find one of his friends trying to get his hand up my sister's skirt. I was or fifteen then, and thought this a bit odd. I thought perhaps my sister had encouraged it, which, of course, she hadn't. I didn't know what to do or think. It was just another part of the whole morass of the abusive dysfunctional family that I was part of.

I discovered what sex was when Kevin had sex with Eleanor; he did sex very explicitly when he was doing a performance just for me. Eleanor doesn't remember any of it, because I've tried to talk to her about it and I think she's genuinely blanked it out. I was when she started having children, and thank God none of her children were around when all this was going on; they were sleeping upstairs. He would sit in a chair and hold her legs open with her back facing him and above him so I could see what was going on. I always remember him saying to me as he was doing Eleanor from behind that he'd like me to do it to him at the same time. That never even came close to actually happening, but I've never forgotten his words, the sick bastard.

He humiliated her. I had normally had alcohol and was sort of mesmerised by it all, and that too was all part of his perverted way of trying to control and dominate me. I've thought long and hard about why a human being would actually do that, and I really don't know. How can someone want to have sex in front of a minor? Yet that's what he used to do. The more I think about it, the more I think the guy should just be obliterated from the planet. He's just scum to the nth degree'.

Eleanor's children have grown up now. As Eleanor's brother, I have a lot to be grateful to her for. I love her, and often wish she were living a happier life. She has been divorced from this man for some years, and these days she doesn't have very good health. She gets headaches, stays in a lot and seems a bit isolated. She is a victim in all this as well and she's referred to other times when Kevin used to abuse her, when her children were asleep. There are no words to describe what he is: a wicked man with inscrutable perverted needs? Every attempt I make to describe him always fails utterly.

Telling the Authorities

Almost two years after my father's death, I went to the police station and reported Kevin. The first thing the policeman said to me when I made a statement, was,

'Did he bugger you?' quickly followed by '… not that we would belittle the abuse if he didn't.' I replied,

'No, he didn't.' Looking back, it seems quite inappropriate to start off with that sort of question. They told me that if that happened as a child, there's an examination they could do. I thought what, odd years later? I have serious doubts about the validity of such an examination. I don't believe that I was physically harmed in any long-term way anyway, as you recover from physical injury. They soon told me that they'd investigated him thoroughly and that he was 'clean'. They also said the following, then quickly retracted it,

'If he'd abused others, they'd know about it', which, in my opinion, is a load of bullshit. So many of the abused are full of self-doubt, and too afraid to come forward. I had expressed my concern about the fact that Kevin was still working as head of the PE department in a school full of kids, but the police warned me not to go to his school where he was still teaching. They said,

'If you go there, you may be arrested.' Nevertheless, I went the very next day. I simply had to. The school suspended him. I offered to testify against him before school Governors, but before the situation could be properly and formally addressed, the bastard resigned (on full pension no doubt). The way the police behaved is just another example of how our society maintains the environment as a comfortable place for child abusers to thrive in. Anyway, when I went back to the police again, they told me the Crown Prosecution Service wouldn't consider prosecuting because none of my family was prepared to back me up. If Kevin's son isn't prepared to take action against his dad, what chance is there of getting anyone else? Eleanor would fall apart, she would be highly unlikely to testify, even about the abuse that she alone suffered. Simon's testimony would be discredited because of his entire life of drug/alcohol abuse, and that would leave just me. One lone voice just isn't enough in cases like that—sadly. It may seem irrational, but knowing what I know about the 'system', there's not a hope in hell of the Crown Prosecution Service doing anything with the case.

§ Optional Questions 21, 22 and 23 §

I feel I did what I could. I suppose you could say that I got some kind of victory by getting Kevin out of that school, but to be honest, that was somewhat unexpected. I've taken things as far as they can go and paid a very heavy price. At one time, I was really very worried about how things were going to turn out. These days, I'm not. I go about my business in a civilised way, am pretty calm and don't get het up about stuff when other people would.

Confrontation

All the same, a couple of years later, even after I was well in to my sessions with an excellent clinical psychologist, the therapy still hadn't erased the weight of Kevin's presence in my thoughts. I could no longer bear the simple truth that here I was, a grown man and still avoiding him, still afraid to go and look him in the eye. By this time he'd been divorced from Eleanor for a few years, but I still had to do something, so I went around to his house and confronted him. I knocked on his front door and asked,

'Why did you do what you did to me when I was a child? Why did you do that?'

He hadn't come to the door alone, and it ended up with his girlfriend holding a gun to my head. The police were called. At the end of the day, the single act that most empowered me in my whole life was just looking him in the eye and saying those words. Of course, I got total denial and abuse in return and he didn't even look back at me in my face, but he knew what it was about. I hadn't expected anything else. What gets to me is that he couldn't even face me man to man, but had to get his woman to stand there pressing a gun against my head. He was hiding: hiding behind somebody else. That is what I detest about child abusers: they are such frigging cowards. I guess that's why they target children, because they need to have power over something. Something became restored in me that had been taken away a long, long time ago. Simply looking him in the face and being unafraid of any consequence has set me free. And after forty odd years, I feel I can put aside the burden of guilt that we all carried from all those years as a family group, not just for me, but all of us.

The reason I don't go after him further now is to protect members of the family who would suffer one way or another. The fear of a family scandal is very real. Some of my family (niece Katrin, and nephew Jack) still don't talk to me. I didn't speak to Eleanor for years, probably because the burden of our shared past was just too uncomfortable. Other members of my family, like Noreen and Simon, asked,

'Why bring it all up?'

Whenever I do talk to family, all sorts of emotions come up. Kevin is such a coward that if I was to go after him again in a legal way, in court and everything else, the first thing he would do is start on the family by manipulating and threatening them. He can be very powerful with his brand of verbal abuse, and he'd make their lives hell. So I don't persist in going after my ex-brother-in-law purely to protect the family from that. Kevin has an unusual surname, which my nephews Simon and Jack share, making them traceable, and I fear for them because of the expected embarrassment. There's a lot of misguided rubbish in the papers about a tendency for child abuse victims to become abusers themselves, and who knows what else might be said about them.

I've thought it over loads of times, and a few years' more suffering would not be worth it. To me, in the end, it's a matter of action and faith. It may sound like blind ideology because I know how nasty people can be, but I've found that evil has a way of burning itself out.

I really believed what Kevin used to tell me when I was a child. When you're a child, it's bizarre that you're under the power of somebody you look up to. The psychological stuff did more to destroy my soul than anything he could ever have done

81

physically. Anything I wanted to achieve, anything I wanted to talk about, I sadly used to bring it all to him, and I took whatever he said so much more than whatever my father said. He was highly respected as head of a department in a large school that had sporting connections and Church links with other schools all over London. I looked up to him, and no matter what I came out with, Kevin used to put me down, in subtle and not-so-subtle ways.

Kevin comes from a family of highly successful academics and sports people who played sports internationally; I understand one brother was an army colonel. Back in the fifties 1950s, teachers could scrape into teacher training college with four 'O' levels, so Kevin was at the bottom of the heap in his own family. When he met me, he transferred his feelings of inadequacy to me, and did a very good job of it. One of the reasons I chose to become a teacher and still work as such, was because he used to tell me how stupid I was. He would continually tell me I was not very bright and would end up working in an office or doing something menial. I looked up to him and wanted to be like him, but all the put-downs and the relentless negativity burned into my ambition like acid, destroying everything I had. Nevertheless, something arose in me in my mid twenties; I became motivated to become a teacher, because I wanted to prove him wrong.

Prophecy

I can give examples of a few self-fulfilling prophesies. I had a great interest in bike racing. At fifteen, I was naturally gifted in what I could do on a push-bike. A couple of ex-professional cyclists and others told me,

'You've got a lot of potential, Michael!' I never believed it, because I never got that message from anybody in my family, least of all Kevin. When he could see I was taking my cycling quite seriously, I can remember him sitting down with me one night around at my sister's. He went into a tirade and said,

'You'll never be any good at any competitive sport, because you just don't have it in you!' It wasn't the first time I'd heard that sort of thing from him, as week after week he'd always told me I had no aptitude for ball games out on the rugby pitch.

Nevertheless, soon afterwards I took part in an early-season bike race. I was up against quite a good field of riders, including the previous year's junior national champion. For most of the race I hung on and on, never believing I was going to come anywhere. Approaching the end, I suddenly realised I was probably stronger than most of the other riders. I started to make my way towards the front of the field, and by the time I hit the front bunch of riders there were only twenty or thirty yards to go, by which time the first two people had already crossed the line and it was just that little bit too late.If the finishing line had been one hundred yards or even fifty yards further on, I would have won easily. I came third and the national champion of the previous year came fourth. I was elated! At first I thought it was great, but as I was riding back home there was a weight on my mind. I hadn't got the psychological make-up that could make me go on to become a success. I always think back to that day. If I had disproved him at an early age, he would have had to acknowledge that and step back.

Of course, it wasn't something I was given any great credit for. I had always expected my parents to have very low expectations of me...they seemed to totally lack ambition for all their children and none of us have ever understood that. I didn't get a pat on the back about it back home and that was the end of that.

Likewise, I dabbled with the idea of becoming a priest, which was very close to my heart. I had a strong relationship with my god, and foolishly talked about that one evening around at my sister's. Kevin said,

'There is no fucking God.' And he went into a tirade about that. The following morning this guy gets up and goes to Mass, and to this day goes to Mass on Sundays. There were no depths to which he would not descend to destroy anything I attempted to achieve and believe in. I took up a sport. He tried to destroy that. I had a belief. He tried to destroy that. He totally corrupted my relationship with my family. He corrupted my relationship with my Dad by calling him a coward, and my Mum stupid. Whether that was true or not, you don't say that to poison a son against his own father, but that was what Kevin used to do; he would attack everybody and anybody around him and never take responsibility for any of his own actions, his perversions or inadequacies. His way was to go after a little boy and take it out on him. Even when I was getting on in life, at twenty and twenty-one, I was in some ways still under his power. School was all over, but he was still a close member of my family.

§ Optional Questions 24, 25 and 26 §

First Love

At nineteen, I had a brief love affair that fizzled out when I went off to work in Africa. Later, at twenty-one, I met a girl and fell madly in love. She was the French relative of a family friend from Togo in French West Africa. We spent four or five weeks together over one summer, when we were never out of each other's sight. I was still living at home and working in an office and she was over staying at her aunt's, in Finchley. She didn't stay over at my Mum's too often, but as soon as work finished, I was straight there at her aunt's and I used to sleep there. My Mum has always had strong feelings about any girl who was involved with me, and these can be summed up in one word: 'hate'. She always hated anybody who dared to have an interest in her precious children, particularly her boys. When Mum and Dad were away on holiday for a week during that summer, Michelle had been staying over at our house with me for a few days, when Mum and Dad returned. I introduced Michelle and they were very pleasant, but Mum was pleasant only because she didn't know that she was my girlfriend, and anyway, I'd never taken a girlfriend back to our house before.

Soon afterwards, I was in the garden with Michelle, and we were sitting on the fence together, holding hands. Mum spotted us and turned suddenly ,

'I want this girl out of my house! Who *is* this girl?' She'd suddenly gone from being quite pleasant and polite to 'How *dare* this girl hold my son's hand in the garden!' Of course, I felt horrible. That was always the pattern with my Mum and anybody I had a relationship with, even with my current wife, Sue. She behaved like that with Jackie, my first wife, and I asked Mum why, but she refuses to say that she has any bad feelings although clearly, she does. I've been with Sue for seven years and for the first four and a half years she referred to Sue as 'that woman'. Only in recent weeks as she's slowed down and become quite unwell, has she started referring to her as Sue, and not 'that woman'.

It took me about eight years to get over Michelle. When she was leaving for France to start university I told her I was madly in love with her, and was devastated. She said,

'Of course we can keep in touch. I like you very much as well, and I think maybe I love you.' A week before her departure, we bumped into Kevin in a pub on Richmond Common. Kevin eyed her very carefully and was probably thinking 'She's rather nice.' She was. Not only was she very attractive, she was also bright and artistic. A day or two later, I found myself with Kevin, walking up the street. Kevin could never say anything without bringing sex into it, and turning it into a crude, twisted perversion. As we made our way along the pavement, I knew some part of me was just about to cringe. He said,

'Oh yes, Michelle. She's a very attractive girl...' in an incredibly insincere tone. Characteristically, he continued to press on in his sarcastic style,

'Yeah, a very *attractive* girl, lovely bottom...she'll *never* marry someone like you, Michael.' By that time he was sniggering,

'She'll end up marrying a doctor, or a pilot!' At that moment I remember thinking,

'He's right. Of course, she will. She's intelligent, she's beautiful and she's going to university. She speaks different languages, so she's not going to be interested in a waste of space like me, that left school with nothing and no qualifications.' I totally believed that.

A few weeks later I met another woman who I just threw myself at, and vice versa. It had been me who pursued Michelle, but this relationship started with a lot more interest from the other party. After we'd met one evening, she made contact with me again, and the very next time I saw her, I asked her to marry me. She said 'Yes!' and that was in early 1979. I was feeling so bad about having lost Michelle when Jackie came along, I felt like grabbing anybody who might want me and love me. Soon after asking Jackie to marry me, I realised that it was probably going to be a huge mistake. In a couple of weeks I got a letter from France, the first I'd had from Michelle. It said,

'Aren't you gonna come over and spend some time in the summer with me in France?' and, 'I look forward to seeing you....' I can't tell you how gutted I felt as I read that letter, because there I was, engaged to somebody on the rebound. I was full of mixed feelings. I wanted to get away from home, but couldn't see any way out. I was just a low-paid post office clerk with little money. Jackie lived up north and had great parents who were nice, and had a nice house. It was a different world, far more exciting than mine. Michelle was still waiting for me, yet it was too late. I kept that letter for a few weeks and eventually tore it up thinking,

'What have I done?' which has been the story of my life, having choices and making decisions based on believing that good things couldn't ever happen to me. Also, it took me years to see this, but my pattern of relationships was that I could never be on my own. Even when I got out of my marriage, I hooked up with somebody else.

Getting Help

Only a few months after my father's death, I started trying to find help. My reflections upon all these aspects of my life started to touch ground when I eventually found a therapist who I could work with, but the search wasn't without frustration.

Through knowing a lot of other abuse survivors, various techniques were suggested to me, including group therapy, individual therapy, psychotherapy, counselling, and Prozac. I was drinking a bit excessively in 1995, when my GP referred me to the local hospital. I spent an hour and a half with a psychiatrist who told me I had survived something awful, had done well to survive, 'must be incredibly strong', and if I didn't touch alcohol for six months they would put me on their waiting list. I still can't fathom how he didn't connect my excessive drinking with my pain and loneliness, which was due to the fact that I wasn't getting any help.

I couldn't wait that long, so visited a local 'counselling service'. The counsellor spent about an hour telling me how great and well qualified he was, and I didn't go back. He'd also been to the same grammar school as I had and 'hadn't been abused'. Good for him. After that, I went back to my GP to say I was a bit desperate. I then got referred to the Mental Health Unit of the nearest large teaching hospital, in North London. I saw a most interesting doctor there, who was Head of Psychotherapy. She asked me why I hadn't 'stopped the abuse when I was a child'. Oh yes! I was eight and about five stone, whilst Kevin was about thirty-two, stone rugby player. Yes! Why didn't I stop it? She asked me if I 'enjoyed it'. Yes, of course, I enjoyed a huge drunken bastard lying on top of me yanking away at my little penis! It was awful. She asked me about my religious views, and said,

'Have you considered going to confession? It can be very therapeutic.' She wagged a finger in my face and suggested that my abuser's remark to me, that I was 'stupid', may not be far off the mark. Looking back, I find it hard to believe I sat through two sessions of this and refrained totally from striking back. I subsequently discovered that this doctor was a supporter of the British False Memory Society and acted as an 'expert witness' to get alleged abusers off the hook. Need I say more? I considered stepping under a bus as I left the hospital, but thought better of it.

Whilst teaching at another London college just a few months after the events above, someone suggested a local 'Catholic' counselling service. My boss kindly ensured my timetable was freed up for that one hour per week, and, at last, I thought I was on to something. I had to pay but was desperate, so did so. After only a couple of one-hour sessions, my therapist started to nod off. I know it must have been a bore listening to me, but hey! I was paying for this. We parted company after a few months. That really finished me off with the private sector. No wonder those people make so much money. I pay and he sleeps? No thanks!

A couple of years later I still wasn't making any progress, I changed jobs, moved house and changed GPs. In this surgery it turns out, the doctor was very sympathetic. I told her about my background and she revealed she 'knew something about abuse from her past'. I couldn't really handle my work as a teacher, and my GP said it was not the best place to be in, given my current state. I was then put on the local mental health waiting list and waited and waited. I was drinking and getting ever more depressed. When you feel down, drink makes you feel temporarily better, and then a lot worse. Then the drink becomes the problem. Despite the offers, I assiduously avoided anti-depressants. I really didn't want to swap one drug for another: I just wanted to heal. (Not that I'm knocking them – sometimes they do help, I know.)

I called the counselling unit to see where I was on the waiting list, and when the doctor there was in the middle of explaining how static the list was, he mentioned that I may 'prefer to go private'. That made me angry. I went to see him and he realised I was so angry by what he said that he actually said, 'I've made you cross!' He was damned right, I was.

About two weeks later I got the call. That was the start of my fourteen months of therapy with a young female clinical psychologist, doing self-healing therapy. She was cool enough to state from the outset that in her book child abuse was never the fault of the child, and it was good to get that out of the way. I talked and talked and talked. She listened, but knew when to interrupt and when to challenge. Sometimes, I left feeling very good, sometimes I left feeling down, and sometimes I wanted to cry but held back: my stiff-upper-lip upbringing, perhaps. I did feel comfortable with her, but didn't fall for her, as lovely as she was. I'm told that sometimes happens with your therapist, but gladly it didn't happen to me!

I've found that when it comes to healing, you have to do it yourself. A good therapist or counsellor can only facilitate the process. Misuse of power and the abuse of trust happen to children, but these things also happen to adults who are trying to heal their childhoods. I just want to give the reader a word of warning, in that people who are abusive are going to be attracted to positions of power and jobs that provide access to vulnerable adults, and to children.

In trying now to explain how I got to be here, I'm looking at a life that's been a succession of strange choices, and it's been messed up big time. Jackie, my ex-wife, is five years older than me and we've been divorced for years. I have a lot of respect for her, we're great friends now and we make a pretty good team as parents. I don't fear being on my own now, but then I''m and I've sought help, had therapy and time to think. I'm not going to give Kevin the credit for wrecking all of my life; still, most of the credit has to go to him. I know that the best thing for me now is to stay settled down with Sue. She is a fantastic person who has really been a rock to me and I know that I could never meet anybody nicer than her.

Speaking of blessings, shortly before my father died something quite wonderful and totally unexpected happened. Dad admitted it was probably a mistake that he'd used corporal punishment in the way he had; he was simply repeating what had happened to him, and what he believed was right at the time. Never in my life had I once contradicted him, and I was really surprised; he just came up with it completely off his own bat. He conceded that whacking kids isn't the way forward, and it was very brave of him to admit that. So Dad and I got close just before he died, which was so many years too late. Even still, those words of his shortly before he left eased much of the harsh burden of my childhood years, and they're something I'll always cherish.

A few days after his death, when I told my family about the abuse memories coming up, they accused me of bringing it all up at a really insensitive time, and of trying to wreck the family. I was the spoilt boy again, asking for too much. Their reaction surprised me. And even though Kevin abused his own children too, my family has never broached the subject of abuse: only I prompt it. Eleanor is divorced from Kevin now and knows about it, with disdain. She has a boyfriend who calls about once or twice a week but never stays over, and perhaps this shows the lengths she will go to, to protect herself and the one remaining child who still lives with her.

I get pushed around by my family in the same way as always, although Dad has passed away and only Mum''s alive. She's ninety 90 years and still likes to put me down whenever she gets the chance. That comes from forty-six years of practice. My mother always wanted me and her other children around her, not really for healthy reasons, but for her own need. She fed, clothed and provided us with a place to grow up, but it's still difficult for me to credit Mum with very much I'm afraid.

Noreen doesn't have the kind of strong emotional attachment with Mother that the rest of us do. There have been family rifts in the past and may be more in the future. None of the family, particularly Noreen, has ever been happy with my interest in matters of child abuse. Perhaps it's a constant reminder that all my family let me down in a big way as a child, which didn't occur to them for years.

§ Optional Questions 28, 29, and 30 §

I can gratefully say that I've created my own family now, and get a lot of support from friends and all different kinds of people who've come to share my life. I give what I can and I have so very much to be grateful for that I couldn't even begin to list all that here: it would fill a book. Faith comes in to my daily life and I'm still indoctrinated by God, by whom I feel guided, and my therapist said that's no bad thing. It's *people* I don't really trust, and it's the higher power that keeps me on the straight and narrow. There is some hand here, some invisible power that's helping out, because a lot of good things happen, and that can't just be down to me and the people I bump into. I know that's daft logic, but having been hurt by so many people, I believe in something that can't hurt me. Every now and then I think of my job as department head as a kind of therapy: perhaps it's a way of getting back at Kevin. I do a job similar to his, but with a view to caring for young people and empowering them, not drowning them with authoritarian derision and abuse. Indeed, it is hard work, but if it is any kind of therapy, it's a very full and rewarding one at that.

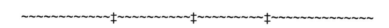

Optional Questions

1. What was it that Michael wanted and needed most of all, at various points in his life?

2. What states did he experience as a child that the adults around him were unable to see?

3. Can you imagine how many playtime hours he got outside school? Where did he go to spend this time?

4. How much time did he spend with Eleanor?

5. Who, amongst Michael's carers, enjoyed the simple fact that he was a little boy?

6. Who might Michael have played with most?

7. How far do you think Michael was allowed to speak freely, and how far did his parents listen to whatever he said?

8. Who, in Michael's world of relatives, friends and acquaintances could he bond with positively and trust?

9. How much exposure did he have to this person (or these people), and how long did his relationship(s) with them last?

10. On a count from 1 to 10, how afraid was Michael at home? How much time might he have spent in a state of anxiety or fear before the time Kevin, his abuser, came into his life?

11. Did Michael's parents play with him?

12. How much praise or encouragement did he get at home?

13. How much opportunity did he get to play as a kid?

14. How would you describe Michael's mother?

15. As a child, did Michael have any rights? If so, what were they?

16. What did he understand his position was, within the family?

17. Taking a guess, how good was Michael's physical health and vitality as a child?

18. On a count from 1 to 10, how afraid was Michael at school, and how much time might he have spent in a state of anxiety or fear?

19. Are children currently protected from this abuser?

20. What could be done to protect other children now?

21. How were the positive aspects of the bonds Michael had with his family, affected by Kevin's abuse?

22. Michael said, "They told me that if that happened as a child, there's an

examination they can do. I thought what, thirty odd years later?'

Although this policeman did not interview Michael very skilfully, what he said is actually true. There are adults who still have internal and external scar tissue and evidence of damage in and around the genital areas, and this can affect their physical and mental health throughout their lifetime.

23. As he was growing up, did he 'shut down' within these bonds? If so, with whom, and how far? Roughly, how old was Michael when those various 'shutdown' stages occurred?

24. Why do you think that nobody pulled Kevin up for his behaviour, ever?

25. Regarding Michael's memories of school and how the Catholic authorities merely relocated child–abusing priests to other schools following parental complaints, what do you think his ongoing perspectives towards the Catholic authorities might have been through the years?

26. How might that have affected the better aspects of religious foundation he got from his culture, his relationship with his family, and his personal relationship with God?

27. Was Michael's family concerned about the possibility that he might be suffering because of things that happened within the family itself?

     Why?

28. In terms of Michael's place in the family or place of origin, how comfortable does he feel now in relation to his relatives?

29. How much more comfortable might he be in that setting, had the abuse from Kevin never taken place?

30. Has Michael's life been a success or a failure, and what do you think Michael might say about that himself?

Reflections on Michael's Story

It seems apparent that here is a child who was loved and cared for to an extent, yet, when he was only behaving like a child, he was seen as being deliberately defiant. His childlike behaviour was rejected, and attempts were made to modify it with severe force. Whenever this authoritarian force was absent, this little boy seems to have been criticised, mistrusted, and ignored a lot of the time when he needed attention.

His siblings appear to have been raised under much the same sort of circumstances. One wonders what they would say to him. Perhaps,
'There's nothing special about you...we were *all* hit ...'

In school communities now, whenever the police give talks to children about what abuse is, some of the children come up to talk to the police officers afterwards. It often transpires that what is normality to them is, in fact, abuse. Some children and adults believe beatings of varying degrees are the norm, and they too have absolutely no means for comparison. This was commonplace fifteen or more years ago, but such behaviour will still go unchallenged today. However, intervention is possible. As long as they know how, people can address extreme authoritarian attitudes around a child. Positive inputs can gradually assist children and get them the protection they need.

If we look at the context of corporal punishment in Michael's family, whatever damages one child may not appear to damage another in the same way, but it's damage that may be less obvious. If we look at how this family behaves today, what quality of relationship do they now have towards one another, and how closely does that reverberate with the behaviour they received and expressed as children? We cannot know for sure, but if we take Michael's middle brother Simon, or Noreen, the eldest, their attitudes may have mimicked those of their parents. Older children, being more experienced than younger siblings, often hit or patronise in the same way they perceive their parents hit and patronised them. Your perceptions as you grow up could well be quite different compared to the youngest. Even your most basic attitudes towards people as an adult later on could be quite different. Michael grew up knowing that the power of physical pain came from the entire group of bigger people he lived with, and depended upon. If he had hit back, they were bound to win. Pain made him submissive. His external world didn't necessarily communicate anything to him or encourage him to communicate anything back, and this was all happening in the midst of the most appalling communication breakdowns.

Abusers get plenty of opportunities from families where children live within a threatening authoritarian environment. Due to the absence of proactive protectors in Michael's circle, Kevin moved in. Abusers can easily bring in their own brand of authority over a child, and get open approval for doing it. Michael had little sense of self hood, and low self-esteem. It was how he had been treated in his family that made him become Kevin's target.

Children sense a great deal going on in the relationships around them, and it may not be all that obvious how Michael also carried the burden of his sibling's abuse. Eleanor was often intimidated and on the defensive around Kevin. Michael may have thought it was up to him to pretend Kevin wasn't a monster, and through his ongoing suffering, protect her. Wrong though it is, this survival mechanism can provide a sense of place, and source of belonging, as soother and protector.

Child Abusers: - Perverts?

For aeons, child abusers have been believed to be unable to function as equals in an adult heterosexual relationship, yet they often do. For many, it seems mind-boggling how child abusers perpetrate their abuse within an ordinary home. It seems implausible how they often sneak out of their marital beds in order to get at a child during the night. Why wouldn't a wife or partner *notice* such behaviour? Because it would simply never *occur* to a partner that they might be in a relationship with a child abuser. It's never been a question that adults asked themselves, and they often justify it as being beyond the realm of possibility because their partners act so 'normally'. They have so much personally invested in their partner, that they wouldn't risk the humiliation of even considering it. All kinds of excuses can be used for sneaking out of the room in the middle of the night. Abusive personalities can be superbly good liars. They can be so intimidating that questioning or challenging strange behaviour becomes too painful; so much so that it's better to keep the peace and say nothing.

Are family patterns of behaviour based upon the values imposed in childhood? Such reverberations from the past were perhaps felt at the time Michael's father died. The whole family was together, yet he was not met with any concern for him. Michael was seen as attention-seeking, and perhaps somewhat of a nuisance. Perhaps this was because his brothers and sisters were brought up under a replicated form of cold, strict authority. They too didn't get any 'special' attention or care as children, and Michael should know they would reject the idea of expressing concern about things that happened so long ago. The family would rather never have known. These patterns may well continue into the next generation without question, and be accepted as normality.

I pressed Michael as we were working towards the final draft, asking him about Eleanor, as she was his other 'mother' in so many small ways, as the closest and most caring elder sister as he was growing up. Despite the fact that her ex-husband Kevin also abused one of their own sons, I was assured that she does not wish to be reminded about the abuse in the family. In terms of his relationships with his parental family, Michael knows he can't push them any further. He keeps in touch at Christmas and other family occasions, and remembers them in his prayers. Despite the hurt, he knows full well how things may never change, and he's accepted that now as best he can.

Justice Today

At the time Michael went to the police, Kevin was not brought to justice because the correct procedures were not in place. Michael did inadvertently succeed in stopping him from working in his old school. He wanted more than that, and today, the referral could be made to the Multi-Agency Public Protection Panel for a strategy to protect the community. This can be done even though there was no prosecution. Following a risk assessment, it may lead to a referral to the Protection of Children Act List (POCAL) to prevent further employment with children.

Survivors carry the burden of wanting to protect other young people, and seek justice not just for themselves, but for others. Reporting something in order to set off an action to protect other children can in itself be part of the healing process. It can add to a positive sense of self-identity, but can work the other way when very little happens as a result of their efforts. Survivors need support to fight the devastation and depression they could feel when, despite their best efforts, children remain unprotected from an abuser they know about. It is difficult to brave the justice system, but when adult survivors do this they relieve children from having to give evidence. Police and social-work professionals often seek adult survivors in order to shield child victims from the trauma of court processes. Michael tried hard, and certainly achieved something under the circumstances. He is obviously very concerned for other young people, and today, there are more channels available.

Story Two

Events in this story remain unchanged, making this a correct and truthful account of a childhood; people and place names have been changed.

Vicky

Vicky has always sought to develop her talents and use them not only to her best advantage, but to everyone else's too. She works today as a partner in a business consultancy and she says her work teaches her a lot about people, their motivations, aims and backgrounds. It involves working on many projects at any one time, ensuring that no two days are the same, let alone minutes or hours! With an outgoing personality and quite a vocal sense of humour, she has a pleasing mixture of old and new friendships, all of which are good on the whole. She met her husband when she was twenty, and now eight years on they are happily married and working towards a great future.

When Vicky was eight, a fourteen-year-old boy who was the son of one of her parent's closest friends, began to abuse her. When she reached sixteen and her abuser was around twenty-two, Vicky was becoming a young woman, and she wrote a fairly balanced letter to him, fully detailing what abuse he had done. In the letter, all that she asked by means of reply was that he said sorry. Understandably he never answered, probably because he thought it would incriminate him, yet all Vicky was yearning for was simply some kind of closure, because the memories of what she had gone through as a child were still very much with her, and they were tearing her apart.

In our home there were four people; my father, mother, and brother Martin who's four and a half years older. My major carers were my parents. Our first house in Cambridge had four bedrooms, two bathrooms, a hallway, two sitting rooms, one dining room and one kitchen. When I was nine we moved to a new house just a mile away, so it did not affect school or our friends. The second house had one less bedroom but otherwise it was just the same. The first house was on three floors, the second on two.

I certainly did need some kind of discipline and control throughout my childhood, and there was always swift, firm verbal direction when we were in public. That usually worked, but if it did not work then a private verbal 'telling off' was definitely on the cards. If there was an important point, like why they wanted me to do something different from what I was doing (for example, always be careful when crossing the road, or whilst playing in the street) my parents would sit us down and have a reasoned discussion as to why. I was hit infrequently when I was growing up, but even then it was a light tap, not actually causing pain. It was more the action, which symbolised proper trouble! I can't really remember this very well but up until I was two, I got a smack on the bottom or sent to my room. Then until I was five, there was more of the same, but a bit more verbal explaining. By the time I got to six, there were taps on head, or again I was sent to my room.

"You are very naughty!" and,

"Go to your room until you have learnt to behave!" continued into my early teens on occasion. From the age of ten till thirteen there was more of the same with a further progression of verbal explaining. By the time I got to fourteen, there were considerably more verbal arguments, as I was pretty strong-minded! Then on till I was twenty, things changed into more of a reasoned debate, as I had by then left home for university. As I got older, the words I heard were more like,

"How could you disappoint us like that?" This was much more effective as it made me feel guilty!

When I was younger, the adjective 'cheeky' very accurately described me, and in certain social settings it probably still holds true today! I think this came from my natural inquisitiveness. Also, as the youngest member of the family group perhaps I was 'getting away with' certain behaviour, and asking the sorts of questions that wouldn't otherwise have been tolerated.

Similarly at school I always had the self-image of being ultimately well behaved and certainly a nice child, but one that perhaps gained particular favouritism from several teachers because I was also full of quick quips. In general I am someone who seeks to break down barriers and open up social interaction, and I continue to do so to this day. Mother did at times humiliate me, although most of the time I hardly think she meant it. Martin used to tease me by being sarcastic and dishing out patronising comments. When I got to adolescence, Mummy used to bully me on account of the length of my school skirts! In a similar way Daddy could be quite insulting, without meaning to be perhaps; you see in the teenage years I was a bit more sensitive and suffering from teenage appearance angst! When I was a teenager, on the whole my parents could be patronising about my behaviour, but then, that's just the way most adults would appear to petulant adolescents!

Humour always played a major part of our family life. All of us were able to be cheeky to each other and poke fun, and gladly, humour still does have that same significance for us all. Everybody had a nickname. Mummy had several, from 'The Boss', to 'Queen Tut'! The 'Boss' came from one day when she was particularly stressed out, when as she was asking us all to complete tasks ... she kept saying,

"When you're done, report back to me!" She didn't live down these words for years and father, brother and I would jump into a mock salute and say,

"Yes 'Boss'!"

Daddy was referred to as 'Grumpy Toad' on account of him sitting in his chair and making grumbling noises. My fertile imagination saw him sitting there, looking for all the world like a toad. We often reminded him of his toad like alter ego to lift him out of his bad humour. Martin was, 'The Vicar'. Whenever he had been naughty he was so good at looking worthy and 'good', you'd think him utterly incapable of doing anything bad! Martin had several nicknames for me; for example 'Miss Ratty' summed up my mood perfectly whenever he found me in an impossible state!

They never resorted to sarcasm, but through the eyes of a child or an adolescent the banter could be quite humiliating, bullying and insulting. In the eyes of an adult, they were not actually being unkind. Mummy always resorted to reasoning over and above other forms of control, and one time I remember her shouting in total and complete exasperation,

"I don't *care* what other people do!"

As I've said before, she hit me infrequently, but it was deserved at the time, and I mean genuinely!

§*Optional Questions: 1, 2, 3 and 4* §

For my own defence, I would either adopt their suggestion, or act like I did by saying the right thing. In other words, I told them what I thought they wanted to hear. I was pretty good at making my parents think they knew exactly what I was up to but in reality I did keep certain things to myself which, had they known, would have worried them. When I say that, I am not talking about the abuse but rather the phase that began from when I was twelve years old and more, of going out late, dabbling in soft drugs, hanging out in nightclubs and so on. I first smoked drugs when I was thirteen and I started going to clubs and so on at fourteen, which is when I started smoking. As a pre-teen child I was often denied something as another kind of punishment. For example I was denied a favourite food until I had finished tidying up my room, or until I had finished eating some food as expected, I was not allowed to do anything else. As a teenager there was much less denial punishment. I was never grounded for example, and perhaps because we cared so much about each other, it wasn't really required. After I had done something that really annoyed my parents (or perhaps the whole family) I had to work hard to be really cheerful and helpful until the mood in the house shifted! You see I was most of all afraid of the 'cold shoulder' treatment where things that my parents had been tolerating reluctantly, suddenly started to really bother them. This withdrawal meant I was permanently being told off, and there was nothing worse than that.

Positive Bonds

When I was a very young child, it was my mother that I felt closest to. I really think that up to the time I was two I was certainly made to feel safe and secure at bedtime, and really, I felt loved. The same is true right up till I was five, and beyond that I can remember being six, seven and eight and just getting hugged and cuddled. This was not necessarily connected to little accidents, or me hurting myself, but rather it was spontaneous affection, particularly with Daddy, because up till the age of eleven, I was a real 'Daddy's girl'! That is … until the dog usurped him in my affections!

From then on plenty of hugs and affection was on offer although it was decreasing as I hit secondary school at eleven, when I was getting more self-conscious. From the age of fourteen onwards, I had mainly friendly relations with my parents, it was certainly a more communicative situation than it was between several of my other friends and their parents. At the time, although I definitely suffered from the 'my parents are so embarrassing' syndrome, today I enjoy their eccentricity. From when I was seventeen onwards, it was all more of the same as the years progressed, with the relationships in the family increasingly changing into friendships rather than being confined to the parent–child bonding scenario. As for mentors and influential adults around me, one of my mother's best friends, Louise, became someone really special when I was ten years old and onwards. She stayed with us for a few weeks from time to time. This is a friend of the family who lives in Belgium but was over regularly with her academic research.

I only had one sibling to choose from; nevertheless it was still he, Martin whom I could trust most. We used to fight and argue when we were growing up, but once I had hit my early teens I did not fight with him much more after that. To me, he was also one of the adults in my life. That's how I actually felt about him. We have always got along very well and been close. Perhaps surprisingly, I didn't resent him in the abuse matter despite the fact that as a child, for a long time I thought he must know what was going on. Because I thought he knew, I believed it had to be okay, or tolerated. I say 'surprising' as I resented my Mummy so much just for inadvertently putting me in the situation where I was abused, and keeping me there. But then again she was the adult and the protector whilst Martin, despite being older, was still a child. Although he was six years ahead in school terms, he was only four and a half years more in years.

Mummy

My mother is a very hospitable, friendly and kind person but bizarrely matter of fact with emotional things that might concern a child. In the past I've had weird feelings of resentment towards her that took some working through. I felt that she should have protected me against my abuser. It wasn't that I expected her to know; it was rather that I resented her brushing off my pleas not to have to play with this family's children. The parents were very good friends of hers, and she used to blame me for being the horrible one, and tell me off for whining. As a result I think I shut her out and was a bit mean to her at times during my teenage years. Perhaps then, there were times when she wanted to be close to me and I rejected her because I was so angry, although at the time I would not have analysed my behaviour – I was pretty convinced I was just always right!

I therefore can't really pick on any specific examples, it's more that retrospectively this feels like it must have been the case. This is because when we now have 'close moments' and 'deep chats' about how her relationship is going with Daddy (it is good but like all relationships, it has its frustrations!) or how we feel Martin is doing, whatever, she responds very positively and is always open to my feelings. Her enjoyment of my thoughts and feelings seem to suggest this, I too also warm to that. But throughout the ups and downs whilst I was growing up, her lack of emotion meant she wasn't that empathetic to a child's, or teenager's highly sensitised state.

§Optional Questions: 5 and 6 §

Louise was more 'in tune' with my needs; perhaps not as a family member but just as someone who knew us all well. She was a helpful provider of perspective. It was largely during the time when I was between thirteen and seventeen years old, when she stayed with us regularly. We would discuss all things that included matters I would not discuss so readily with my parents. For example boy friends, what I got up to with them, what it was like going out with my friends and so on. Perhaps what she did most for me, however, was to empathise with me, in that my parents weren't always entirely reasonable. In retrospect I should imagine she agreed with most of my parents' actions but was kindly helping out as a go-between.

Definitely Louise made me feel there was a different life out there for me later on, not in a major change type of way, but she respected some of my gripes about my up bringing, as if they were justified. I would imagine I conducted my conversations with Louise in a more mature fashion than I often did with my parents, which I guess must've influenced her response to my concerns too. On the other hand, Louise spoke to me altogether differently from how my parents spoke to me, by expecting me to be capable of a mature response. Even so, I still never have discussed the abuse with her to this day and I only started to discuss it at all, several years down the line.

As for my godparents Madeline and Luke, I have always been very close to and regard as my 'second parents'. They are extremely kind, warm people. They fall into the same category as my parents though, I would not want them ever to know about my abuse as it would ruin for them what they thought had been at least a partial contribution to a happy childhood, which in the main it was.

§ *Optional Question: 7* §

My school friends changed through my life stages. Pre primary school I was best friends with Sophie who lived down my road, but she then emigrated to America. At primary school I was part of a group of three; there was Mary, Grace and me, and we were all close. One of them I would see every Tuesday, then we would all spend many days together in the holidays and several term time evenings. I kept in touch with them but we gradually drifted, when I began to change into a tomboy, then an image conscious teenager whilst they remained tomboyish. So they became a bit 'geeky' for me as my social likings became quite picky a little later on!

I went to an all girls' secondary school and I hung out in a large group of five to ten other girls, with two special girls in particular. By the age of fourteen I had become best friends with a girl called Melanie; she is still one of my closest friends. We went home together every day and would meet up most weekends.

Between the ages of fourteen to sixteen I expanded my social group to include the other classes in my year. Holidays started to involve friends, because spending more than a week away on holiday with only my family became a little boring when all my friends were back in Cambridge, so from the age of thirteen onwards I started to holiday without my parents. This included starting off going on 'exchanges' with a French family with whom my family had a long-standing relationship, and then as of fifteen, I would spend time away with my friends. At sixteen, I moved to a boys' school that took girls for 'A' levels, and two girls I already knew came along too. Another girl joined and we formed a tight group and added a group of five boys into our circle. I would go out with this group every weekend and we spent a couple of evenings a week together too.

§ *Optional Questions: 8, 9 and 10* §

Then, our punishments were pretty similar although most were 'grounded', so for a temporary period they were not allowed to go out socialising, or else had to be home very early. That never happened to me, yet my parents were more 'strict' than most when it came to getting my own way. For example getting to go to nightclubs, go on holidays without parents and so on were pretty difficult, but I worked out how to placate their security concerns so that I could do what I wanted to do anyway! I do remember talking with my friends about the naughty things that we did, and what the punishment was that we might get for it; but the whole point of talking about that at all, was figuring out how to get what we wanted and avoid punishment altogether!

School

My very first day was at a nursery school, aged two. This is probably my earliest memory. I was very upset and refused to speak to anyone and I had to be collected by my mother early. When I got home I was sent to my room. I remember standing on my bed looking out of the window and watching the laundry van collecting laundry. The driver was really friendly and I thought about sneaking out and just living in his van and going around with him all day. For my first day at primary school, I was excited but nervous. Originally my name was Willemina, and having a regal name like that was difficult, as it took me years to even spell it! Actually it was when I was trying to spell it that I ended up changing it to Vicky, or Vic, and my parents were okay about it. Now absolutely anyone who knows me from school, university or work calls me by that name. I always hated being called Willemina.

When I was between five and eleven years old, I was afraid of the headmistress and the deputy head. Also, two of my form teachers were nice, but strict. I loved one of the form teachers in particular as she was very warm, kind and fun but you also respected her as the boss. I didn't really hate any of the teachers at primary but couldn't help being very scared of the headmistress, who was a disciplinarian, but very bright.

At secondary school, the thing I was most afraid of getting punished for, was not doing homework. Luckily I didn't do it often enough to get into real trouble, as I always had an excuse which was just about plausible and sometimes true! For me, talking was always a favourite pastime! On more than one occasion I was sent out of class for talking too much. Whenever I broke a school rule I was sent to the deputy headmistress, which was pretty intimidating but it didn't actually result in any major punishment, but just staying an hour or so extra after school. I didn't really feel afraid of most of the teachers at school, because I liked it there. Martin was faster at running, better at playing the piano, and better at mental games. I was pretty competitive but couldn't match him, as he was too much older than me. I admired him as being the fount of all knowledge when young, and I wasn't at all afraid of him. There were also my godparents, but then I was almost always immaculately well behaved with them because I was so happy to be with them.

My parents took a very keen interest in my education and listened to what the teachers said about me. This always happened once a term for my formal review. They did care about what happened to me at school a lot, but I did notice that they would believe the staff at the school over me, pretty much every time. Asides from one term of pseudo rebellion, I always loved school. I was also a little cheeky, but even then I never really had any big problems on that score. My parents got an update on how I was doing at school, both on the behaviour side and the academic side, and making the most of school was very important to my parents. The teachers probably didn't pay particular attention to my parents because whilst they were interested, they didn't look to involve themselves with what my parents did and their focus didn't stretch beyond a formal review.

§ *Optional Questions: 11, 12, 13 and 14* §

As a six to nine year old I went to the Brownies. I loved it as it involved playing lots of games, being outside, and earning badges for good deeds! I didn't ever join any other clubs or groups though after that. My parents cared very much about what went on at any clubs, or institutions outside the home. They also cared about how I felt about what happened there, quite a lot. They were probably quite right to ignore daily grumblings, yet when I think about it, it took quite a lot for them to believe you, rather than the adults outside the home.

Finances

Compared to my school compatriots our family was in the middle bracket in terms of being well off. Compared to society as a whole, we were comfortably off. My father was the Managing Director of a division of a large corporation, and he became self-employed in the same sector when I was fourteen. He wasn't happy at work, at least particularly not in the big company. He really enjoyed his own business but let it take over too much. That definitely impacted on my parents' relationship for a while which, although strong, was strained by this as my father could not switch off. My parents managed money very carefully. They were good at that and took a cautious approach so there was always money for the important things, like the private school fees they had to pay for.

Our family had inherited a country home, which was like a second childhood home for me, as well as a great retreat for our family. During the holidays we spent most of our Christmas and Easter breaks there and usually one or two weeks in the summer. Like most children (and adults!) I really enjoyed the holidays. We started to travel abroad more regularly once I reached the age of six or so, most often travelling to France where we would stay in a hotel or rent a holiday cottage, which was almost always by the sea.

I had piano lessons from when I was eight right up till I was seventeen years old, and from eight to twelve years old I got to go horse riding. If I liked any school sports, they endorsed that and would get the equipment. I always had a bike, even if it was a hand me down from Martin. When I got a new bike for my ninth birthday that was very special, and is one of my better memories. They were fair in the way they spent money between Martin and me and never showed favouritism, or administered punishment by not buying something they had previously promised. They were astute enough not to use anything material as a reward or as a punishment, and were always consistent and fair with giving me whatever they could afford. They never squandered money, and they hated being in debt. They were pretty open with us about money, and told us as much as we were interested in knowing about. They were straight and honest about money and the sharing of possessions on a very consistent basis.

Scott

I was abused by the older son, Scott, the teenage son in a family whose parents were very good friends with mine. He intimidated me from the beginning as he had a very combative verbal and physical 'play' style with his younger brother and sister. I was afraid of him, and sometimes in awe of him, as he was older than me and very strong. I was seven, possibly eight when the abuse began. He was six years older than me, and occasionally I admired him in a weird way, I'd say it was more like fearful awe than anything else. In the beginning, I thought that as he was an older boy he must know better than me. When the abuse started there were no conversations; he just started doing things without asking.

It was regular abuse that happened sometimes as often as once a week, and at a minimum it was happening once a month. After a while it did become somewhat routine and I knew what to expect. It was usually in my bedroom at my home, or else it might be in the spare bedroom at his home. Scott's family used to join us at our country home for the odd weekend during the school term. Whenever he and his family came to spend the weekend there; he had many more opportunities to abuse. He and his family usually went abroad during the longer school holidays, but on the few times both his and our family went abroad together, he had more opportunities to abuse. Initially it was all more deeply confusing than distressing, and the confusion seemed to feed the situation as he misguided me into thinking it was something I had to accept.

§ Optional Question and Comment 15 §

When I was in public and surrounded by the family, and maybe other children, I felt a bit in awe of him and a bit frightened of him as well. When I thought of him in bed alone at night, I felt nervous so I tried not to think about him and was quite good at blocking it out. I definitely thought about it and worried about it in advance when I knew we were going to be seeing him. I would think about it for short periods and then try hard to stop.

Not long after the abuse began, I remember him saying to me,
"Do you mind if I do this?" I don't know what I said back to him, but I didn't respond very much, I rather mumbled that I didn't know, that I didn't mind but in any case I clearly wasn't positive about it happening. I remember him saying to me,
"Do you want to keep your underpants on – what do you prefer?" I used to reply, that I didn't mind, or know. This remained the way things went on for a long time. It was only nearing the end, and perhaps the main reason why it ended, that I started to answer back and work out ways of not doing what he wanted.

§ Optional Question: 16 §

He used a game of hide and seek as the method. I would play along but only recognise that whatever he did with me was all just part of the game. We would be the hiding 'pair', and Martin and Scott's sister Jasmine and brother Tom would get together as the other group. We would go and find somewhere to hide in the house and it was their job to find us, or vice versa. Whenever it was our turn to hide, if we heard any noises and somebody was approaching, we stopped whatever we were doing and ran and hid somewhere. Usually after a few goes however, the other group got distracted and ended up watching TV or playing a game of cards. They wouldn't come and find us immediately, which gave Scott his opportunity to be alone with me.

§ Optional Question and Comment: 17 §

I am pretty sure I was not required ever to take the top half of my clothing off. I must have had to pull down my own trousers or take them off, because as a tomboy child, I never wore skirts.   Throughout the three or four years duration of the abuse, from the beginning of the time he abused me right up until nearing the end, the abuse remained pretty consistent in its content. It usually started with my underpants on, but sometimes they were taken off right at the beginning. When I was a child I would use the word, 'kiss', but in adult terms he would perform oral sex on me and also finger me. If my pants were on, then he would probe with his hands and his tongue from the outside.

§ Optional Question: 18 §

Apart from those times when we played 'hide and seek', he got increasingly bold and would touch me inappropriately when other people were just through the doorway, or in the next room. He would not say anything on these occasions; he would just make sure he had a reason to be close to me; like he would pretend to be reading a book for example whilst sitting on the sofa, and then he'd move in by putting his hands inside my pants, and touch or finger my vagina. It was only in these instances that I actually cautioned him to what he was doing, like "They are only in the next room!" but I never actually shouted for help.

For approximately just over the last year of the abuse, when I was nine or ten years old and he was fifteen or sixteen, things started to change. He wanted me to get involved. This is the part of the abuse I remember most vividly. We were both naked and he would want me to touch his penis and 'kiss' his penis. Really, he wanted me to give him a hand and blowjob. This was when I really started to resist. I didn't resist in an obvious 'No – get off' sort of way. I did it by acting 'dumb', and pretended not to understand what he wanted me to do. For example, if he wanted me to kiss the base of his penis or he just wanted me to pat it or rub it, or suck it, I would do something different. I cannot remember whether he performed things on me at the same time, I am pretty sure he didn't, because I didn't enjoy any of it. I think instead he would abuse me because that turned him on, and then when he'd finished that he would want me to do things to him.

Occasionally Scott was very nice and friendlier to me than he was to others, and I felt like a favourite when that happened. Most of the time though he treated me like he did most of the others, which means he was physically quite intimidating (eg throwing stones at me, and every non-adult) and being very verbally intimidating at times too. It's funny that he didn't humiliate me in a group, because he was a bully to most people, and he was pretty difficult with his elders. I wouldn't even say I got more abuse than anyone else in public.

§ Optional Questions: 19, 20, and 21 §

102

He told me not to tell anyone, but that what he was doing was all right. The only time he got a bit threatening was when I started to resist. He didn't insult me particularly, aside from how he tried to trick my childish innocence into accepting what he did. His words were used more like a pressure, applied on me to make me do things. In the earlier days it was done through asking questions like

"Shall I do it with or without your pants on?" or

"Shall touch or kiss?" Just the requirement to respond, and the act of responding made me feel paralysed, and embarrassed, as I didn't want to answer. I didn't 'want' anything at all, but also felt somehow complicit. I made out I didn't understand what he wanted me to do, when in fact I did, especially in the final stages when he was much more demanding. He would give me exact instructions of what I was to do. He would force me, by moving my head and hands if I wasn't doing it how he wanted.

The session I remember most vividly was in the spare bedroom. I was ten and he had started to want me to respond by touching his penis and giving him oral sex (not that I had that type of terminology in my vocabulary at the time). We ended up in the bed, which is somewhere we never normally went. I'd say the incident lasted thirty minutes. It was always in the middle of the sessions with him, where I was made to take part, and by that time I had gone the whole journey from feeling placidly accepting to feeling scared and disgusted. He'd push my head down to make me do what he wanted. Those times were the most painful of all and I felt really physically disgusted, I can remember hating the taste of his semen and the smell of old urine.

§ Optional Questions: 22 §

I found out about the 'facts of life' pretty early, largely as a result of the abuse but also because I had an older brother whom I could ask. Bizarrely, I prided myself as a knowledgeable person upon the subject. But it was also true that I didn't 'know' anything about the facts of life either. There was dark stuff going on inside a secret world that I couldn't bring out into the light of day. I couldn't relate it to the people around me or understand what it meant; I was still a child.

§ Optional Questions: 23 and 24 §

By the age of twelve I was fully aware of all the things that adults do during sex, and I had known about the 'facts of life' for a year and some months before everyone else. I can remember times at school when we were all discussing sex, but hopefully had no practical knowledge. I wasn't concerned about hiding my practical 'knowledge' during these discussions; nobody would dare to assume that anyone had any. Those discussions seemed light years apart from the incidents that happened with Scott.

§ Optional Questions: 25 §

I thought my brother Martin knew, so that confirmed to me I just had to accept what was happening, or that maybe what was happening was like a kind of game, and it happened to other girls as well. The fact that Martin and Scott were around the same age would have had something to do with it, plus I trusted Martin one hundred percent and saw him as someone older and wiser. I got no help or support when I asked not to have to be with him, particularly when we were taken to the holiday house that our family had in the country. This only confirmed further it was something I just had to accept, or put up with. I remember feeling really uncomfortable and embarrassed which, thinking about it now, is one of the reasons why he did things like ask me whether I wanted to keep my pants on or not. Really, I found I couldn't cope with the question.

The question itself seemed to have some kind of power over me. I was also scared at times both of him and of being found out, I was entirely sure about that. I accepted what was happening because I had to accept it, despite the fact that I knew it was wrong. I didn't even know why it was wrong, but I knew it was wrong and somehow, I felt complicit. As things progressed and in the latter stages of the abuse, my usual feelings went from fearful awe, bewilderment and uncertainty to blood pumping fear and upset which I think helped drive me to start rejecting what was going on in the end. For the majority of the time it was he who took action in abusing me, with me being in this confused state interspersed with occasions when he would get more bold and this would frighten me more. It was the final third or so of the time that got much more distressing as I was being required to reciprocate.

The entire period of abuse lasted three years or so, and as a regular social relationship it lasted around four years because he, his brother and sister gradually ceased coming round, as we got older. My parents and his still are very good friends.

Getting Out of It

Throughout the years when the abuse was going on, I felt confused, scared at times and desperate to get out of the situation. Thinking back to when I was a child, it's very hard to assess whether or not I would have kept what happened a secret anyway, even if my abuser had never told me to keep it a secret. I have no clear memory of him telling me to keep it a secret. I know that I was afraid of him, and my feelings about this are hard to assess. I think it was a mixture of him pushing to keep things secret coupled with me thinking Martin knew and that I had to accept it. The combination of these made it very unlikely I would have actually told anyone. That said, had my mother probed as to why I didn't want to play with Scott, maybe I would've said something, but probably not as all I seemed to be able to say to her, was that I didn't like him and didn't want to play with him, which she probably quite rightly didn't accept as a good enough reason.

My way of dealing with the abuse whilst it was going on was to come to the conclusion that is must be OK. Basically it was a constant justification exercise. In the last phase of it, it clearly felt wrong but I had to accept it. As things moved on I started to think up ways of avoiding the situation. One way of avoiding it was to 'act dumb' when the situation arose. One self-justification route was to think that Martin must know, and that because I trusted Martin I used to ask myself,
'Should I therefore just accept this?' The other question constantly going on was,
'How can I get my mother to understand I don't want to be near Scott?' After sifting through endless impossible solutions, my conclusion was,
'I must simply behave, not cause any upset and get on with it.' Then it would go back to 'How do I try and stop it?' And then the whole thing would start all over again. I knew if I told anybody about it, there would be major repercussions but I wasn't sure

exactly what those would be. I thought I'd also get into big trouble, plus there was a possibility that no one would believe me. I was afraid of no one believing me, most of all.

§ *Optional Questions: (comment) 26* §

Over the years that the abuse was going on, I felt like I was part of some complex web that I didn't understand, yet I found myself compelled to be a part of it. When I looked around at all the faces around me, I wished they could help me. I thought, if only they knew what was happening, would they believe me? Yet I was full of self-doubt. Was I over-reacting? I was very unsure. I didn't have a low sense of self-esteem; in general I was pretty well adjusted. I fitted in amongst all these people like this. I was the little kid, the youngest, quite boisterous at times but ultimately I was the one who had to behave, to follow the lead and accept my part as the youngest. Only Martin was better than me, and I mean that in a sweet kid-like way when I say that. He was a faster runner, he could play the piano better, he knew more things and so on. Although he was a bit older, he was still very sweet to me. I was just confused as to how far I felt that what the abuser was doing was right or wrong. I was wise to neither really, it was when it was all nearing the end that I knew it was wrong. I was eight at the time when the abuse began, and I didn't know it was wrong, then in the middle when I was about nine, I was neutral, then in the end when I reached ten and eleven, I definitely knew it was wrong.

§ *Optional Questions: 27 (comment)* §

Telling

All my feelings about letting the secret out as a child, are complicated. Just writing about it makes me feel stressed and glimmers of old, chest tightening palpitations are still there. I'm fine with the fact I didn't say anything, that is I don't blame myself and I've dealt with the fact that my mother could've been a bit more perceptive. I really believe now that it would be unreasonable to attach any blame to her. Whilst I wish I had been able to speak up, in another way I'm happy I didn't. I have decided that I will never speak of this to my parents, as I wouldn't want to ruin our relationship. What's the point of causing such horrendous upset? I'm okay now. I've reconciled myself to knowing that it would perhaps (and only perhaps) give me a second's worth of selfish self-help but it certainly would result in years of regret.

Over the years, I wanted to tell some of my close girlfriends about my distress. At the time it finally happened, two friends and I were there in the bedroom at one of their houses. I was sixteen, and we were all wrapped up in the kind of 'deep and meaningful' conversation you like to have when you're a teenager. Bits of it started to come out. I started to cry a lot, and I really couldn't stop when I first told them about it. Things had already been starting to bubble up in my mind because I wanted to confront my abuser (I guess I had a need to do that) and I needed to speak to someone to see what they thought. One of my friend's mothers was a therapist and she had picked up some of that kind of way of listening and expressing herself, from her mother. They were very comforting and helpful. They were not guarded in their response; they encouraged me to talk, and they were quite open with me. I told them the basic details, I didn't go into much detail about the actual physical stuff itself. They were shocked and upset for me, but they comforted me. I had blocked it out for so long that it stumbled out in disjointed pieces, and this still happens sometimes even today.

Even so, I told them most of it but I missed out the physical detail of the abuse and just referred to it in more abstract terms. I didn't feel it was fair to put that upon them, and I still feel the same way now; plus it's a particularly distressing part of the situation for me as a whole. It was a few months after that when I wrote a letter to Scott, talking about the abuse in graphic detail and asking for an apology. Although I detailed what abuse he had done, I tried to keep the letter balanced. I told one of the girls I wrote the letter, but I didn't show it to her. My key feeling at the time was just the need to reach out for acknowledgement and an apology. He never responded but then again thinking about it I guess if he had, he might have thought I had an ulterior motive and taken it as evidence to the police. In fact it wasn't like that at all, I simply wanted an apology.

§ Optional Questions: 28, 29 and 30 §

From then onwards, I think my friends were more considerate whenever topics related to this ever came up. They tried very hard to comfort me but then again I didn't want to talk about it much, nevertheless they were there when I did. Afterwards I felt grateful, even though I regretted slightly I'd let my secret out. Their response didn't surprise me as they were, and still are good people. We've since lost touch but I have spoken to a couple of other good friends subsequently and mostly to my husband, who has been my real rock in this. When the abuse surfaces fully, I feel a well of emotion inside as if I'm about to burst and all the stuff inside just literally pours out. Every time I have an outburst about it even today, after the strength of the emotion has settled down I just wish I hadn't talked about it.

§ Optional Questions: (Comment) 31 §

I wasn't afraid my friends would then go on to tell anybody else, and they didn't do so as far as I'm aware. I didn't want them to tell anybody else, but anyway I didn't think they would. At the time, that would have been very damaging to me in my standing amongst the people that I still had to continue relating to on a regular basis. Generally, my confidantes offered help and a shoulder to cry on. They sympathised and probably trusted me more as we shared a special, if sad bond. I'm not sure if their opinion of me changed. If it did change, I think it was that they respected that I'd coped with the situation. You see just by knowing me up to that time, they would never have guessed that I had ever suffered in this way.

After having told them about the abuse, in some ways I felt relieved, in others it heightened my upset as it had all risen up to the surface, for a while. A week after telling them I started to calm down and a month afterwards I was back to normal, and I talked to them whenever I wanted to. After a couple of years we drifted apart as we went to different universities and they went travelling abroad.

Teens and College Years

With adolescence under way, I drank alcohol and got involved in drugs in a way that was normal with my peer group. In fact I held back more than most! I smoked dope when I was thirteen, and smoked dope regularly every weekend from the ages of fourteen to eighteen. I did a little Coke and Speed in that time too, probably about five times in total. After that, I never took anything else. At university I very occasionally smoked dope and did Coke. I always did it with other people my own age, and I felt fine in myself. I wasn't doing it to escape; in fact it was the lack of control with things like Ecstasy that really put me off drugs in the long run. I stopped smoking cigarettes when I was twenty–five, and I wouldn't say I ever have really abused my body, and I'm certainly not abusing my body now.

As a direct consequence of the abuse, my awareness of sex started at a young age. Looking across at my peer group as a whole, losing your virginity at sixteen was normal, but soon after that age I had a reputation for being slightly sexually intimidating. Between the ages of sixteen and twenty–two, I rather enjoyed my image as a highly sexual person. Boys my age thought I was sophisticated and I would 'catch them out' if they weren't skilled enough in the sex department! I also was pretty relaxed about whom I slept with and I moved quickly towards a full sexual relationship with boyfriends, whilst not being particularly concerned about remaining faithful. I guess I did enjoy these relationships, but with the caveats I have written about above. When trying to describe me between the ages of sixteen to twenty–one, I'd say I liked to be seen as being highly sexed, meaning if you were with me you had better perform, well and often. I'd also get much more sexual pleasure if I didn't know the person well; the first couple of encounters were usually the most satisfying. It was only after meeting my husband when I was at university that I started to settle down. At last I grew comfortable with someone, and could begin to let my guard down.

There was a period of between twelve to eighteen months when for days at a time the memories of the abuse were tearing me apart. That started when I was nineteen, when I got pregnant and had a miscarriage all around Christmas time. I was in my first year of university, in my first term. I didn't want to ruin Xmas for my family, so I kept all this to myself, but doing that really didn't help the major emotional roller coaster I found myself on, with my hormones all over the place. For the next three to six months I suffered from very bad kidney infections and I was often sick. This coincided with me thinking about my past, and I couldn't help getting very emotional about it. When I was seeing my local GP throughout the phase of infections, I let her know I was having some emotional issues. She recommended counselling sessions at the University, and that's when my counselling began, in that same university term.

§ Optional Questions: (Comment) 32
§ Optional Questions: 33, 34, 35 and 36 §

A good friend helped me out here with her companionship. She was also going through issues, and she had an eating disorder. But everything in me that had managed to right itself then, somehow all re–surfaced later on in the year. It was as if all these things I'd kept locked up inside were just pushing themselves out and bubbling over. My control over it was limited; particularly as at university there was so much free time, giving me plenty of hours to dwell on things on my own.

I didn't know much about the counsellor, just that she was a member of the university free service. My impression of her was that she was just an open–minded therapist who wanted to help me, and we didn't establish any goals that I can remember. She encouraged me to talk about my memories and discuss my relationships with people today. After four weeks, we had come close to the end of our sessions and she'd helped provide me with some positive images within the negative memories. We had about six one hour sessions in all, and it cost nothing as it was a free service. Otherwise I don't think therapy is really my thing, as it tends to open up more painful memories and feelings than it dispels, which in turn causes me to over-focus on the pain. I do think it has real value for people though, particularly those who don't have other connections or outlets elsewhere and suffered truly awful things. It gave me a valuable outlet at the time but it's not something I'd keep returning to.

When I met my husband the following February, I was still going through the main personal turmoil of dealing with my abuse. In some ways I was beginning to recover from everything I'd been through just before Christmas. To all the world I looked like I was doing fine, and at the time I met him, the socially competitive element was still there in my social circle and I was continuing to get lots of attention and enjoy sexual experiences. More importantly though, quite soon after meeting him, I quite quickly let him in on what was really going on with me. It was impossible not to as I was getting quite emotional on occasion, although most of the time I both appeared and felt 'normal'. Even through that turmoil though I was in fact pretty happy deep down, because I knew that for the first time in my life ever, I'd met someone I really really liked at last.

Support and Intimacy

Over the years my husband has managed to make me feel 100% secure and comfortable talking about it. He manages to encourage me to talk freely when I want to, and he's brilliantly perceptive when a conversation that might have some sensitive 'trigger' points is going on (he just squeezes my hand or catches my eye), but he doesn't over–load me with it. I talk when I want to, and not when I don't. He would never raise it unless I did. I really like that as others can tend to see you as a bit of a 'interest case' and, for decent motivations want to ask you loads of questions and assume it's constantly on your mind. They also can make assumptions about feelings, which can be very irritating, but my husband doesn't do that either. Basically, he goes along with whatever decisions I make but provides advice whenever I ask for it and a big shoulder (literally!) to cry on.

§ Optional Question: (comment) 37 §
§ Optional Questions: 38, 39 and 40 §

About a year into our relationship I relaxed after a while, and could actually speak about sex. Rather than just suggesting we have sex, I was more inclined to say what I liked and what I didn't like, whereas before I used to avoid any kind of conversation about details of my own sexual preferences. I also was able to be happy giving oral sex to my husband about two years into our relationship. You see, I had been unable to do this since I was seventeen or eighteen years old and it turned into a major mental block, I think because that had been the worst part of the abuse.

108

We have an active, healthy sex life where I enjoy giving him pleasure and him to me and we are compatible physically. I love just being with him and feel completely relaxed about my body and myself. The words lover and spouse mean the same thing to me, and we are very happy. We don't have any children yet, but look forward to having them later on. I feel really lucky, as I am a genuinely happy person who feels fulfilled at home, with my family, friends and work. Whilst I might have appeared super confident as a teenager and woman in her early twenties, I was actually a bit insecure.

Now I know I am genuinely content and confident and hopefully people don't think I'm arrogant. A big reason for this is the happiness I've found with my husband. I think we are particularly lucky to have found each other, as we're both strong outgoing personalities that happen to compliment extremely well. I feel we're extra lucky somehow and we both know we have a much better situation than most, added to which we both have successful careers and good relationships with our families and great friends. So now my abuse only comes back to haunt me on occasion, for example in a conversation, a phrase someone says will trigger it usually without warning.

Worries

I have wondered whether Scott's younger brother and sister might have suffered abuse from him as well, but the thing that still really plagues me about it today, is if Scott is doing it to other children now, and that would really kill a part of me. I pray he isn't and hope it was a phase he was going through before he reached adulthood. Part of me knows this may not be the case but also I know that I would destroy several lives now if I were to go public about it. There's nothing the police could really do, so whatever I did, he'd be free to act anyway.

§ Optional Questions: (Comment) 41 §

The Future

My plan now is to use what happened to positive effect. By doing this contribution to the book I know I am making a difference. In future I would like to help charities in some form or other, by helping survivors of child abuse and preventing child abuse from occurring. I do think about how I could use my own life more effectively towards that cause. After my parents have died I do intend to be more public about the work, although I'm aware I'd need to think about Martin though, as he still has no knowledge of my abuse. I'm thinking along the lines of being a spokesperson, because I could use my public profile to that charity's advantage. In the meantime I am happy behind the scenes as a donor, and helper in raising funds, and raising awareness about abuse survivors and child protection wherever possible.

Doing the Project

The questionnaire was very helpful as it helped marshal my thoughts. Only a very few questions seemed a little out of place, but once I read the information all pulled together into a draft, I could see what those questions were doing there.

Writing the story was a bit cathartic and unsettling for me as it opened up old memories, but it helped me clarify my thoughts. When I wrote the more detailed 'difficult' parts, I experienced delayed anguish and upset. Surprisingly, the words flowed pretty easily once I started writing but whilst doing so I felt a mix of triggered emotions and stress, and I did get flashbacks. Digging up the past made me feel worse, and now and then I felt inexplicably down. I was also pleased though, as setting out the story on paper has been a weight off my shoulders.

As for my husband, I told him about the finished draft and left the decision entirely up to him about reading it, as I didn't want him to feel pressurized either way. He did, and said he found it really helpful to have context around the actual abuse and how it all occurred. It mirrored what I'd told him but filled in some gaps, answering some of the more hurtful questions that he didn't want to ask. He now knows the 'physical details' without me having to articulate them. Ultimately, it seems to have been an a positive experience for both of us.

For now at least, I won't be showing anyone else the draft, and I'll be getting on with the rest of my life as usual. I don't know what's different since writing the story, but I suspect and hope it'll be the start of me being more up front about it. It's important to me to do something positive in relation to what happened, so I'll be on the lookout for things I can do to ease the suffering that so many people around us experience, because of child abuse.

~~~~~~~~~~~‡~~~~~~~~~~‡~~~~~~~~~‡~~~~~~~~~~~~~

Optional Questions

1   As you read on, who, in Vicky's world of relatives, friends and acquaintances could she bond with positively and trust, whereby she could feel reasonably confident about feeling safe?

2   Did Vicky's parents play and interact with her?

3   How much opportunity did she get to play as a kid?

    A   How much praise or encouragement did she get at home?

    B   How much exposure did Vicky have to the people she bonded with positively?

    C   She said her mother resorted to reasoning with her; how far did Vicky's parents listen to whatever she said?

    D   Up to now on a count from 1 to 10, how much time might Vicky have spent in a state anxiety or fear?

    E   How good was Vicky's physical health and vitality?

As you go on, keep in mind how her positive relationship(s) were and how long they lasted, in general.

4   How encouraged was she to have friends? Have a guess how many play time hours she might have got outside school.

5   Did Vicky's mother ever think Vicky might be vulnerable to abuse in this situation?

6   What sort of attitude did Vicky's mother have, when it came to controlling, versus understanding children?

7   How could Vicky have gained help to tell her Godparents and to gain support from them rather than her keep the secret?

8   As for Vicky's friends ... to what extent do you think her family encouraged her to have friends?

9   How high on a scale from 1 to 10 would you guess was the quality of Vicky's playtime, and the quality of her friendships as she was growing up in and around her family?

10   How far might Vicky's friendships have contributed to her development as a person?

11   How supportive were Vicky's parents in her efforts to achieve at school?

12   How good a job did Vicky's parents do, at disciplining her and providing a fair atmosphere at home?

13   How far do you think Vicky's parents had confidence in her talents and

abilities?

14   Vicky seems to come across as quite a confident person, why might this be?

15   How could Vicky have been strengthened in her thinking that the abuse was wrong, and therefore not have been a victim of the abuser's distorted thinking?

This situation exemplifies the importance of school 'keeping safe' programmes. Children need to be encouraged to be confident in protecting themselves and their body integrity, and assured of their right to say 'No'.

16   The abuser asked Vicky whether or not she wanted to keep her pants on. This represented the abusers deceptive techniques in allowing Vicky to think she had some control in the abuse situation. She may have been led to think that she agreed to the abuse in some way.

   What might have helped Vicky to know that she as the child, was not at fault?

In the circle of people she know, there were no proactive protectors who she could tell.

17   The abuser minimised the abuse, defining it as a 'game of hide and seek'. How could Vicky have been helped to see that there are some games, which are not acceptable for children because they are abuse?

(It is common for abusers to define abuse in terms of games and nursery rhymes or use   cartoon characters. This makes it harder for the child to gain belief when describing events to an adult and it makes it easier to convince the child that the abuse is acceptable.)

18   Vicky minimised the abuse by defining it as just a 'kiss' – how could she have gained the knowledge and understanding to know how serious the abuse was?

19   Did Scott ever think that what he was doing might do Vicky any harm?

20   Scott was barely a boy when he started abusing, did the adults around him ever guess that he might, just might be capable of sexually abusing anybody?

21   What were Scott's reasons (either conscious or unconscious) for not fearing discovery, and not fearing any consequences for his actions?

22   Vicky describes the abuse as not quite as invasive as rape. Is it possible to rank types of abuse as more or less serious ?

23   Given that at this point, it is now four years since Vicky's abuse began, throughout all that time on a count from 1 to 10, how much time might Vicky have spent in a state anxiety or fear?

24   Where was she, when she felt most vulnerable and in stress?

25   Vicky learned about the facts of life from her older brother, as well as other sources. Why is it that she didn't connect that knowledge with her abuse?

26 *'Martin must know...'*

This is a common complexity of the secrecy surrounding child abuse. The child may think everyone else knows about it and is party to the abuse. In Vicky's case, she did this independently. Abusers use this and may even lie to a child and tell them another adult or sibling knows and approves of what is happening.

27 *'I felt I was part of some complex web.'*

How could Vicky have had a clear concept of what was and was not acceptable behaviour from other children and adults? If she wasn't sure, how might she have tested her views and explored with trusted adults about what abusive behaviour was?

28 How far could the adults around Scott and Vicky have benefited from some aspect of sex education, whereby they understood adolescent boys can begin sexually abusive behaviour on their own, quite independently?

29 Might Scott have benefited from sex education that made him aware that adults were aware about these things, that addressed the role of sex within a healthy relationship, about the consequences of abusive relationships.

30 How much could the adults around Scott have gained from educational guidance about child protection? If they had known what the long lasting consequences of either perpetrating sexual abuse, or being a victim of that abuse during adolescence usually were, how differently might they have behaved?

31 Friends often hold the secret, yet are rarely interviewed for 'evidence'. They can and do help bring abusers to justice, by standing as witnesses in criminal courts.

32 Vicky mentions 'bad kidney infections', but this physical impact of abuse is often ignored. How might the GP have made the connection between the physical and emotional signs of the abuse? Although often not definitive, physical signs are often the first indicator of abuse and may lead to investigation.

33 Going back to Vicky's family as her haven of support, how were Vicky's more positive family bonds affected by the abuse?

34 Did she 'shut down' within this bond? If so, how far?

35 Today, is there any way her relationship towards the family could improve? How?

36 In terms of Vicky's place in the family or place of origin, how comfortable do you think she feels now, in relation to everyone there? Use a 1 to 10 measure if you like.

37 *The response from Vicky's husband is wonderful. There are some support*

groups for relatives of survivors, which can be a transformational force for good not only for a partner, but also within the family as a whole.

38   How far is it possible that a survivor can have their wounds completely healed from the past?

39   What did Vicky attempt to do, and succeed in doing with each attempt at self-healing?

40   What was it that she needed, in order to move towards having her wounds healed from the past? Where did she find it?

41   Vicky's comment, 'There is nothing the police could do.' is wrong. For Vicky now as an adult survivor, it's important to stress the importance of referral and action to protect other vulnerable children from this abuser. Here, Vicky needs to come forward, yet not endanger her own well being in the process. The survivor must be aware of all possible outcomes, and with adequate support, retain some sense of remaining in control. If we take the scenario of Vicky as a child who is suffering abuse now, people can rest assured there are tried and tested child protection procedures that do work.

Reflections on Vicky's Story

Vicky disclosed her abuse at a comparatively young age. Even then, it was difficult and quite painful for her to tell those she felt she could trust from her peer group. She's already made a firm decision never to tell her birth family for the rest of their lives, and has made peace with the situation quite consciously on those terms. One can respect this decision as an adult, but one wonders how close her behaviour is to that of a suffering child.

The survivor looks out at the world from within thick walls of thought that comprise of,

'The truth of whatever happened to you will destroy us, and be devastating for you too'.

It's better known now how children are so horrified, confused and ashamed by the experience of abuse that they 'split', and their experiences are buried in their unconscious. What's not so fully understood, is how many others just like Vicky clearly remember their abuse. In the face of destructive force or violation, a child will seek to balance that destruction by sacrificing itself. Children either want to, or are forced to go along with protecting the rest of their family and their abusers by remaining silent, and hide their confusion and disorientation.

For generations, survivors didn't divulge anything to a living soul until death took their secret with them. Aspects of this silence quietly beg our respect, almost like there's an endemic need to leave matters well alone. Vicky feels that exposing herself will hurt her family. Perhaps she anticipates the sort of questioning survivors often dread. When the silence is first broken, they are greeted by a barrage of questions that often miss the point, *"But why didn't you **tell** us at the **time**?"*

Familiar Environment

Many a police officer can tell you how adult rape victims often take days, weeks, months and sometimes years before they come forward. Why the delay? Often it's the sheer sudden shock and trauma of attack from someone introduced to the victim by their friends or relatives; someone who has been well acquainted within their intimate circle. The head of the Association of Chief Police Officers' Working Group on rape, says that between 80 and 90% of rapes go unreported. It's those ill-fated victims of violent rape by a complete stranger who come forward much earlier. *There's something about violation that happens within a **victim's familiar environment*** that we haven't examined closely enough. If we did, we'd feel more enabled to respect and learn from our response of silence. As we glance across to situations of battered wives, battered partners, and battered and sexually abused children, this sacrificial response is so universal, age and 'maturity' clearly have nothing to do with it.

Shame

One universal aspect from within our own human makeup that offers some answers, is shame. It's the main element from within children's silence that goes so far beyond history or social setting, that it may even be more resilient to change than the outer social environment of denial. Shame seems like a featherweight emotion, something that might make you blush or put you at a complete loss for words, but shame is an existential part of experience. It carries an unfathomable inbuilt memory that stretches way beyond the early years, having immense leverage upon a whole mass of strong feeling of regret and helplessness that will affect our most major relationships, for life. When Vicky's abuse started, the shame concealed the shock, and then bit by bit cast its shadow over her life. Any expectations of protection from the bonds of unconditional trust and dependence all around her were shattered. The resulting silence stretches universally between sexual and non–sexual emotional and physical abuse, and you can trace the same behaviour over to the adult rape victim's response mentioned earlier on.

Hiding inside the Main Carer's Bonds

For Vicky, Scott was her parents' best friends' son; a young boy that her parents had probably known since infancy. Vicky's whole family felt deeply obliged to respect and accommodate him. Scott's parents probably knew nothing, and Scott deceived everyone by disguising his abuse to Vicky's parents and siblings, who were the people who cared about her the most. He felt safe to abuse because Vicky's brother and mother openly trusted him; he had the right to be there. When an abuser, or abusive adolescent (like Scott) is already linked, or becomes linked (even indirectly) to the child's main carer, they automatically have complete access. For example, Vicky believed her brother Martin approved of Scott, and her big brother Martin is completely enmeshed with her parental bonds. Vicky believed Scott had an important relationship with the bigger people and parent(s) she loved most in the world. These bonds made Scott important enough to have an almost unlimited leverage over how he could treat Vicky.

The child's bonds of dependence don't stand upon the parents or the abuser as individuals, but upon the web of relationship between them all. Bonds parents have with whichever sibling, relative, teacher, lover or friend, are what really matter, and children imagine all manner of things about bonds and fear their power immensely. Even when a child appears "petulant" (to use Vicky's word) or rebellious, their uncompromised loyalty towards their parent's happiness exists well over and above everything.

Vicky's parental bonds stretched down to her in answer to her need to be loved, but equally, these bonds are about Vicky's need to love back safely in return. In order to do that, Vicky needs to have a right of place and know her presence is allowed and accepted. Ironically, it was Vicky's shame that twisted her natural need for parental intervention and protection. Instead, it transformed into a desperate need to protect her parents from the terrible knowledge of who and what was hurting her. Everything changed in a way that seems irrevocable … and yet …

Vicky's comment, 'There is nothing the police could do.' is wrong. For Vicky now as an adult survivor, it's important to stress the importance of referral and action to protect other vulnerable children. Survivors have a choice about who they tell and when. The difficulty is that within the law, the pace for them to manage this process emotionally may not be comfortable. Vicky may not be ready to go public, and this presents her with a dilemma. It can require a high level of professional skill to support a survivor. Here, Vicky needs to come forward to protect other young people from Scott, yet not endanger her own well being in the process of going public. The survivor must be aware of all possible outcomes, yet have a sense of remaining in control.

If we take the scenario of a child like Vicky suffering abuse now, people can rest assured there are tried and tested child protection procedures that do work.

Vicky has decided that it's not primarily her, but her *family* that would lose most if they knew about her abuse. I beg to differ, and think there are ways that families can address things in order to heal those betrayed and wounded bonds. Through lightening the load of ignorance, families can become equipped to face their pasts, allowing survivors to come forward and get support.

Most survivors are not takers; many want to give their support to any relatives who have also suffered. By so doing, isolation may end and for Vicky and many other families like hers, making it far less possible that another child of their clan will ever suffer again.

Story Three

Events in this story remain unchanged, making this a correct and truthful account of a childhood. People and place names have been changed.

Jim

Jim comes from Plaistow in the east London area, and he's as active as they come. This is a man in his prime who doesn't like to sit around and prattle, he likes to get right to the point and get on with things. He used to drive all over London working as a taxi driver, but he's shortly due to switch jobs and start work as an ambulance driver. He knows there's less money in it, but quality of life counts for more than that. He wants to work in a team and he feels he has a lot more to give. It was impressive to listen to him telling me about the voluntary work he's been doing locally at a children's charity for the last eight months. He said, "I hope to get qualifications so that I can work there more seriously in the future." In aid of this charity he recently took part in a sponsored bike ride from John o' Groats to Lands End as the support driver. He enjoyed taking part in it and several thousand pounds was raised.

I couldn't help but reflect upon what I already knew, about how this man had been hurt as a child, yet what he cares about most is using his time in a way that's going to mean more to him. He wants to make constructive relationships; that is, more constructive than those he's had before. He's the first to admit that he's come a long way from where he was three years ago, which was when he was coming to terms with his own child abuse.

At the point I realised I needed help, it was either get help or go down. I felt as if I had a big ugly worm wriggling around inside my brain. Suicide was the constant thing that I thought about. It was the logical thing to do, although I never actually got to the stage where I was close to physically doing it, it was something I couldn't stop thinking about, and I understand why people want to commit suicide. If I'd never reached my crisis point, I probably never would have got help and I'd have gone ahead and done it. In a way I think, "Thank God a crisis did happen." You see, I was always trying so hard to hold on to the thought that I was *all right*, but in the end I had to take action. The first thing I did really was get some books out of the library. The things that were being described in those books had happened to me, and I read that some rape crisis centres actually helped men as well as women and I went to the one nearest me in London. During counselling, the emotions that came out were overwhelming, even though it was all because of something that happened thirty years ago. It was like a bloody monster was trying to push his way out through a civilised person. After a couple of years of counselling and then group work, I can honestly say the monster is gone. I'm never going to be OK about what happened to me before as a child, but I can be OK about who I am now.

I was born in 1969 and my parents split when I was approximately one year old so I only really knew one parent; my mother. I had a young mother, and I always lived with her. She'd actually run away from home at fifteen and she had me when she'd just turned seventeen. When I was about two my little sister Josephine (we call her Jo) was born. I grew up living with my mother and Jo till I was two, and my sister Amelia, and my brothers Bernard and Toby, and with their various fathers who were around for different lengths of time. I'm the eldest in a family of six kids headed by a single parent mum, and all my brothers and sisters have different fathers.

I thought Jo's father was my father until I was about fifteen, but he only lived with us till I was about two, which is when he and my mother had a divorce. I never knew my real father and probably never will. After the divorce I stayed on with my mother, and my little sister Jo went to live with her father. Then when I was five my mother got herself another boyfriend and my sister Amelia was born. Her father was my first abuser, but he was only around till I was about seven or so. When I was ten my brother Bernard was born by a different father who was quite a nasty piece of work and my mum had a particularly hard time with him as well. Then just under two years later, Toby was born.

As a family, it has never bothered us that we all have different fathers, it's just the way it is and undoubtedly my mother was the major carer overall. And by the way, the youngest in the family now is my second sister Amber, who was born when I was nineteen. So that's the family tree to date.

Up to the time I was about four we moved about a bit, living in bed sits and small flats around Plaistow. Then we lived in one council house until I was about eleven, then we moved to a new house in a new area and we stayed there till I left home altogether at eighteen. Both these childhood homes were three bedroom council houses.

My mother worked sometimes but over the years mostly we were on benefits. We didn't have holidays much. Not till I left home was there much in the way of luxuries. We used to play sports, general school sports like cricket and football and so on out in the park. We used to get birthday presents and something for Christmas and that sort of thing, and there was just about enough to go round.

§ Optional Questions: 1, 2 and 3 §

My memories of my childhood are quite sketchy. Apart from the abuse memories, which are very clear, I don't really remember much that well. At the time you see, hitting kids was a pretty normal form of punishment and all my friends were treated in much the same way. I suppose I just tried to be good, and then whenever I failed, I was being hit. We were hit when we were caught doing stuff that we shouldn't be doing and mostly my mother dealt with my punishment.

I wasn't beaten regularly, just every now and again I would get a beating for stuff I'd done wrong. I remember being hit from about six upwards, probably up until just the beginning of the teenage years, because I don't remember being hit at all after that. But it wasn't just getting hit either ... there were some other quite humiliating events. Verbally, punishment was described as threats really, I guess we were warned and

121

threatened with how we were going to be punished if we did something wrong, as a way of stopping us from doing stuff. My mother would make comments about my behaviour. I think it was an attempt to show me right from wrong, anyway all in all I was hit most often really by my mother. As far as physical violence from the blokes who came and went, I don't think that was really a problem. I don't remember what I did for my own defence, apart from trying not to do anything wrong.

At school after about the age of eleven it was quite common to be humiliated by the other kids and by adults as well. I wasn't hit at junior school, but I was caned and slippered at senior school as punishment.

§ Optional Questions: 4, 5 and 6 §

I do remember getting kissing and cuddling, but I don't remember how often or what ages. If I hurt myself, I do remember being comforted and hugged and that sort of thing, but I don't remember it being a common thing. I ran away a couple of times from the ages of six to eight. When the police found me again, my mother got very emotional and I got a lot of hugs then. Between the ages of thirteen to sixteen, I was probably not comfortable being hugged at that age. I was getting into trouble with the police and all that from fourteen onwards, and with the schoolteachers as well for not going to school.

Occasionally the teachers would speak to my mother about truancy, and after the age of fourteen I just didn't go to school much. In my last couple of years of secondary school, I thought my mother would have preferred me to be at school but she didn't seem to mind my not attending.

§ Optional Questions: 7, 8 and 9 §

I seem to remember having a reasonable relationship with my mother at that time. I was doing things wrong but I wasn't all that extreme. Later on from seventeen to twenty I was a tearaway pretty much of the time, and out of control for several years. I don't remember how much attention I was being paid by my mother. I still felt I could trust my mother and it was her I felt closest to. Perhaps because we didn't live together from the time I was two onwards, I never felt particularly close to Jo or her father. When I was about seventeen or eighteen the relationship with my mother was starting to change. I was feeling a bit more independent and resentful at any attempts to discipline me. I felt differently I guess, because I was becoming an adult.

As for school, I can't remember my first day. Apart from a very vague memory of teachers from primary school, I don't remember any at all and I don't remember being anything other than an average kid. I don't remember feeling afraid of adults at that time; in fact I was a bit of a class clown. I didn't get in to any particular trouble, just got told off, but nothing major. I remember having a good time in the playground. Up to eleven, school was good, I enjoyed school. But when we moved house and I had to change to senior school, after that it was a different world entirely. We moved to the other side of Ilford, beyond Plaistow to get away from my brother's father. He wasn't abusive towards me, but towards my mother and she needed to move away for safety reasons.

When we moved I found myself in a totally different environment. I felt like an outsider to everybody else. To go from junior school at eleven and find myself in a much bigger school where I knew absolutely nobody was just horrible. I had always been a bit of a class clown and tearaway and there I was, dropped into a hostile environment. I did notice that the friends I made had similar home lives to me; they had a broken home kind of background like mine. We were all tearaways basically, and we had a laugh. We didn't dare dream of talking about the punishment we got at home from our mothers! In the first year of senior school I was pretty well behaved but no teachers stand out in my memory. By the time I was in my second year I was getting into trouble a hell of a lot.

§ Optional Questions: 10 and 11§

I was starting to stand up for myself and I was always fighting. I was subjected to some humiliating things. I was definitely an object of derision and a target for people to make fun of, even though throughout I managed to make friends as well. I remember my physical appearance was amusing to some, and people would make fun of me quite a lot and make comments about my face. On one occasion a note was passed round the class saying, 'Jim Walker prays that he can please not be so ugly'.

When I was eleven, shortly after we moved house the whole family started going to church. Then when I was about thirteen or fourteen, I used to go to church on my own, because I believed what I was told and thought I should go.

§ Optional Questions: 12, 13 and 14 §

There are some people from school that I'm still friends with now, and I spoke with a couple on the phone just the other day. So although I did have a hard time at school, I was able to make friends as well. In the end I absolutely hated school and basically I stopped going when I was fourteen. I started messing around, usually in a group. I didn't like the head of our year. He humiliated me a couple of times but I don't remember actually being afraid of any teacher as such. It was not a particularly harsh school, in terms of how the teachers were to the kids.

I don't go to church any more now, as I have no interest in religion, I will go to weddings, christenings etc... but that's all. Basically, today I don't believe in God but I do believe in good and evil.

From the years of seventeen to twenty I felt suicidal, depressed and downright horrible. When I was drunk I could cope. I did enjoy myself. And I did get into trouble with the police; I was shoplifting, committing petty crime and doing several other things during my teenage years that if I'd been caught, I would have been banged up. I am quite lucky that didn't happen to me. I got into drugs, cannabis, LSD and all that.

From eighteen till about twenty-one I was depressed, my mind was in complete turmoil and I could think of nothing but bad things. I'm sure it was the drugs that were bringing it out. The drugs tapped into the damage and the effects of the abuse, it just tapped into that. At twenty-one onwards I stopped smoking the stuff. I drank a lot and I was using that to cope, convincing myself I was happy. I had to drink just to socialise with people. The shyness I had was chronic – so much so that I sometimes think I never got the opportunity to choose a woman to settle down with and have children.

When I was in my teens, there was another adult I felt I could trust, he was twenty years older than me and I think he was rather a role model. Like I said, I got in trouble with the police and that sort of thing. We were into smoking dope at that time, and I would go round to his house to kill time. I suppose you could say he was a friend of sorts, and I did get to know him reasonably well. I would say that he was one adult outside the home that I trusted, but today I wouldn't say he was a good role model. That friendship started when I started to drink alcohol, smoke cannabis and take speed, from when I was about fifteen. Drugs stopped when I was about twenty, twenty-one. The drinking still goes on but not so much.

Jerry

My abuser was my mother's boyfriend, the father of my sister Amelia. His name was Jerry Howell and he abused me from roughly the time that I was five. At first he seemed like a decent bloke. He used to take me out to places, like take me swimming or to football and he did play the role of the stepfather, but he used to have this strange habit. He would slip his thumbnail underneath my thumbnail, as that used to amuse him. It didn't matter to him one bit what he was doing to me, that it was uncomfortable or that it bloody hurt. While my mother was on the nightshift, he used to baby-sit me and that's when the abuse took place. I remember when I was sitting up watching TV with him at night, he would offer me a sweet and just before I took it he said,

"If you take the sweet you have to go to bed." This statement has always stayed with me all this time. I had to make a choice; I could either not take the sweet, which is pretty much an impossible thing for a child to do, and stay up watching telly, or take the sweet and go to bed. I wanted to do both and I can't remember which I chose. It felt very painful and paralysing for me as a child because the prospect of going to bed when we were alone together in the house, was anything but nice. That was something I'd try to resist.

§ Optional Question: 14 §

I don't remember being terrified, but I used to try and pretend I was asleep and be absolutely still and quiet and hope that he would just go away. You see, I actually believed that if he thought that I was asleep he wouldn't disturb me. I wasn't really afraid until the abuse started, just after it started was when I became really terrified.

I don't think I admired him; I just didn't want him to do anything. I don't think he told me to keep it a secret and I don't think he said anything about it. I just done what he wanted to do and after it was all over, it was as if nothing happened. He never spoke to me about it. It was just that when we were alone together these things happened. I don't remember anything being said about it whatsoever.

I don't remember him treating me badly or talking to me badly in front of other people, yet every night he would have access to me, and after a while I did know what to expect. Each encounter was horrific, yet I don't remember feeling strongly at the time. Whenever he did get into the bed, I wanted so much for him not to do them things again, but he always did.

What I'm trying to say is that it's funny that as a five year old kid, I don't remember dreading these things at other times during the day as well, because I think I blocked it out, I really can't remember being disturbed or upset about the abuse at all during the day. It was like it was happening to someone else. Because there were different things that went on during a typical day and there wasn't just sexual abuse between us, the distress varied depending on what was going on. It was only at nighttime that I always anticipated there could be something different, something new and horrible and even worse than what had happened before. This abuse with this Jerry Howell lasted a couple of months. I think my mother was working on this nightshift for a couple of months and when she became so heavily pregnant she couldn't go on working, the abuse stopped.

I felt dirty. I think I felt cut off and numb. I think I just wanted it not to be happening and because it was happening I wanted to forget it, just not to acknowledge it. I remember being a smiling laughing kid and having a good time but at night it was a different world, it was a nightmare. I just kept it to myself and I don't know how to explain it. But I think I can understand it as just a poor little kid having horrible things done to him who doesn't want to talk about it. It didn't even cross my mind to tell anybody.

§ Optional Question (and Comment) 15 §

My counsellor described my abuse as being "particularly brutal". Jerry Howell had complete access to me, and he made me suck his penis and swallow the semen. I remember when he done it to me, I felt that he had urinated in my mouth, as that's all that I understood. The abuse went on for I would guess a couple of months, and obviously it was only when I grew up that I understood what was happening. Being made to do such a thing with his penis was bad enough but my worst memory was when he lowered me into a bath of freezing cold water. I did a shit in the bath. When he saw what I'd done, as a punishment he made me pick up the shit and he made me eat it.

§ Optional Questions 16 and 17, with Comment §

As I said I was roughly five years old when it was going on and then my sister was born and my mother was back in the house all the time again, and the abuse stopped. In the end, he was forced out of the house because he was such a nasty piece of work. For example I remember once I threw up on the floor. I was standing in front of it and he made me kneel down and lick it up off the floor. It's almost unbelievable that he was able to do this to someone, and further, I cannot remember anything being said in a violent way. It was as if what was happening was a normal form of punishment or discipline. It was like that with everything.

§ Optional Question: 18 §

It wasn't something I ever thought about telling anybody and that was it. It was like I was just there to be used when he felt like it. I don't know whether he had malice towards me, I just felt that he was in total control over me. He didn't even need to make threats. He didn't seem to care, he just done what he wanted and it didn't matter. He wasn't afraid of anything, being found out or that. He didn't care.

He behaved as a normal person would behave with a child in their care. He didn't treat me as a favourite or give me special treats or things like that. I didn't know what to expect from him. I don't remember what kind of conversations we had. I was only five. I don't think I even looked at him unless I was being spoken to, and I didn't acknowledge his presence unless I had to. When I thought about him I just felt fear and I was just scared of the next time he might come into my room. Maybe it was because I felt it was dirty and it was bad that I didn't think about him as a child unless I really had to.

It's a different story now, because as an adult, I find I probably have thought about him a good deal more often than I'd have liked to. I knew it was wrong definitely back then. But then I didn't have the capacity to understand what would happen when the secret got out, all I knew was that it was unthinkable and impossible to talk about. At the time I understood everything to be okay, there was just something happening at night, and generally when I was that age, I felt okay about myself, like I was enjoying myself when I was with my friends. I remember feeling very strong at that age, for example really really feeling that I wanted to be grown up, I felt that I couldn't wait to be a big boy and to be older, bigger and stronger so that no one could touch me. Anyway as I say, eventually Jerry Howell was forced out of our lives.

More

The other abuse incident happened to me when I was nine. There was this seventeen or eighteen year old guy we knew when we were kids. He would often come and visit us, and play in the house. He was called Ahmed. He used to like wrestling, and he told me he would show me how to defend myself. He told me to take my trousers off and he would get me to lie face down on the bed. He pressed himself against me. I felt, yes, right this is hurting. Then it stopped. Then this stuff was running down my legs and I didn't know what the hell it was. It was semen. Then a couple of years later when I grew up I realised what it was. I can remember him trying it on with other boys. He tried to make me convince another boy that it's not dirty; that it was a way of defending yourself. I did tell the other boy that there was nothing wrong with it, because I didn't realise what he was doing.

§ Optional Questions: 19, 20, 21§

By the time I was nine I'd known two sexual abusers and I'd had oral sex, anal sex and I knew what spunk, shit and puke tasted like.

Telling Others

I didn't confide in other people for a very long time. Finally it came out one night when I had been drinking, to a close friend in my early twenties. I can't remember a time before then that I talked about it. It was just a matter of blurting it out. They were shocked obviously but pretty supportive and they were just trying to say things to be supportive. I didn't tell them everything. I wouldn't want them to have pictures in their head. I just told them the words "I was sexually abused." without going into graphic details about what had happened. The sexual abuse was bad enough but there were other things that happened as well that I felt were horrific, but I didn't tell him about

126

them. I felt our relationship was okay after that. I thought that I should be able to tell a friend and the response didn't surprise me and he took it as I was hoping he would take it.

§ Optional Question &Comment 22 and Question 23 §

However, just a couple of years ago he did start telling other people. This was at a later stage, when it suited him to. This was a massive betrayal and I will never forgive him for doing that. I had to take steps. I had to tell my family, my sisters and my mother what had happened. Pressure definitely was a factor in the telling of my story. I was under a lot of pressure to tell my family at a time when I didn't really feel ready to do so.

§ Optional Question: 24 §

To be honest I've got more pity for him than anything else, because most of the people he told my story to, well, some of them have definitely been using it as a juicy piece of entertaining gossip. As I say, it was just recently, a couple of years ago that he started telling these people. That's over ten years down the line from when I first told him, but in any case, these were the people I didn't care about because they were the kind of people who were not able to accept this was a terrible thing to happen to a child. I wasn't interested in their opinion. I remember I did tell the girlfriend that I was involved with at the time, and basically she hugged me. Our relationship was not a long term one, but in any case it felt good when she hugged me.

It's been a couple of years since I first started talking about it to my counsellor, and doing that has helped me to venture into the graphic details. Now I can share the disgusting things that happened to me with whatever people who want to listen, and not be ashamed of what I'm saying. Because I'm not a victim of what happened to me anymore, and I know it's a step towards stopping it happening to other people.

When I was telling my counsellor about it I could barely say the words and what had happened. When the individual counselling finished I went into a group. In the group, it took me a couple of weeks between deciding what to say and then actually saying it, but I did feel better about myself after saying it. I can say it all now because it was nothing to do with me. It doesn't make me disgusting or dirty. It is on his soul or whatever and now I can say it without even flinching really. The only thing it brings up in me now is disgust and anger that someone could to that to a small boy.

I haven't really discussed it further with my family, since telling them when I had to tell them because it started to get banded about. The whole family responded by being shocked, upset and worried about me. They struggled to find words because they were devastated. At the time, I was receiving counselling and I reassured them that I was okay. I told them that the act of telling them was for the good, and would probably help in the healing process.

§ Optional Questions: 25 and 26 §

127

Family

Although us six kids have different fathers, we all grew up together so I consider my siblings as complete sisters and brothers. It means nothing to us that we've got different fathers and we're a pretty strong family. After my wilder days were over, I helped my mother out and chipped in financially wherever I could, and we're all like that, all of the same kind of mind, if you like. We all have a lot of respect for mum, and she's always interested in each and every one of us.

If there was a way for me to pursue the people who abused me, I would. At one stage, I was thinking constantly about taking out my revenge upon Amelia's father who did those sickening things to me when I was five. The thing is, it appears that somebody else already has. Someone hurt him so badly that he is now brain damaged. Sometimes I think it could so easily have been me who did that to him, but it wasn't. As you learn more about child abusers, you get to know how one abuser often abuses scores of children in one lifetime. Understandably it follows that another person that he abused as a child probably did this to him, for revenge.

But there you are, I didn't have to do it. Frankly I think it's just a shame that he's alive and wasting people's money to take care of him. As for the other one, I can't get to him. I've been through telephone books and been to the police and that sort of thing. There is no trace of him. That's a shame because I would like to be responsible for getting abusers to pay a price for what they've done. If I were to witness abuse happening I truly believe I would lose control. The abuser would be in serious danger, and the only thing that would stop me is concern for the child. I would like to hurt them and scare them. I have been through periods where I would have been prepared to take the law into my own hands. I have fantasised about torturing abusers, and I like to hear that abusers are beaten up in prison and they live in fear for their lives; I have no sympathy, they deserve it.

Relationships

I was really looking forward to having a sexual relationship of my own right from when I was fifteen, but I had chronic shyness and never really started to have an ongoing sexual relationship till I was thirty three but I did enjoy it when it started. It's just that there were other aspects of the relationship that were pretty problematic.

I've had a lot of relationships where people abuse and hurt me and I know now it's supposed to be a pattern with survivors of child abuse, and I recognise it in my own life. A friend of mind settled down and started having children. His relationship broke down with his first wife and he had another child through another woman. When I was in my mid twenties I became that child's godfather, but the problem is the woman I got involved with was the child's mother. We became lovers and she wanted to have a relationship with me, even though she was married to my friend. I'm not claiming to be an angel, but when my friend found out, I started to get blamed for the entire situation. I became the scapegoat and now I no longer see my godson. I tried to get a contact order through the court, and as a result they made very serious disgusting allegations, which really shocked me. Part of their grounds for denial of access was that I was abused myself as a child and because of that, I'm supposed to be a danger to other children. Then they won the case and I couldn't keep contact with my godson.

My godson and I had such a good, close relationship. I was enjoying his childhood and making him laugh, and we spent many happy hours together. I'll never forgive them for taking him away from me, and me away from him. It gives me the absolute horrors that they think I would ever abuse him, because I probably know how to be his protector better than anybody. Nobody could be more vigilant because I know exactly what to look out for. They know what they have said are lies, but they are prepared to do anything to get their way. I'm absolutely gutted. At the end of the day I know I tried as hard as I could to be there for him, but on the other hand I feel I have let my little friend down because it's my duty to protect him. He's a fun loving little kid who has a lot of friends, and I contributed to the development of his pleasant personality. That's a real achievement and I know that if six-year-old kids were given choices in these matters, I know he would choose to have me back in his life.

I can say to my abuser now that good relationships are what I value in life. I have a beautiful thing that I know is there, that I know I created and there's nothing you can do to take that experience away. I can get rid of all the rubbish, because the rubbish belongs to him.

Future

Hopefully I can start to have a more settled decent life if I can stop people abusing and hurting me. I've met people who treated me badly in the past, as I've said it's not uncommon for people who've been abused to find themselves with abusive people around them. To give you another example, just recently I was arrested because this woman who I was involved with made false allegations to the police. After they spoke to me I was released without charge. People, who are hurt and quite damaged themselves, seem to find me a target for their own problems and they take it out on me. You start off with a good relationship with them and somewhere along the line they turn into horrible people. I've had to take action to defend myself and it's time to start mixing with decent people who don't make themselves feel better by abusing other people. So I'm taking steps to change those I associate with and make changes with the people I am close to. Having said that, as I said before I still have some friends from school and it hasn't been a complete disaster. Hopefully them days are over and I can look forward to love and happiness and feeling good about myself.

I think after the upheavals I've been through I feel I'm in position now to take advantage of the good things in life. I am not responsible for the bad things that have happened to me and I'm looking to the future. I want to get married and have children, and create a happy family. Over the last couple of years there have been some relationships that have broken down, but most of the people in my life now are fine. I've got really great family relationships now, and I am interested in going forward and having a relationship for life with a partner.

If I can do anything to help other people to stop these things happening I'd gladly do it and gladly do whatever I could to make this world a safer place for children. I've got a deep, deep hatred for people who do these things and I think it's appropriate considering what's happened to me. My counsellor tells me it's OK to hate. I've made it. I've survived even though I've come close to ending my own life. I'm one of the lucky ones. I've got there and I just hope that I can encourage other people to talk about the things they need to talk about. That's why I'm contributing to this book and hopefully it'll make some sort of difference. After seeing other people talk about their abuse and sharing my history with them, it showed me that there is a way through it. It is hell on earth but it's well worth it in the end.

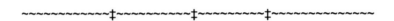

Optional Questions

1   Who did Jim bond with positively and trust?

2   How much exposure did he have to this person (or these people) whilst he was growing up, and how long did his relationship(s) with them last?

3   On a count from 1 to 10, how afraid was Jim at home, and how much time might he have spent in a state anxiety or fear?

4   Do you think Jim's mum played with him?

5   How much opportunity did he get to play as a kid?

6   Can you guess how many play time hours he got outside school?

7   'she didn't seem to mind me not attending school'

Although Jim wasn't sexually abused during this period of time, this is a common gap for child abusers to step into. How could a child abuser exploit a child in this position?

8   It was when Jim was between the ages of six and eight that he shocked his mum by running away from home. Once Jim's abuse had started, how much less safe would he have felt at home, compared to how he felt before?

9   Did it occur to Jim's Mum that he might have been vulnerable to a child abuser? How far do you think Jim's Mum would have listened to whatever he said?

10   How much interest do you think Jim's mum took in his school, and in his school work?

11   How much would Jim's mother have respected his school, and respected outside authority, like the police and such, compared to how she respected Jim as an individual?

12   How much praise or encouragement do you think Jim might have received at home?

13   Can you guess how much shouting, and how many rough words he heard from the adults around him at home?

14   Jim's abuser offered him a sweet. But what was he really trying to do, and how did he deceive Jim?

15   It is common for survivors to feel dirty. If a child or an adult survivor was to tell you this, how would you respond? If you say,

'Of course you aren't dirty!'

That smacks of denial about what's really going on, and it doesn't move towards the survivor on their own ground, so it's better to offer acknowledgement. For example,

'I can see that you really do feel dirty after what has happened to you. What can I do to help you feel better about yourself?'

16 Jim is describing the most terrible forms of child abuse. As listeners, how can we make sure we are open to thinking the unthinkable and believing the unbelievable?

17 'I felt that he had urinated in my mouth...'

This is a common misperception in children who lack sexual knowledge. It is not uncommon for children to lack sexual knowledge, but interviewing children on these issues is a highly complex and specialist task. Otherwise, it can all lead to confusion when interpreting the child's account. Professionals sometimes make mistakes too. For example one child spoke about white pee. They thought the child meant semen but in fact the abuser had urinated on the child as part of abuse. Clarification is really important here, as is stepping out of the habit of making assumptions. When talking to children, we have to enter the child's world in a big way.

18 Overall, try and imagine what Jim's mother was like as a mother, as a family member and as a person in her own right.

19 As Jim was growing up, did he 'shut down' within his parental bonds?

20 If so, roughly how old was Jim when those various 'shut down' stages occurred?

21 How and where and to whom was this shutting down expressed, if at all?

22 Both adult survivors and children tell in their individual ways as best they can. This may seem extraordinary to the listener, because sometimes their story comes across in a matter of fact way, or as a joke, or spoken with seeming confidence. It may well not be as we would expect, with the child (or adult) in a tearful and upset state.

23 Think about how Jim was able to speak of his child abuse. How might other adults and children tell?

24 Jim's friend told other people without Jim's agreement. How did this add to the abusive experience and Jim's sense of exposure and betrayal?

25 How do you think the positive aspects of the bonds Jim had with his family might have been affected by his abuse?

26 How far do you think he wanted to spare his family the pain of knowing, and why?

27 Do you think this was a just outcome?

28 'Part of the grounds for denial of access was that I was abused myself as a child.' This should never be any justification, unless it is clear that there is evidence of risk to children. It would be the worst insult to all survivors of child abuse to suggest they may, as a result of their own abuse, go on to abuse children themselves. There is no evidence to suggest this is the case.

How might Jim have been affected by all this as an adult, in terms of feeling stable enough to go on and make better relationships in the future?

29 For a child who has had to put up with such a lot of rough treatment, how far do you think Jim's abilities to be comfortable with positive people versus negative people, may have been affected?

30 Why is it hard for abuse survivors learn to fill their lives with more positive relationships, and learn to connect with their true feelings and instincts?

Reflections on Jim's Story

It was talking to Jim that showed me glimpses of an attitude that it's okay to hit. It seemed to me that although his mother loved him and did her best, there were plenty adults around both him and her during his childhood who made him feel that being threatened with violence was normal. Indeed, there were phases when it was normal for his mother to be treated like this, just as she probably was as a child.

When a child is fond of someone, they are willing to give all that they have, and when they're being blatantly pushed around and manipulated, we can only dread the ways they might suffer. They could be made to give in a vast variety of ways. Strange mixtures of promises, rewards, and forceful lies get dreamt up on the spur of the moment and used experimentally, just to see how well they work. Whilst an abuser is grooming a child, a well-administered progression of these can constrict and control a child tremendously. Fear and control work their way into the child's understanding of who they are, what they are allowed to say, to whom and in what ways they should be obedient, and to whom they are either allowed or forced to be intimate with. These things make children ideal subjects for abuse and sexual exploitation, and children are a pushover for anyone who knows how to wield power over them.

Jim doesn't think that it occurred to his mother that he could be sexually abused as a child, especially not by someone trusted as a boyfriend and lover. Sadly, it's often the case that a parent just doesn't realize what danger they might be putting their children in. They are seduced by the person, and they aren't 'in the know' about how easily child abusers can break into to the bonds of relationship between parent and child. This is equally true for all parents who never give a thought to the possibility that even a life long relative or a well known friend could perpetrate harm. Child sex abusers who get professional help, and undergo probation and supervision admit that targeting single mothers is quite standard. They can rarely recover from being child sex abusers; they can only manage their behaviour, for example by reducing their opportunities to abuse.

Jim told his mother about his abuse because someone in his community was spreading rumors, and he wanted to be in control when his family found out. As statistics circulate in our society without context, child abuse survivors (especially men) can easily get laden with other people's assumptions. One assumption is that if you were sexually abused as a child, you will go on to abuse children as an adult. This can transform into something malicious wherever there's ignorance. But perhaps it's a pretty good example of how, at the point when a survivor discloses their child abuse, they have very little on the positive side to gain.

Jim's Mum was devastated when he told her his big sister's father abused him, but the whole family got together, and they've supported him as best they can. If we look into that more closely, we can possibly see why. Jerry Howell was rejected from the family by Jim's mother just under thirty years ago. If this man had gone on living within the family unchallenged, Jim may well have had the hardest possible situation to live on with, even now. As well as the child target, abusers groom whole families whereby every member experiences an enormous sense of betrayal. In Jim's case, his family's response was to confront the abuse, and this enabled Jim to heal.

134

Story Four

Events in this story remain unchanged, making this a correct and truthful account of a childhood. All names have been changed.

Lillian

When I met up with Lillian for our interview, she was just about to go off on one of her weekend visits to see friends. She has friends inside and outside work and enjoys other long term fulfilling friendships; some going back to her university days. The closest ones know what kind of childhood she had, and also share their problems with her. She works as a book editor for a publishing firm, working on reference books like medical encyclopaedias and first aid books. She's well read and was always very successful academically, which has proved to be a vital source of income and freedom in her adult life; also a strengthening force that helps her see problems not only through emotional experience but in a freethinking objective way. In her mid thirties now, she told me about the things that have kept her going. Her interest in social change and politics has provided her with role models that include three former politicians who she calls her "three wise men". She sees each of these men as interesting, wise and lovable in particular ways.

Whilst she enjoys exploring natural wild landscapes on horseback, like Exmoor and other places, she used to love watching Concorde so much that she often went to the airport to see it come in from New York! Her home is her sanctuary, and she loves London, feeling that it protects her like a huge warm overcoat; she particularly likes the river, which she says is beautiful and gives out huge amounts of gentle energy without her having to do anything.

This appears to be a portrait of a trouble free life, yet Lillian is nevertheless weighed down with the spectre of a childhood that catches up with her when she suffers another bout of self-harming, or when she does nothing to resist a bullying situation in her professional life. Perhaps some of the clues to these things lie in her story:

The people I grew up with were mum, dad and my brother. Mum and dad were about twenty-six years old when I was born in 1967. My brother Robin was born in 1969; he is twenty months younger than me. We moved house several times. When I was born, my parents had been married for less than a year. They lived in a caravan park in Sussex and by the time my brother was born, they had moved to a bungalow in a nearby town. I started playgroup while they lived there. When I was three, and my brother was about one and a half, they moved to a village in Cambridgeshire.

Dad graduated from art school specialising in graphic design, got a job as a graphic designer, and still works as such. Mum graduated in English and used to get sub editorial jobs for various magazines before my brother and I were born, and she went on to do office admin in a staff agency. For about a year, when I was about four, my grandmother (my father's mother) also lived with us. She had also lived near my parents before my brother was born, and used to visit mum a lot. She looked after my brother and me, and as my parents tell it (and I vaguely remember) she favoured me above my brother, but this was only because she thought the eldest child in a family was "the most important". That didn't have anything to do with me as a person; she did the same thing to my cousin. I didn't feel any particular connection with her, and she has never known what has gone on in our family. In fact, she is a bit of a "baby Jane" character, she's never really grown up and the rest of the family have always protected her.

§ *Optional Questions: 1 and 2* §

Mum was the one who saw to our physical needs. Dad worked full time and, when my brother and I were young, Dad often arrived home after we had gone to bed. Mum did most of the "parenting" and nurtured my brother. When I was eight in March 1976, we moved to a farmhouse situated by itself in the fields, some way out of the village and we were there for two years. When I was ten, I went to boarding school because my parents had just moved abroad, to the Middle East. I was there for about a year and a half. During term time I spoke to my parents on the phone, but my main concern was my life at school. Although I had a couple of friends, I was ostracised and bullied there. This was at the hands of my housemistress as well as many of the other pupils, and was so bad that other parents heard about it and told mum and dad. In the eighteen months there the holidays were stressful. I had to face my father's pent-up frustration because he hadn't had access to me, and my mother's ugly moods as a result.

My brother Robin was at his prep school for a year. Then when I was twelve, and he was ten, my parents took us to live with them in the Gulf. I lived there until I was eighteen, when I went to university. All the houses we lived in really varied in size, from my parents' first tiny caravan to the farmhouse, which was gigantic and had about five bedrooms and two bathrooms. It was quite old and dilapidated, but much loved by all of us. We moved several times while in the Gulf; each time we lived in a one-storey villa with two or three bedrooms. One of the villas had a swimming pool.

Mum and dad used to have fairly extreme arguments and discussions in front of my brother and me, but told us how we were to interpret what went on. I remember my mother saying, once,
"I don't want Robin to go back to school thinking we're going to divorce behind his back, and I don't want Lillian thinking it is all her fault."
That was a horrible surprise to me, as I had ignorantly seen it as all my parents' problem and nothing to do with me. Those strange ideas of my mother's sounded like the real truth, and I couldn't help feeling I'd done something wrong.

The problems at home existed for as long as I can remember – possibly even way back before the sexual abuse started. Mum controlled all of my behaviour by shouting at me and belittling me. She used to rage at me and hit me a lot. Even the smallest thing that I did could send her into volcanic rages. Mum hit me most often of all. I was much more terrified of her than I was of my father. Mum used to criticise and correct every aspect of my behaviour, down to the way I stood, sat or breathed. When I was small she was always shouting at me for not keeping our bedroom tidy – she used to call me a "slut".

§ Optional Questions: 3 and 4 §

My brother used to tease me when he was small; he didn't understand what he was doing but just thought it was funny. I used to get in a rage and hit him. He would cry out and mum would come in and shout at me and hit me. I was jealous of him because I felt mum loved him, not me. I was also frightened of him because of the power he had to make horrible things happen to me. Dad used to smack me occasionally, if I had done something he thought was wrong. I wouldn't say I got swept along in a wave of getting hit, and hitting out myself, because I felt in no way equivalent to my parents and Robin. They were human beings – I was just nothing. In any case, after a few years of hitting out to defend myself, I found the consequences were so frightening, I gradually stopped and the pain just went inside. Yet the violence towards me continued, regardless of what I did or didn't do. The smacking died out almost altogether by the time I was about eight or nine. Mum's verbal attacks still went on, though, for the whole of my childhood, and even continued when I was a student.

Mum loathed everything about me. Her derision would start with something really small. For example, that I hadn't put my brother's and my toys away, and it would build up into a storm of bellowing. Sometimes it didn't even make sense. I remember her shrieking at me one day that my favourite colours were "pink, red and green", and on another occasion that I "relished potatoes". I would only have been about five or six years old at the time. Obviously, looking back on it, I can see that these episodes were absurd and rather pathetic, but at the deepest level I still feel pain, rage and terror about them. I just remember this constant rage and screaming. Mum would tell me her criticisms were
"for your own good!"

I was very very good, so that I could be as sure as possible of not doing wrong. I also tried to keep still and quiet – again – so that I wouldn't do anything worthy of blame. I grew very good at analysing my own intentions and motives minutely in case I did anything that could possibly cause offence. Sometimes I managed to avoid trouble by second-guessing my parents; sometimes I didn't. I was equally afraid of the tongue-lashing and the physical violence. I was just afraid all the time.

§ Optional Question: 5 §

Basically, I almost never got any kissing and cuddling from mum. Dad was all over me a lot of the time, but that was just cold groping and snogging. That started at some non-specific time during my childhood. It was unpleasant. When I was in my teens or even a student, the attacks wouldn't even be sarcastic, it would be an outright attack on what I looked like, what I was wearing, what I happened to be doing or not doing at that moment, even how I stood or breathed. I couldn't see any pattern to the attacks, or work out what I was doing to cause them. I became so careful not to do anything to bring it on, and this is the thing that nobody understands. I really was like a ghost; I was so "good" I was almost invisible.

The thing that other adults said about me most often was, "She's no trouble – you hardly know she's there." Apart from one or two incidents that stick in my memory, I never retaliated or 'acted out' any bad feelings in response to what was happening to me. From quite early in my childhood I learned to weigh the possible consequences of every word and action very carefully indeed, so I could never, ever, ever act on impulse. I am still like this today. I am sure it saved me from feeling even more pain than I had to cope with already, but as a result I cannot allow myself to express human feelings or impulses. Even when I try to explain my situation to other people, they completely fail to understand, and this makes me feel more alone. The abuse is still poisoning my life.

Mother's Family Origins

She was just angry with me because that was the way it was. Mum had had it tougher than me in some respects, but much easier than me in others. When she was little, her family lived in South Africa, and it looked like rather a charmed life. Mum didn't see much of her parents, but was brought up by her paternal grandmother, who was a stable and loving presence in her life. She also had adoring uncles and aunts, and servants who looked after her. The family were mixed–race but well off. That changed abruptly when the family had to leave South Africa and come to England. There was isolation, as there was no existing community to come into in London, unlike (for example) Caribbeans. Mum had to face racism from some people for being too "black", but also experienced racism from black people for being 'not black enough'. They left South Africa because my grandfather was fighting against the apartheid regime and the authorities were after him. Then life became much poorer for them, and Mum had to go out and work from the age of about thirteen, to help support the family. There was no pressure on her older brother to do this however, he was thoroughly spoilt in comparison to her.

§ Optional Questions: 6 §

When I was growing up she wasn't attacking me because she was jealous that I was becoming an attractive young woman in comparison to her; I really was ugly. I looked like Kermit the frog. When Mum was in her teens she was much more attractive, and very much more confident about her appearance than I was about mine. There are some photos of Mum and I, each taken when we were about seventeen years old. Mum was posing on a ladder somewhere in Italy. She's wearing a tight top and tiny shorts, and showing off her figure. In the picture of me, taken during my gap year between school and university, I am wearing a dress that looks like a sack, and my hair hasn't been styled for many weeks. I look like a vagrant.

Regarding my father's work in the office, I think Dad basically liked what he did, but his job was also stressful. When we moved to the Gulf, there was a lot more pressure involving deadlines, budgets, advertising standards and publishing laws whilst skirting around the ever–changing political situation. Mum didn't seem to have any professional preferences, and went through university because her father made her. She started working in an office, but told me she stopped it because I was physically sick every morning when she got ready to leave. She never seemed to make the connection between the sickness and how much I needed her.

The sexual abuse went on nearly every day, and I don't know when it started, but the first instance I remember was when I was about four. We didn't really have any kind of conversations in the beginning. He wasn't usually very "fatherly" and I only really noticed him when he was molesting me. Dad was a bit of a shadowy figure – I never expected anything from him. I just wished he would leave me alone. He just groped me and took what he wanted from me with no human interaction at all. (When I hear of what has happened to other abuse victims, though, I am almost glad that there was so little interaction.) I didn't feel like his favourite – I didn't feel anything from him, except occasional bursts of intense hatred later on when I was in my teens. I was a Mummy's girl, in that I wanted a mother's love more than anything else in the world, not a Daddy's girl.

When he was molesting me, at first I accepted it because I didn't understand it, but when I got to school, and got to see other people (such as babysitters with their boyfriends) I understood that it was weird. There were no words. I don't recall saying anything myself, and the reason I don't, is that Dad didn't say anything – he just did it. He used to have a sickly smile on his face, or be looking into space or looking at me with a "love-sick" expression when he was wanking. When he wanted me he would whistle for me, like someone calling a dog. If I didn't go to him, or if I showed any sign of disgust at what he was doing, his sickly smile would turn instantly into a cruel, disgusted face, and he would pull my clothes back into place in a very exaggerated way that left me in no doubt about how much he hated me. I just remember being in the bathroom with him, with him wanking himself (and me as well). He would be jerking himself off, and fiddling between my legs.

I remember telling Mum about it soon after I became aware of it, but she said I was talking rubbish. It used to happen everywhere at home, including in the toilet, the bath or bed, and also in public. He did it so much, there wasn't really time to think about it. When my father and I were out, and surrounded by other family and/or other children of my own age and I looked at him, I felt either blank if nothing was happening, or terrified and helpless if he was molesting me. I was safe when I was away from him at school or on the bus, then I could block it out of my mind for a few hours. I still love buses, trains and aeroplanes now, because I feel safe on them. Nobody can get at me there.

I was only safe from being molested when I was alone. There was nobody, no other adult relative or friend, that I felt close to outside the home or that I could trust. I only remember Dad using the "our little secret" gambit once. He didn't need to tell me to keep it secret, because he knew Mum wouldn't save me. I would wish that one of the teachers at school, or one of my parents' female friends, would take me under her wing and look after me, but there was nobody. My grandmother, who lived with us for a year, was nice to me but I didn't have a particular bond with her and she had no idea what was happening to me. I was a little girl with a whole procession of imaginary "mothers", including aunts, family friends, teachers, dinner ladies, and I even imagined that Princess Anne might comfort me one day instead.

§ Optional Questions and Comments: 7, 8, 9, 10, 11 and 12 §

Regarding friends, while I was at primary school, middle school and boarding school, I had only two or three, if any. Then there were other children who were not chosen friends but my parents' friends' children. I didn't have a close friend until I was twelve. My friends were not very curious about my home life.

Throughout my childhood, I never discussed my home life with any of my friends, even when they told me things about theirs. As I got to my teens though, I was aware of problems in my friends' lives. My best friend at school had anorexia and then bulimia. I knew that her family had arguments, and that her father, like mine, drank a lot. In fact sometimes, her father and mine had drinking bouts together. Some of my friends used to get shouted at a lot in their families, and in one family the parents were always criticising the children severely. Nobody seemed to get the intensity of punishment that I did though.

School

I started school at four years old; it was the Easter term, 1972, I think. I had a favourite teacher at primary school. She was quite unlike one of my fantasy figures like Princess Anne, probably because she paid some attention to me in real life, and in the way that a five-year-old child can love a mother figure of sorts, I loved her. Mum kept well in with her, so we looked like the perfect family. She was friendly and took the time to talk to me, although she had no idea about what I was going through at home.

The family went to church nearly every week and we went to sunday school. Dad, though, says he is an atheist and didn't like us being brainwashed. The people at church were all friends of my parents and had a lot to do with them. The teachers got on extremely well with my parents and because I was good at schoolwork and not much trouble, they seemed to think that my family was ideal. My parents, especially Mum, enjoyed the fact that I did well at school because the teachers were so complimentary to them about it. The only thing that worried any of them was the amount of bullying I got from other kids, but nobody thought that was a major problem.

§ Optional Questions: 13, 14 and 15 §

I was usually so engrossed in schoolwork or in my fantasy life, that I didn't feel anything about being in the classroom. I suppose I must have accepted the situation at school totally. I was nervous of one teacher (who picked on all the children, not just me) and most of the dinner ladies, but not really frightened of any of the adults. I didn't get hit or belted at school by the teachers at all; I used to get slapped occasionally but probably much less than other kids. In the 1970s people weren't as sensitive as they are now and we all came in for it from time to time. I did, however, come in for a few problems from one teacher at primary school and one male teacher at middle school, who didn't like the fact that I got so many things right and could guess what they were going to say!

§ Optional Questions: 16, 17 and 18 §

At primary school in deepest Cambridgeshire, where people from five miles away

141

were strangers, bullying was a huge problem for me, right from playgroup till I left there. At first I was bullied because I was a different colour from the other kids. My brother came in for some of this too, and the other kids used to call him and me "blackie" and "nig-nog", and tell us we came from Africa or China. It used to get me upset when they did it, but I wouldn't say it scarred me. My brother was accepted though, but I wasn't. Looking back, it seems to be a "chicken and egg" situation. I acted oddly, therefore I wasn't accepted and because I wasn't accepted I retreated further into my fantasies and became even more peculiar.

The bullies were actually younger than me. They knew how easy it was to intimidate me because I was afraid of everything and everyone. All they had to do was come up behind me and whisper something – even just my name – and I would flee. I would hide in the school building every break time, and if any adults tried to shoo me outside I would make up excuses about having a cold or something like that.

I never fought back, apart from one occasion that remains in my memory. I was standing on a chair in a classroom, having an argument with another little girl called Kathryn, who was also standing on a chair. I pushed her and she fell off. I was sure I was going to be punished severely, but nothing happened. The thing that stopped me from retaliating every other time was the fear that I would be "found guilty" when the adults got involved. I appeared to be a goody-two-shoes, but I wasn't – I felt guilty before I'd even done anything. The bullying went on at state school (middle school) and boarding school as well. The only place where I was free of it for any length of time was in the Gulf. Even then my best friend turned against me for a year (I didn't blame her – she had family problems). Towards the end of my year and a half at boarding school, just before my parents moved us to the Middle East, I told the headmistress that I was unhappy at being taken away (although I didn't tell her exactly why). She told my parents and Mum hit the roof. That was the closest I ever came as a child to telling someone in the outside world that I was unhappy at home.

§ *Optional Questions: 19* §

When I went to university in the north of England, I found, to my great delight, that I could get on OK with people. I had friends right across the university and got involved in lots of activities. I was a wardrobe mistress for drama productions and I helped run various other projects. I got on with almost all of the lecturers. Even there though, there was one lecturer who didn't like me. He wasn't keen on young female students anyway. I know I was lucky, as from what I've heard it could have been worse. Classical Arabic was usually taken by mature students or Arab people and he thought that I was a snotty teenager who had no business doing this high-flown academic work. I got the highest marks of all the students in my first year, but by the end of the second year this man had destroyed my confidence so much that I thought I was useless, so I changed subject to Anglo-Saxon and Old Norse. The lecturers in my new department, though, were lovely and encouraged me as much as the other students. I ended up with a 2:1. I didn't expect to get such a high grade; I thought I would fail. I had to ask one professor whether the examiners really meant it or whether they were just being nice.

I have also come in for bullying at work, on several occasions, each of them lasting for several months at a time. The last episode was last year. I think all these people picked on me because I looked weak, and onlookers assumed that I lacked character, or "asked for it" because I didn't stand up for myself. I suppose when you are scared of everyone it must look contemptible. I think I've been conditioned in some way so that I act out some kind of behaviour purely due to the trauma I suffered as a child at home and then in the outside world. If I had been treated differently I would have had the full range of emotions, including the less attractive ones, and would have developed much like anyone else. I really wish that someone had understood my situation back then when I was a child, and recognised that I was undergoing almost constant violation, victimisation and trauma. The way I am now is a reflection of this fact, not a sign of weakness or lack of character. I hope people are more aware today so that no other young person has to suffer as I did.

Molested

I was sexually abused by Dad almost every day until I left home. When I was little it was sexual molestation, such as fiddling with me, making me wank him or watch him wank, and licking my cunt. I couldn't get away from him anywhere – even when I went to the toilet, he would follow me and fiddle with my fanny when I peed. Mum stopped this when I was about eleven, because she was afraid of him making me pregnant.

Mum had always been perfectly aware of what he was doing with me in the bathroom. She professed not to know the details for years, until Dad blurted it out one night in a drunken rage, but she had always suspected it was something to do with sex and that's when she actually declared she was worried about me getting pregnant. Mum said to Dad, and also confirmed it to me later, that if he didn't stop what he was doing she would tell his father and his brother. Years later, though after the sexual abuse had stopped; she told my brother it wasn't that bad because Dad had never actually had sex with me. My brother has separate memories of her getting furious when Dad took me away, but this was anger and jealousy directed at me, not Dad. Dad had a very strong ally in my mother. Robin also told me about one occasion he remembers from several years ago, when Mum told him that I had been "having an affair" with Dad when I was nine.

I was only about five or six when I knew about the facts of life and pregnancy, it feels like there was never a time when I was free of this knowledge. I even used to put on plays with my dolls where I would stick a little dolly up a big dolly's dress and then pretend that the big dolly was giving birth (yes, really). When I was being molested as a child I knew that what Dad was doing was wrong. Thankfully I was never raped, but I knew that what he did was bad as well as unpleasant. I didn't think about me getting pregnant. It was not something I remotely associated with myself. I never wondered or imagined what it would be like if my father forced himself upon me and actually raped me, I was overwhelmingly frightened enough as it was, and I didn't need to torment myself with any further thoughts. He never talked about actually having sex with me personally, and in this way I know, I am much luckier than many other abuse victims.

§ Optional Comment 20 §

Financially my parents always seemed to be struggling, even when we were in the

Middle East. That may have had something to do with the fact that Dad was very honest, and never took bribes from anyone, so although we didn't have a fancy house or a new Mercedes every year, that was no bad thing. Mum did find administrative office work in the Gulf, and they earned a good salary between them, but most of it went on property, education, or living expenses. We did go on foreign holidays, but to places that interested our parents – e.g. the Maldives and the Seychelles, rather than Disneyland.

My brother and I both had piano lessons, and music was just a thing I had to do, like schoolwork. I was never very keen and was hopeless about doing music practice. We both had second–hand bicycles, because that's all my parents could afford, but we liked them. We also had things like tape recorders, walkmans and digital watches. I don't recall wanting anything very flash (apart from a horse – but I had imaginary ones, so that was OK). I was eight when I started horse riding lessons and I loved it and used to go riding nearly every week. The people at the stables did not know my parents, and that was the only area of my life that was separate from my family. Although my parents did let me do horse–riding when I was a teenager, Dad was jealous of the horses and used to go into rants about "throbbing stallions" and "getting your leg over a horse". He did get up horribly early on Saturday mornings to take me to the stables, but I can't say I have any lasting guilt about that. He also had a pervy colleague who used to buy paedophile magazines showing pictures of naked little girls on ponies. All this though just wasn't an issue for me. I was much more concerned with what my parents actually did to me.

They were very open with us about money, and used to tell us all about their money situation, right from when we were children. Sometimes my parents were more open-handed to my brother, for example when he got to do sixth form at a public school, which was quite expensive; and sometimes they were more open-handed with me, for example, I did horse–riding when my brother didn't get to do some of the things he enjoyed. I don't recall them using gifts to "buy" us. They were mostly consistent and fair, although they resented my riding a bit because it took me away from the family. I wouldn't say my parents squandered money, although Dad did buy and drink a lot of alcohol while we were in the Middle East.

§ Optional question: 21 §

He used to get drunk a lot there, especially at the weekends, and rant and rave at Mum and me because she wouldn't let him have sex with me.

§ Optional Questions: 22, 23, 24 and 25 §

It was unfathomable to me what caused mum's moods and dad's frustrations. I was terrified by the lust, viciousness and rage that apparently sprang up out of nowhere. I couldn't identify anything that I did, or didn't do, to cause these things. Really, it was the abusive behaviour that caused my terror and confusion, but I didn't realise that at the time.

Dad also did things to make us feel frightened and isolated, like pulling out the telephone cord so Mum couldn't phone her parents in England. He could get really nasty. He wasn't an alcoholic, but used getting drunk and being apparently out of control as a way of frightening Mum and me. Once he got drunk and wrote me a poison-pen letter full of venom and hate about how I was such a useless daughter and he was going to buy another one from Sri Lanka. He also used to do things like "stalking" me in the house, such as lurking outside the bathroom, or my bedroom door when I was getting changed. He would tear up a picture of me with one of the dogs and shove it under the door, or go outside and throw stones at my window to scare me. Every form of abuse was equally terrifying, no matter what form it took. Every single day I wanted to get away from him and Mum. I only remember him hitting me once out of his sexual frustration, and his behaviour towards me varied between outright viciousness and sexual harassment, such as groping, sloppy kissing or attempts at French kissing, pressing his dick into my bum and filthy talk. This largely stopped when I left for university, although it still happened sometimes in the vacations.

§ *Optional Questions: 26* §

I still see my parents occasionally, but don't like seeing them. I never enjoy it. When I was little I found it creepy, and when I was older it was really frightening. I never in my entire life looked to Dad for any emotional nurturing, because he was so cold about getting what he wanted and no more from me. I looked to the imaginary women instead. I even tried to pretend Dad was a woman once, to make it easier to cope with. Just for the record, I don't consider sex filthy, just my father.

When I was a young child, Dad and I didn't talk much. He only noticed me when he was using me. When I was older, he used to "talk dirty" all the time, both when I was alone with him and when Mum and Robin were there as well. He never had much to do with me as a person, and I got a strong impression he really didn't like me. He had always talked dirty to me right from the start.

At first it just happened when he was molesting me. He'd say words like "fan" and "rude" and "sexy beast" to turn himself on. Later, when he was finally stopped from molesting me by my mother, it got nastier and more threatening. He was always talking about sex and genitals and telling rude jokes. It was a constant stream of talking about sex. He also used vicious words and silences to punish me for not doing exactly what he wanted.

Brother

My brother saw my father's interactions with me right through his childhood, the 'love sick' father groping me in public as a child, and the 'talking dirty' sessions every day, but obviously he didn't understand what was going on. I guess if he thought about it at all he just believed what Mum told him about Dad and me being "in a relationship" or whatever bollocks she came out with. I only told my brother what had happened to me when we were both in our late teens. I was about twenty, at uni, and he was about eighteen when we both started confiding in each other and discussing our family situation, and began to trust each other to some extent.

Sometimes my father would humiliate me in a group. When I was about fifteen, we were all in a car with some other people, really squashed in, and he tried to French kiss me, and when I turned my head away he sneered
"Difficult to kiss, aren't you?"

145

When I was about twenty or twenty-one on holiday from university I remember being out with a large party of his workmates. Whenever dad was drunk, he was never as drunk as he liked to make out and he was pawing all over me. He had always liked groping me in public places anyway, because he enjoyed getting away with it. There was no particular thing I was especially afraid might happen; everything I most feared was already happening anyway.

§ Optional comment and question: 27 §

Telling

I constantly wanted to tell someone about it, but never dared because I believed that nobody could possibly care about me in real life. (I remember once, when I was staying at the house of some family friends, the woman kissed me goodnight and I was astonished, because I thought I was disgusting and didn't understand how she could bring herself to kiss me.)

§ Optional Comment and Question: 28 §

When I got to my early teens and learned how other families have serious problems too, I was disgusted at myself for being so disloyal and cowardly and not putting up with it more. From then onwards I really believed that I had failed my own family. I felt I "should" put up with as much as my parents wanted to heap on me – rape, beating, whatever. I wasn't even human; I was infinitely worse in relation to everyone else. I was brought up with Christian values and taught to be kind, understanding and forgiving to others, especially people who bullied or abused me.

I didn't have "internal conversations" about it when I was a child, except for feeling very unhappy at what Mum was doing to me. When I got to my mid teens, I particularly loved one teacher, and every day I used to fantasise about throwing myself into her arms and telling her everything, and having her protect me.

In the family there was no secret. Mum knew from the start, but was overwhelmingly angry with me, not my father. My brother said that when we were little, and Dad used to take me into the bathroom, Mum would crash around in a rage. She also told him years later, that I had been having an "affair" with Dad when I was nine. She was always making out to other people that Dad and I were some sort of romantic couple, saying things like "they can't keep their hands off each other" and reinterpreting what was happening as me having some guilty liaison with him, even when the molesting was happening right in front of her and she could see exactly what was going on.

She saw it all but flatly to my face denied that I had been resisting it, even when she could see I was scared and distressed. I think she simply wasn't interested in either the truth, or me. It suited her that I was being molested because then she could be the Madonna and I got to be the whore. I had to soak up the horror so that she and my brother could have their happy family lives. I have to be so careful not to project that anger on to other mothers today, but sometimes I can't help feeling it intensely.

Mum and dad used to sit my brother and I down from the time we reached about eleven or twelve. Mum used to "interview" me about this "affair" I was supposed to be having with Dad in a Kafka-esque kind of trial. She said things like,

"Lillian has obviously superseded me in the family" and "I'm going to leave and take my Ben with me, and Lillian can stay and be Dad's concubine" (God how that hurts, even after all these years). She also got Dad to say what he thought about it, and he would go on and on about being "infatuated" with me. Mum also used to have discussions with me alone. She used to say things like,
"You must think very carefully what you are doing, because you could hurt a lot of people." and
"The onus is on you to control this situation". Her most common phrase was,
"Use your discretion."

§ *Optional Questions: 29* §

Even now I have no idea what she meant by this. I also remember once, when I was about fourteen, Mum was talking to Robin and me about how Dad needed us more than we needed him, so we had to look after him. At that time she also told me that she knew she had a choice between protecting me and protecting Dad, but chose to protect him because he was more vulnerable and more in need of care than me. I guess that was her Christian values kicking in.

The fact that Mum told so many lies to me and to others, for me, just confirmed the distinction between my parents' fantasies and the truth. I was aware of the lies. But my awareness didn't help me at all, because Mum and Dad controlled all the information about the family that reached the outside world. Everyone believed them, not me; or like my headmistress from boarding school when I was eleven talked to them, instead of taking instant action to protect me. It was like living in a totalitarian society.

All I needed was just one person to care for me as I was. They didn't necessarily have to do anything heroic, such as confronting my family – they just needed to see me and care for me as a person, not just as a robot designed for passing exams. That care would have made me stronger and less timid, and the fact that someone else cared for me might have made my parents more cautious about what they did, or else the outside world would have seen what was going on. In my life now, this is something I do find myself thinking about quite a bit; perhaps because it was crucial to my protection. I can see how important it is to apply this awareness in our ideas about protecting children now.

§ *Optional Questions: 30 and 31* §

It never occurred to me that anyone would find out, and even if they did, they would take my parents' side, not mine. I had to bear it alone, not because of an intrinsic loyalty that I had towards my family, I simply couldn't tell and simultaneously, I was constantly desperate to tell someone. The consequences would be so terrifyingly violent that it was safer just to put up with it. I suppose this is why I now talk about it so much – I have an extra twenty years of human life to catch up on, by breaking through the silence.

When I was seventeen I was in my gap year between school and university and staying with my parents. One time, Dad had been out drinking with a friend and he came back in a filthy mood. He started attacking Mum and I think hitting her as well. I couldn't see them but I could hear him saying, over and over,

"I'll break your fucking arm!"

This was particularly horrible, as Mum had been ill for months. She'd had an operation to remove a brain tumour a few months earlier, and was in no condition to be treated like that. I had reached the end of what I could bear.

There was no way I could escape, since I didn't even have the money for a taxi, never mind a plane ticket. I suddenly wanted it all to end. Even the thought of going to university wasn't enough to stop me. I went into the bathroom, took about a dozen Pro-Plus (caffeine) pills, which was all I had in my possession, then lay down to die. Twenty minutes later, when I didn't die, I got up again. I went into my parents' bedroom, where Mum was, and told her that I thought I needed to go to hospital as I'd taken an overdose. She threw herself on the bed and started crying.

I stood there like an idiot, not knowing what to do. I know it sounds ludicrous and of course I know now that I was in no real danger, but as far as I was aware then, I really was dying. My mind just felt completely blank. In the end I went to bed and stayed awake all night, feeling my heart beat like a pneumatic drill. I heard Mum shouting at Dad, calling him a "stupid drunk", but neither of them came in to see me. I speed-read a whole book in about three hours. I read sections of an art history book that I didn't like just to keep my mind occupied. In the morning, my parents were very subdued. They took me to my secretarial course, where I spent a perfectly normal few hours. That morning was even more frightening than the previous night, I had done my utmost and it had made no difference to my life. I felt as if I had really died and come back as a ghost.

§ *Optional Questions: 32, 33, 34 and 35* §

Self-harming

A couple of years later I started self-harming by cutting myself with knives and razor blades. This began one summer when I was staying with my grandparents; on my mother's side. They never abused me and very kindly let me stay with them for the long summer vacations, although they also knew nothing of my problems.

Mum and Dad were still living in the Gulf at the time, but Mum flew back to England for a short visit and managed to upset me. She said various hurtful and untrue things to me, about how I was "useless with people" and things like that, and the cutting started quite unexpectedly just after she'd flown back. It started with a really trivial incident. My grandfather wanted me to make him some soup, as he wasn't feeling very well. I was in the middle of watching a programme featuring one of my favourite politicians. I was frustrated and angry at having to stop watching this programme as it was comforting me a lot, especially after my time with my mother. But I felt guilty about wanting to disobey my grandfather, so I went into the kitchen and cut my arm several times with the bread knife. Nobody saw anything though, and I carried on as normal.

With cutting, at last I had somewhere to go with the pain. Usually, I just caused scratches or thin scars and could hide the evidence. One day, though, a few months before my finals, I cut myself with a serrated knife and unthinkingly used such force that I cut into my arm right down to the main tendons and nerves. I lost a fair bit of blood and had to walk into town to get to the medical centre. I then had to go to hospital to have it stitched. I have almost always self-harmed alone. A few years ago

148

in a club, I did it in public. I was already feeling upset and some guy wanted to dance with me and he wouldn't take no for an answer. He wasn't nasty or anything, but he was so insistent that I picked up a lit cigarette lying nearby and stubbed it out on my arm. He backed off immediately.

§ Optional Questions: 36, 37, and 38 §

I have had two prolonged courses of antidepressants, but these didn't stop the self-harming. Today I still have the urge to self-harm quite strongly, but I usually only do it occasionally, just once every couple of months. I use a form that doesn't cause problems, like hitting my belly with a heavy object or stabbing myself to make a small but deep wound. Periods are my usual flashpoint time, because I so hate being fertile.

Telling

It was only when I reached university though that I started talking to friends about the abuse; I also talked to some of the lecturers and tutors in my college. I wanted to tell the various women that I encountered and loved about my distress, and during my time at university, I continued to love the teacher from my school in the Gulf. She and her husband had moved back to England, to a village in the West Country where Dad was born. Her husband still has some relations there, so we got to see them in England. I did stay with her a few times while I was at university, and just before my finals when I was twenty-three, I told her what had happened to me.

When I started telling her we were in her house. She was guarded in her response with me, although she did listen. At first she said,
"You don't have to tell me if you don't want to", then later in the conversation she said,
"You should have shouted more". She must have told her husband that night, because the next day he made a vague, embarrassed reference to it and said,
"Your father must have been under a lot of stress".
I tried to be brief and not burden her with a lot of detail. Afterwards they acted just the same as before with my parents, although she did occasionally do things like patting me on the arm when she thought my parents weren't looking. But really, I only ever told her the brief outline of my past. I didn't tell her all the stuff about how frightening it was and how intense. I never told her how completely I loved her – I didn't want to burden her. I wasn't afraid that they would go and tell anybody else, and I don't think they did, as far as I know. Initially, I felt glad that I had told her, although I didn't want to labour the point. I also felt ashamed of feeling so needy.

§ Optional Questions: 39, 40 and 41 §

Later that year, though, when she was nearly forty, she became pregnant. I was devastated because I felt usurped, and I was horribly ashamed of being a grown woman and having such feelings. It was as much of a shock as bereavement.

During the time she was pregnant the self-harming became really intense, such as smashing my face with a boot. I was suicidal. I wanted to slash out my own womb. At odd times, such as when I was on the bus, I would find myself crying, tears gushing down my face, and this was so embarrassing, like pissing myself in public. I literally punched a hole in the wall of our lounge. I had got through all my teenage years by not

149

asking for anything from her, but stupidly hoping that one day I could be hers, instead of belonging to my parents. That door had finally slammed in my face. The molestation, the violence and terror were all the childhood I was ever going to have. It was never going to be all right.

I saw them a couple of times after the baby was born. The first time, she took me up to the nursery and talked to me while holding the baby in front of her, as if to get me used to the sight of the child. To me though, the baby just looked like a very small human shield. I went out with them once, to see some horses, but in the years since then I have only seen them about twice. This was largely my doing because I couldn't bear to see the child, and was afraid of losing control around them. She and her husband still keep in fairly close contact with my parents, and this feels to me like the ultimate betrayal.

Love

I really didn't want to know about having a sexual relationship of my own when I became old enough to do so; I had sexual fantasies from my twenties onwards which involved either men or women, but usually women. What I really wanted, though, was someone to care for and protect me, but I was so disgusted with myself for wanting this. I feel I'm surely much too old to be protected and cared for in that way, so these cravings make me feel really stupid. I don't hate sex, but it just feels "unreal".

I dread the social aspects of sexual relationships more than the sex itself, like other people's expectations. I would hate to be part of a couple, especially if I had a relationship with a man! I couldn't bear to be with someone who wanted children, and I might feel a bit better about it if I was sterilised. Now I'm thirty-five and apart from one or two fleeting sexual contacts with women, I have never been sexually active. I still have fantasies, and if I met someone who felt right I might risk it, but my feelings of love come out in other ways.

I spent several years being in love with my woman boss at work; I did tell her about my problems, and she was as kind and supportive as she could be given our working relationship, but again I couldn't go too far. I'm afraid I was also jealous of her children, but I never let on to her. There was another woman whom I loved for two years, a friend who is unconnected with work, but she was straight.

Therapy

I have had so many different therapists, it feels like there are too many to list here. Two therapists compelled me to analyse my own motives and consider the situation of everyone else involved in the painful events that happened to me. These are things that I have always done anyway. These requirements actually formed part of the abuse; they meant I could never "be myself" but always had to consider other people's feelings instead.

Also, because I had problems at school, university and in my work and social life, as well as in my family, I now distrust the very underlying social structures within which my suffering took place. Other people seem to take social structures like marriage for example, for granted. I don't see why I should have marriage, or a family as a goal. I question everything, including what therapists tell me. I have been in and out of therapy since I was at university. I have had various forms of therapy – hypnotherapy, psychoanalysis, Gestalt, group therapy and so on. I have liked some of the therapists a lot, and found it comforting to talk to them, but I still have little or no trust in the actual process of therapy. Although there is still a lot that I don't remember, particularly the psychological stuff, I have always known that it happened and I was fully aware of it as it was happening, so I don't expect any further big secrets to be revealed in therapy.

I don't admire therapists per se; however, I have always admired people who created their own institutions out of nothing, like my beloved teacher and her husband, or the original boss of my company, or Helen Bamber (who runs the Medical Foundation for the Care of Victims of Torture). I also admire people who break down existing institutions to start afresh.

Confronting the Family

I see my own family as little as possible – about two or three times a year. I wrote my parents a letter, several years ago, in which I set out what had happened, said how I was trying to cope with my life, and described the effects of the abuse on me. I kept my tone calm, trying as hard as possible to be factual, and certainly not vengeful. Dad was actually more sensible than Mum about reading it, although he said he wanted to put a meat cleaver through my head for upsetting Mum.

He blamed me for causing mum's distress and attacked me for upsetting her. He spoke a lot about his position in my life as my abuser, just the same as he had all those years earlier during the dreaded "family meetings" that happened intermittently way back when we were children. He described how painfully frustrated and angry he was when Mum stopped him from having me; he said it was like being forbidden to eat a delicious slice of cake, or take an enjoyable drug. To his credit, he has never denied what he did. I think this is because of the lovely liberal family myth that if he just talked about it, the slate would be wiped clean and everything would be OK. He said he carried out sexual activities with me

"… to make you into a more interesting person."

§ Optional Questions: 41, 42 and 43 §

He also told me to stop referring to his activities as "abuse", but I said that is exactly what they were. He said that he wanted the whole issue "buried". My parents both wanted the slate wiped clean and wanted to be "good friends" with me. My mother said she cried and cried when she read the letter, then said she burned it and felt much better. I was upset but not really surprised. I wish I could have been left to live my life without having to explain myself to them, but at least I think I was fair. Mum said that her feelings on reading the letter were,

"Why has Lillian done this to us?" and "We've got so much to worry about already". She was upset for herself, because I had criticised her. Burning the letter was her way to make all the things I'd said, "go away".

She sent me a typed reply, written like a business letter with bullet points etc, in which she justified what she'd done and explained how she saw herself, not me, as the rejected one. I do still have a copy of the letter I wrote them, as well as the one Mum wrote me.

151

A few years ago my brother arranged a family meeting to discuss the matter again, I think as an attempt to heal it all up and lay the thing to rest.

§ Optional Questions 44, 45 and 46 §

The cigarette incident in the nightclub happened the night before this family discussion, and I probably self-harmed because of the stress and anticipation about what was to come. In the end, I found it very upsetting to be on the receiving end of my parents' anger and accusations. They started inventing bizarre stories to "prove" I was a bad person. Mum talked about an incident that was supposed to have happened when I was about nine. According to her, the woman who helped her in the house asked me what a Hoover was for (a hint that I was supposed to clean my room), and I said, "For you to clean with". I don't remember anything like this incident at all. I also think it was most unlikely that this woman would expect a nine-year-old child to use a Hoover. If anything like this happened at all, I think it's most likely that she was innocently making a funny remark and I innocently didn't get it. I can't remember the "example" that Dad produced, but it was along the same lines. In the end Mum got very angry that I'd "divorced" the family, in her words.

§ Optional Questions 47 and 48 §

This meeting had only happened because my brother was becoming worried. Mum had been phoning him and been really vicious about me, saying I was no daughter to her and so on. I hadn't been home for Christmas and I hadn't let them visit my flat, and I still haven't to this day. The meeting severely upset me for several months afterwards. I only keep seeing my parents only because I fear the consequences of stating what I really want, which is never to see them again. I get on much better with my brother, who is a steadfast friend as well as a dear brother, although he feels sorry for my parents and feels that they need the most care. I feel guilty at putting him in an impossible position. After all, Mum and Dad are his parents as well as mine, and I don't want to deprive my brother of his parents. The family would never be inclined to get some professional outside help. They are quite happy for me to be the one to go to therapy. I don't think family therapy would work, anyway, as it would be yet another audience for them and more pain for me.

If I made any trouble, by taking legal proceedings for example, I would feel responsible for depriving my brother of his parents. My brother wants me to come to terms with what's happened in the past so my parents can, in his words, "start to be parents" to me. He doesn't think I caused it, but tries to find reasons why Mum and Dad couldn't help what they did. He seems to think that my father is "doing his bit" by just talking about it all over and over again, but doesn't realise that Dad basically expects not just to be completely forgiven, but also respected and supported.

§ Optional Questions 49, 50 and 51 §

I feel betrayed by absolutely everybody. Most of all by my parents, but also by my brother and by the people who have heard me but still try to 'put the case' for my parents, as well as those who have used my problems as an excuse for bullying me. I also feel betrayed by society, and by the liberal Christian value system that I was

152

supposed to live up to. I did everything I was supposed to do, and more, but when I was a child I didn't even get the most basic care and protection. Emotionally I do have a sense of betrayal from my teacher from the Gulf, as she and her husband have known about the abuse for fourteen years and are still loyal friends to my parents.

The pain of this is something that I have to deal with alone, as opposed to it being a shared problem between a circle of friends and family who are on familiar terms with me. I think it's easier for them to let me stew in my own juices rather than talk to me, which would mean they would have to start to question their own lives, attitudes and values.

A small isolated 'bubble' in the family, consisting of two of my cousins on my mother's side know and care about me and I also know about the serious problems that they have had. I still have occasional social contact with more distant relations, but they only know the mask constructed by my family, not to me as a person. I don't want them to know because they couldn't cope (they are devout Christians, and it would shatter their world-view) and it would cause immense trouble. I couldn't bear an entire sea of voices and faces all denying me. If they knew the real me, it would cause immense trouble. I'm always living within a state of distanced tension, even with my extended family.

I don't mind children, although I can take them in fairly small doses! The daughter of my beloved lady was a sweet kid, but I am desperate *not* to have children of my own, and my dearest wish for over a decade now has been to be sterilised. I have recently obtained long-term contraception, which has also sorted out my menstrual tension brilliantly. I am really glad I've done this and I couldn't get over the way the doctors and hospital dedicated so much time and resources to me. I'm very grateful.

At work, I have talked with a few of my colleagues about my own problems and try to help them with theirs. Some say that they value my kindness and friendship. I also started an art exhibition for employees at my company so that we could feel a bit more like people rather than production units. I no longer discuss my personal problems with bosses, as I do not want to weaken myself in their eyes. As a book editor, I usually get on OK with superiors, although I did suffer a bit of bullying and I feel that usually they only notice when I do things wrong. I was criticised for being off sick with stress after two very intensive projects, but they don't appreciate what I do right, like working very long hours whenever needed to meet tight deadlines. However this seems to be true for many of us, however, not just me.

I try to be polite to religious people but it torments me to be required to forgive and understand my tormentors. A cycle I share with so many others is to feel resentful, then guilty, then hate myself for my feelings. I was really upset some years ago, when Archbishop Tutu and (former US president) Jimmy Carter brought their "forgiveness campaign" to this country, as one of their aims was to get abuse victims to forgive their abusers. I was distressed that the only time religious people thought about sexual abuse was when they wanted to lay yet more moral burdens on the victims. I also hate the way the word "victim" has somehow become a term of abuse. It simply refers to your position in a certain situation; it's not a description of your entire personality.

Perhaps in an effort to be even-handed, the broadsheet newspapers seem to give a disproportionate amount of space to the "false memory syndrome" and interview members of the False Memory Syndrome Foundation's British branch in an effort to 'balance' other articles featuring child sexual abuse. Perhaps these commentators take it for granted that most people disapprove of child sexual abuse, but from my viewpoint it sometimes seems as if the "false memory" argument is the only one being heard.

Having lived for so long with my left wing, liberal parents' repeated justifications for their abuse of me; such apparent endorsement of their views often leaves me feeling very threatened and isolated. People who have been abused have spoken up about it, and their abusers have gone to the False Memory Society. I heard one person committed suicide because she was falsely accused of lying about her abuse. This shocking idea has muscled its way into society, and society just laps it up. It's all degenerating into an argument where the winner will be nothing more than the person who shouts the loudest.

Abusers live their lives feeling perfectly entitled to go on doing what they do. The greater proportion of those who abuse, have not actually been sexually abused themselves. One third of abusers say they did it because they were abused themselves as children, which leaves two thirds who make it happen simply out of their own minds. People who find little wrong with abuse find it disgusting that people don't buck up and forget it, yet what would anybody possibly have to gain by saying that they were abused? For by far the greater proportion of abuse survivors, taking their abusers to court equates so perfectly to a personal Armageddon, they simply don't do it.

In my life now, I follow Gramsci's dictum of "pessimism of intellect; optimism of will". I cannot bear being confined by aggression, bullying or the dead hand of tradition. I am happiest when I can keep expanding my knowledge and understanding, and am free to live and love as I wish. I still feel scared and hopeless sometimes, but I am constantly curious about what will happen in life next. Despite the bad, misinformed press for survivors, understanding about child sexual abuse has increased hugely over the past twenty years. It is especially heartening that some older survivors are now able to talk to those around them. After decades of silent misery, it may not be too late for them to find a measure of peace, with a more appreciative understanding from those around them.

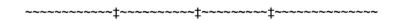

Optional Questions

1   As you read on, see how closely or how distantly Lillian bonded with her mother. What was good about this maternal bond ... and what was bad about it?

2   Where could Lillian go as a child for comfort, to get a feeling of safety and reassurance?

3   Was Lillian's mother able to speak to her in a way a child could understand?

4   What about her father ... how did he communicate to his daughter as a part of the parental team?

5   Who, in Lillian's world of relatives, friends and acquaintances could she bond with, whereby she could anticipate, and look forward to a sense of safety?

6   Did Lillian's mother actually reject her?

    If so, how far and in what way?

7   *"All I needed was one person...* Many survivors speak of 'one person' believing them. This why it's so important for adults to listen to children and survivors. If you are that 'one person', you are very important indeed.

8   Children will often blame an adult carer who isn't abusing them sexually on the basis that they should have known, or did know, when in fact they didn't. The abuser manages and manipulates the whole situation, including the other potentially protective adults in their environment.

    What might have taught Lillian that adults (for example, her teachers at school) can't imagine what is happening and that she would need to tell them?

9   Today, a 'proactive adult' is someone who is aware about child abuse issues, who happens to spend time with the child in the child's immediate family circle and community. This adult has a protective role, and for example could have a position in the family, or be a play leader, teacher, a nurse or a doctor. If there had been protective adults in Lillian's life, how could they have noticed something was wrong?

10 How safe or otherwise did Lillian feel in her own home?

11 Lillian was so scared. What needed to happen so that she could feel safe to tell?

12 What was it that she was longing and looking for?

13 Where, in the end, did she find some refuge?

14 As there was a lack of positive bonding between Lillian and her mother, what did learning, and the teacher who imparted that learning come to represent for her?

15   What was Lillian looking for in her teacher, and in what way did she bond into relationship?

16   What sort of attitude did Lillian's parents have towards her education?

17   How far did Lillian's parents bond with the teachers at her school?

18   How far were Lillian's parents interested in her safety and well being at school?

19   Might Lillian's parents have worried that the outside world would find out what went on at home?

20   Comment "*I am much luckier than many other abuse victims*"

This sort of minimisation is a common survival response. It was awful what Lillian suffered, but it helps her to think others may be worse. Also, this is not quite the same orientation to that of comparison and quantification, as Lillian wants to extend her concern and respect towards other survivors, who she thinks about and feels for.

21   Did Lillian's parents share food, toys, money and resources wisely and in a fair way in the family, or not?

When a potential protective adult assesses a child's parenting, the criterion they choose to judge a happy child–parent relationship can be deceptive. Shows of an equal management of care and resources can deceive the outside world into thinking those parents could not be abusers. Equally, a child might think ... "well, my parents are fair with me (with the things a child cares about such as treats, food and toys). They are fairer than some of my friend's parents, so I can't possibly have bad people for parents." But overall, was Lillian treated as an equal in this family, or was she victimised?

22   What sort of marriage did Lillian's mother and father have?

23   How far was it a healthy relationship whereby each partner felt safe and supported, and could be reasonably happy and fulfilled?

24   Who was more comfortable at home, the father or the mother?

25   How similar were Lillian's parents, one to the other, and how similar were they in their attitudes towards their daughter?

26   As you read on, look into Lillian's experience of being in constant jeopardy at home. From the time that she was born, to the time that she went away to university, did her sense of safety and well-being at home ever get any better as she grew up mentally and physically?

27   Comment and Question

'*He enjoyed getting away with it....*'

The abuse of power is very key for abusers. They enjoy the thrill of deceit and controlling everyone in the situation.

Who exactly did Lillian's father control, and in what instances did he display his daring?

28   Comment and Question

'the woman kissed me goodnight'

Had Lillian ever experience any maternal warmth? Why did she feel confused? How could she, at this stage in her life, interpret a kiss?

Important to be careful about touch with survivors. Check it out by asking permission, otherwise touch may trigger unpleasant things. 'I'd like to give you a hug – it is OK?' Don't pull back from displays of affection but always check it out first.

29   Lillian's mother seems like an intelligent, socially likable, well educated woman. But when Lillian's mother looked at Lillian, what did she see? Did she see a child, or her husband's lover?

30   Lillian's mother was colluding in the abuse by expecting Lillian to stop it. If some protective aspect could have been in place within the social structure at the time of Lillian's abuse, what would that have been? Where could Lillian have found support?

31   In terms of her relationship with the outside world, and her grounding within it, how strong did Lillian feel in herself?

32   Lillian's parents were very affable, and maintained sophisticated relationships with the outside world. Through Lillian's eyes, how did Lillian's experience of pain and abuse balance up with her parent's respected stature in the outside world?

33   In turn, how did that affect her relationship to the civilisation going on outside the family's front door?

34   How did Lillian perceive herself?

35   Why was it that Lillian self–harmed?

36   What feelings did she have going on inside herself?

37   What was the pay–off from her perspective, and how did her experience of physical pain help her?

38   What elements within her might have stopped her from going further with self–harming?

39   Wouldn't Lillian's teacher from the Gulf have known that sexually molesting your daughter is a crime, and against the law?

40   Remember, this woman is a schoolteacher, working with children year after year. Why would she take such a tolerant view towards Lillian's father?

41   What does she stand to lose, by taking the opposite view … which would be to

express her intolerance about his abuse of his position as a father, and his abuse of his responsibility to protect his daughter?

42   Lillian's father is a child sex abuser. Why did he feel so confident to abuse her within the family? He seems quite proud of his sexual attraction to his daughter and the way that he acted towards her.

43   Does he see that he did anything wrong?

44   Does he hear, value or support his daughter in what she says to him?

45   How far does he enjoy perpetrating pain upon his victim, confident that in his position as a respected father within his family unit, he is perfectly safe? How would you describe Lillian's Dad?

46   Thinking about greater society and its dubious knowledge about abuse, for what other reasons would Lillian's father feel perfectly safe to keep going on with such a vocal expression of his behaviour?

47   As a little brother, how would Robin know or learn about what healthy family behaviour is?

48   What sort of behaviour did Lillian's brother see as a child, and why might he have accepted it as normal?

49   Consider Robin's position in this family. How was he harmed by the abusive relationships in this family? What would you guess was Robin's view of his father?

Keep these questions in mind, as more information is waiting further on in the text.

50   What sort of position does Lillian's family want her to have within it?

51   What are her rights within her family, and who is the most powerful person within it?

52   Why is it that Lillian's father is so good at enlisting everyone's sympathy and support in believing he was, and still is harmless?

53   Why is it that that nobody who knew both Lillian and her father when she was growing up, can see where the most major source of her pain originates?

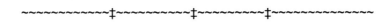

Reflections on Lillian's Story

It's just when you think you understand child abuse, when other facets of relationship appear in the child's world that show you something significant. There can never be hard and fast rules about a child's circumstances. Every case is different, mainly because of the relationships around the child at the time the abuse is going on. But what about how those relationships develop within a survivor's lifetime? They can continue to harm and affect the survivor well after the abuse is 'over'.

Some children are never thought of as individuals in their own right, but as objects, or parental property, for life. For Lillian, there is no time when her abuse began; it was an existential form of recurring distress during every day of her development. Grooming or seduction didn't come into it; she was simply used in the full knowledge of her mother. Some may be appalled that any mother could behave towards a daughter with such jealousy; as if the daughter is a rival lover; but this is believed commonplace in households where the father is sexually abusing to the full knowledge of the mother.

Abusers can get cooperation and support more easily if their partner is immature or insecure as an individual. Partners (who may, or may not know about the abuse) can act as co-abusers. Whilst the principal abuser attacks the child and keeps him or her subservient, the partner supports their mate in maintaining that subservient position. Predominantly, what they often seek to do is dump their stress, and reinforce both their position and their mate's approval within the family unit as a whole.

If we go back to Lillian's story, any abuser who abuses a child emotionally and physically knows instinctively how their humiliations, blows, and threats and can render their victim powerless. They know how society's inability to read into these relationships will ensure that whatever looks like righteous parental authority, can easily conceal far more destructive assertions. It seems that Lillian's father simply wishes to have all the authority in an unequal relationship for life, and she, and his co-abuser could well remain unchallenged by anybody else at all, ever.

Everyone knows that adults can be fickle, even hypocritical to the extreme within their intimate relationships. The John Majors, Blunketts and Clintons of this world can easily provide us with the customary parade of scandals, demonstrating again and again how people take risks and publicly lie to minimise the damage to their public image. The so-called harm that fallen politicians leave in their wake is tiddlywinks compared to the life long devastation caused by a child abuser's power.

Everybody is struck by these survivor's stories in a different way, but I was struck by Lillian's compassion and concern for her brother, who she has no qualms about remaining in contact with. But it seems that now Lillian has grown up, her only route back to power is simply to stay away from her family as a whole; a family that seems co-dependent, and far more concerned about its appearance than its one and only daughter. Lillian's father and his co-abusing wife could well continue as they are if they remain unchallenged. Largely alone, Lillian did challenge them, but one wonders who else could step in within this scenario, even today. This account highlights the importance of finding ways to break this cycle, not just to protect other children from abuse, but in hope of a normally balanced adult life for Lillian, whereby people like her may still find some degree of understanding.

Story Five

John Nygate

John Nygate is a fifty-three year old Oxford graduate from a Jewish background. He suffered unknowingly for years from undiagnosed depression and two (non-dangerous) personality disorders. He spent most of his life unemployed or underemployed. As a child, he asked other parents if he could go and live with them, as he never received any loving behaviour from his family. At school, he was continually in a state of fear, and terrified of being humiliated or caned. In his late adolescence and early twenties he had anorexia nervosa, and has never been able to trust anybody enough to enjoy a sexual relationship. He spent much of his youth living on the fringes, homeless or in squats. He hasn't received adequate help from the NHS or the state. He did skilfully apply his mind to various projects from time to time, but never held down a job permanently. For the last ten years he has been a fervent campaigner for the cause of ending child abuse. He protests actively in public places, raising awareness and handing out leaflets. Currently, he receives no form of state benefit and lives in the same home he grew up in, along with his eighty-three year old mother.

I grew up in Hendon, a reasonably prosperous suburb of north-west London. My family moved house only once during my childhood, and within the same area. When I went to grammar school, I thought if I got good exam results I could get a good job and leave home. That was the only dream I had, and I thought it feasible because I was always the goody-goody at the top of the class. I went on to read philosophy and politics at Oxford, but my dreams were shattered as I came to realise I was too damaged to compete with my peers.

I was born in 1950 and my parents Norman and Doreen were born in 1919 and 1922, respectively. There were four of us: my father, mother and sister Merle, born in 1954. As brother and sister we each had our own bedrooms, and there was a lounge, a dining room and a back garden. To outsiders, we were a respectable, middle-class Jewish family. My mother cooked and took me to the doctor when I was ill, and I was ill a lot in childhood. My father never did anything remotely paternal like taking me shopping or getting me a drink. He provided the income. Early on when the primary school said I was getting behind with my reading, my mother read to me for ten minutes a night. Otherwise, I received no help or encouragement, and neither parent ever read a book to me for pleasure. In most of the photos I look thin and poor. I was

161

clothed adequately, but only just. Basically, I was on my own both in the family, and in life.

My sister and I fought a lot physically, and my parents treated her better than me. My father, mother and sister were one big gang against me. My sister continues to despise me to this day, largely due to the influence of my father. The houses we had were quite decent, and are now quite expensive. My father was a small wool merchant, and quite successful. I have no idea whether he was happy or not in his work. They managed their money well, and we had a nice car in the 1950s and 1960s when most people didn't.

My father could tell the odd joke or two, and was excellent at relating in public. I used to get shown off at family gatherings as the star pupil, the boy 'most likely to succeed'. This was obviously good for my father's image. For five minutes or so I perhaps even felt like a favourite, yet, my father had this strange habit of never using my name. I found this odd, but could never work out why. Once, at my grandmother's, my father said, 'Ask him what he wants to eat' in an incredibly malevolent tone. He'd never say, 'Ask John what he wants to eat.' He always called me 'you' or 'him'. My childhood passed without hearing one warm word from either parent or anyone else, and I cried myself to sleep for days or weeks on end. They were just so incredibly hard-hearted.

I was afraid of my father. There was no bonding in relationships at home, and I got no kissing and cuddling whatsoever as a child – *none*. Even if I fell down or had an accident. I think they generally regarded me as a nuisance and did not want to spend money or time on me. They might have wanted to show me off in public, but put me to bed early just to get rid of me. Once, cousin Frances and her family came around to see us. She was a chubby eight-year-old and I was the same age, but she used to stay up far longer than I. I'd be frantic to find my father alone so I could ask him (without embarrassment) if I could stay up for as long as Francis. He took great pleasure in denying me that small wish.

Early Days

My father's thoughts and feelings were everything, whereas mine meant nothing. Every gesture was underpinned with the threat of violence. However irregular the beatings were, the threat was there all the time. One beating my father gave me with his hand on my backside was really terrible. Soon after, Peggy Wilks, a family friend, came into my bedroom, saw me crying and asked why. My father said, 'We had a little disagreement.' I really resented his hiding what he had done to me. They just wanted complete obedience and domination. I can't remember much in detail earlier than seven years old, but I was shouted at a lot. My mother would say, 'You better stop that or I'll slosh you into next week.' And, 'If you don't be quiet I'll go away and never come back.' She frequently threatened to drop me forever, and I'd often hear, 'Shut up!' and 'Be quiet!' from both parents.

In primary school when I was eight, I caught a parent in the churchyard after school and asked, 'Can I come and live with you? It's terrible there.' This must have got back to the teachers, as my mother was asked to come to the classroom to collect me so they could observe my reaction. The teacher said, 'John, your mother is here,' and I thought, 'So what?' I think I ran away. I went to a clinic where nurses or social workers were observing the interaction between us; my mother was there, but I'm not sure if my father was. I was underweight and often absent from infant and primary school with asthma or bronchitis, and the school inspector would visit. The local authority did have evidence then there was something amiss in my family life. I recently asked them for copies of any records but they said it was too long ago.

I'm not sure I want to recall the earliest memories. I have a vague sense of everything being just so terrible, so not remembering could well be how I deal with it. I can't remember many words that were said, but do recall being bullied and humiliated, largely by my father.

When I went to university at nineteen I resolved this was all in the past and I didn't want to think about it ever again. If the memories came back to me today I wouldn't suppress them, but I haven't much time left and I'm not sure I want to remember. I know I could make things up, but I think the truth is really important. I can remember the overall feelings: The despair, the isolation, hopelessness and anger, and perhaps most of all, the fear.

I'm still scared of the world and people in general, and only for the briefest moments in more than five decades have I felt positive feelings like joy, hope, and happiness. What is a relationship? What, really? I see a relationship on the outside, but never know what it's about. One of my big fears is ending up sleeping in the streets, which is still a possibility. In terms of how I've been affected, my child abuse was severe; in fact, I think it was as severe as it gets.

Once I had left university, I never really wanted to be anything, never wanted to get married, have a girlfriend, own a property or be a success. I ended up homeless. I spent hours travelling around on the London underground just to keep warm. Whenever I met anyone, I just felt embarrassed and apologetic, so I preferred to be alone. I never felt I was in physical danger being on the streets, but looking back, that's when I developed the digestive disorder of ulcerative colitis which eventually led to the loss of my large intestine. I attribute this to continual stress. I hardly visited doctors, and didn't keep the appointments. I finally had an operation in 1999, having been ill for twenty-four years, but somehow I didn't care. I did not understand then why I was like this, but in recent years I found my way to the academic material on child development and child abuse, and at last could begin to understand.

Portrait of a Father

My father was a teenager when the Nazis came to power, and deep down their ideology became central to his core values. My family is Jewish, so someone might wonder how a Jew could be a Nazi, but many of his generation in the 1950s and 1960s were like that. It was more like extreme social Darwinism. Being strong and surviving well was not only admirable: it demonstrated the intrinsic goodness of the strong. To the Nazis, the Jews were an inferior race who would eventually die out through natural selection, so it was OK to hurry nature along by murdering them. My father was not that extreme, but believed unreservedly in the domination of the fittest.

Questioning, sensitive, moral, intelligent people like me were inferior, should be made to know it, and made to suffer. I am hopeless at hiding my feelings, and as a child I was vulnerable, sensitive, and totally incapable of dissembling. I am not a poker player. I can't lie with a straight face, and my father believed someone like that could not survive in the world. He despised me for it. It must have shattered the family myth to pieces when I was unemployed after university. It is very odd how one generation is one way and the next generation totally different. He got himself a son who couldn't help but make him feel uncomfortable. Very strange.

Father and Mother

My parents always backed each other up as a kind of invincible team, and were most keen on politeness, but my father went to extremes. Peggy Wilks regularly visited to play scrabble. She wasn't too bad; she was never violent or humiliating towards me, but cold. I could not really trust her, nor any other loyal friend of my parents. Once, my father told me that if he rubbed the side of his nose during one of her visits, then I should leave the room. I was outraged and said to myself, 'One day your reign will end.' He loved to humiliate me privately and in public by forbidding me things without any explanation. I'd feel worthless as he wielded his power to destroy me just for its own sake. My parents loved watching me cringe as they said to my face, 'Children should be seen and not heard!' They were never curious about how I might like to express myself naturally, as if terrified at my saying or doing anything.

§ Optional Questions 3 and 4 §

I think whenever my father set eyes on me he felt deep contempt. He used to give me terrible lectures, that were always entirely in private. They started when I was eight or nine, and today, my mother doesn't believe me. There was, of course, no question of answering back, as there was always that threat of violence.

I remember one at the age of nine. I could actually feel my heart being broken. I knew that after that lecture I could never reach my true potential. I was often off sick from school then, but was told I had to study and improve my marks for the 11-plus examination. I felt the intensity of hatred in my father's voice, and did improve my marks a lot, but entirely out of fear of him. His voice made me feel like vermin. I felt putrid, like a stinking, infectious disease. I had to better myself, because I was so sickening and detestable as I was. I went to school the day after that, feeling how he had thwarted God's plan for me, which would remain manifest in the ether, never in the world. I would still have my body, still continue living, but with my soul murdered.

When I was a teenager my mother told me she got married to leave her family and get away from her parents who were cold and indifferent. Over the years I found out as best I could that they were not forcefully abusive. One or two years after my mother's birth, her mother died, so the onus fell on her father to look after her and her elder brother. My mother had an unmarried aunt (her mother's sister), Bessie. She became my maternal grandmother, when my mother's father then married her. So my grandfather married the sister of the one who died, and my mother was adopted into a loveless marriage between her aunt and father, and I wouldn't have been surprised if it was a sexless one as well. My mother replicated the same cold, unresponsive parenting style she had received. She was unconscious rather than evil, but my father was positively evil, calling on her unquestioning devotion and support whenever he wanted it.

My father brainwashed me in my teenage years that Bessie was basically one of the rejected ones. I was aware then of some slight criticism that she made of my father, but brushed it aside as being stupid, accepting his view and rejecting hers. Bessie was neither loving, nor abusive, but very damaged. She used to send me £5 or £10 in the 1960s, quite a lot of money today. It's sad that the whole family was so dysfunctional that I couldn't have had much more communication with her.

Spiritual Atmosphere at Home

I am disinclined to share this next bit of my history because people might think my child abuse so implausible that they might reject it, but it's true.

My parents organised seances at home from about 1956 to 1980, once a week or so. Mother and six or eight people would attend, with my father being the medium. Peggy Wilks was a regular. From my bedroom, I would hear strange banging and shouting, and sometimes swearing. I wasn't frightened, but thought my parents were mad. In my teens my mother finally explained that my father would go into a trance, disembodied spirits would take over his body and communicate through him, and one spirit called Phideas ran the whole show. Well, anyone can speak in a funny voice and pretend to be the spirit of a dead person, but I honestly think there was more to it. He couldn't have been deceiving people for over twenty years, never having made any money out of it. But he was involved in the occult, and had malefic power. Today, my mother talks about it a bit then clams up. She's determined to keep it secret, probably for similar reasons to why I am so reluctant to share it today.

Perhaps my father's hostility was deeply connected with all this. His eyes were often empty as if he was not looking out, and his heart was completely closed. Normal psychological explanations for his behaviour are simply not enough. The Catholic Church says that someone who wants to do evil just for its own sake can be 'taken over' by a satanic spirit, and there are books about this, e.g., Malachi Martin's *Hostage to the Devil*. My father is very difficult to talk about and understand, so it's hard to judge, but he seemed to obey 'instructions' from this spirit. At times, he was lost in his own world. He may have had no memory himself of those terrible lectures I now feel were connected to this. People might say my father was just difficult, but I really believe I would have died, had it not been for my mother's loyalty to her duties, to keep me alive.

When the time came for university, my father wanted me to study physics. I tried to tell him (quite rightly) that only ten per cent of students who study physics at Oxford become physicists, but he just could not get this into his head. He went crazy when he learnt I was going to study politics and philosophy instead, shouting, 'You'll come to nothing! Even years later, he'd say with total conviction, 'Physics was your thing.' I often wonder if he had taken Phideas' advice about my career in a seance. He never forgave me for that. I wanted to do philosophy partly to understand why nothing was working with me, and politics to understand the world. I got an excellent upper-second honours degree, but never an iota of praise or acknowledgement from him. The man was half mad really, very odd.

Nothing ever worked for me except books and knowledge, because my father crushed my spirit by taking all possibilities from me except of studying. I could not do money, careers, relationships or housing, but I could do books. And that's not enough for a career in academia or elsewhere: you need to be tolerably well-adjusted as well. I doubt I could have become a physicist, because I would never have had the confidence to give public lectures in my twenties. Developmentally, I was just too far behind everyone else to take on a demanding career.

I was forced to attend synagogue, and forced to go through the Bar Mitzvah at thirteen against my will. I said I didn't believe in Judaism, so why did I have to do this? He said he didn't either, but I had to do it for Bessie, my grandmother. He knew he could get away with this because everyone would think he was doing it for his son's good. In the 1950s and 1960s even fewer people had the psychological awareness they have now, but even today, unless child abuse jumps up and bites them on the nose, most people wouldn't notice it.

I was devastated, hopeless, angry and despairing under this constant pressure, and when I said I was tired of being 'Mr Perfect', he looked quizzically at me. This was something he could never ever dream of understanding. He was quite articulate when it came to forcing me to do things and extracting promises. Whilst he wouldn't swear at me, he would certainly belittle me, shame me and say nasty things in a way designed to hurt and manipulate me.

So again, following one of his lectures, he extracted a promise from me to learn ancient Hebrew. They found an ignorant Jewish private tutor to teach me for a year, so that I could read out a bit of the Old Testament at my Bar Mitzvah. My father's true brand of religious fascination was kept to a very private social circle, so I felt the whole thing was ridiculous. He was doing it for the reputation of the family, but I also felt he did it just to cause me suffering.

§ Optional Questions 5, 6, 7, 8 and 9 §

Outsiders would think we were a happy family since, in public, my father was good at hiding his real attitude towards me. The worst abuses were perpetrated when we were alone, aggravated by ours being a tight, nuclear family.

There are some photos of my sister and me asleep, the bedclothes half on and half off us. He took those photos (not sexual kinds) and put them in an album. My mother and the family friends would say, 'Oh, what a nice man he is, caring about his children so much, taking their photos.' This pretence was deliberately done to isolate me. My father never told me anything about his own childhood or shared his feelings, and was certainly never interested in mine. He pretended to others that he loved me, but he simply wanted to hurt me and break my heart. He was quite a clever, evil man. I felt quite hopeless in public, because no child enduring emotional abuse can express it easily. What *could* I have said?

§ Optional Questions 10, 11 and 12 §

As a child I just used to pray, 'Please God, give me the opportunity to leave this terrible family.' When I thought about my father, I wished he were dead, and he was always at the back of my mind. I was pretty much aware that I was being treated much worse than anybody else. I felt I was more than just unlucky: I felt cursed.

School

I was a very bright kid, the top student by dint of considerable intelligence and very hard work. I cannot remember my parents ever praising me for good exam results, and I suppose I must have got some sort of acclamation from the teachers, but that was unimportant to me. I am always reading books from the public library, often quite difficult books. If I'd had a normal childhood I'd probably have become an academic.

As my parents never used the cane, I was more afraid of being in school than being at home, and right from the age of five, being beaten by the teachers was the thing I was most afraid of. Although I was never actually beaten with the cane, I spent the first ten years of my schooling in perpetual fright. I thought, 'Well, if I don't exist, I cannot be beaten, can I?' My tiny handwriting took up as little space as possible, and I tried my best to do the same.

From the age of nine I had to have this horrible tutor for the 11–plus examination. If you passed it you went to a supposedly good school and if you failed you would have a life with no prospects. Exams were everything, the key factor being that my father left school at fourteen and my mother at fifteen, and never had an education themselves. When I was ten there was an option about which out of three grammar schools I should apply to. My father always chose whatever would cause me the most pain, so decided on the most authoritarian school.

From 1958 to 1962 I attended St Mary's Church of England Junior School in Hendon, North London, near Greyhound Hill. I can't remember my first day when I was five, or even the individual teachers very much. They generally got us through our schoolwork by humiliating and threatening us, and I always kept a low profile. There was nobody I was *not* afraid of, and Icertainly didn't look up to any of them. The headmaster was E. W. Grant, who may be dead now but nevertheless I was terrified of him and consider him a wicked man. There were brutal beatings with the cane, a flexible stick about a metre long and a centimetre in diameter. Grant took delight in caning children in front of the whole school. He loved to summon a boy for a beating at assembly, and say, 'Bend over and touch your toes,' and administer several hard strokes to the boy's backside. As he swung the cane, It cut through the air with a loud swish that could be heard throughout the school hall. Sometimes Grant added insult to injury by demanding that the child shake his hand after the beating. I believe some pupils never recovered from the experience of a public caning. I had a friend, Jeffrey Chesnick, who was beaten by Grant this way and it damaged him greatly. He was really quiet throughout the rest of his school days. I remember making a vow to myself when Jeffrey was being beaten: that when I grew up I would refuse to contribute to the wicked society that treated my friend like this. I have largely kept this vow.

I didn't talk about the punishment I got at home to my schoolmates or anybody else. I think I was treated far worse than my friends at school, although any attempt to communicate about it was out of the question. My secondary school was Orange Hill Grammar School for Boys, Edgware, where also boys were caned on the backside. My problems were certainly compounded by the cold and harsh atmosphere there, where we were only known by our surnames. On the very first day at Orange Hill, our class was told it had to recite the register by memory. The teacher expected each pupil to call out his name in alphabetical order. I can remember it quite clearly: Long, Maass,

Martindale, Martin–Ross…

When a boy was told he was to be caned, he was to go to the headmaster's study, knock on the door, ask for the cane, and bring it back. Everyone witnessed the humiliation as he walked carrying this instrument of pain. Then the teacher took the cane, told him to bend over and carried out the beating in front of the whole class.

I will never forget Mr Reffold, a teacher of French, who I lived in terror of for years. If you took great care to obey all the rules at Orange Hill you were generally safe from beatings, but not in Reffold's class.

It was the first lesson of the autumn term, 1962. Reffold was our new French teacher, whom we had not met before. We were in class waiting for him to come, making a bit of noise. We stood up as he entered, this being the rule. He was very angry at the noise, told us to shut up and sit down, and made us sit in complete silence for about five minutes.

Then he told us of a new rule. His class would be conducted in complete silence. No boy would speak unless spoken to by Reffold (usually in French). If any boy spoke or made a noise (like dropping a pencil) without his request, he would be caned.

I was terrified. Then Reffold joked around a bit, talking in French and English. This relaxed the class a bit, but I was still terrified. The class had been laughing with Reffold for a good five or ten minutes, and he didn't seem offended. He joked around a bit more, and a boy, Rennie, I think it was, said quietly, 'Very funny, Sir.'

Reffold said, 'Rennie, go and get the cane.' We all laughed quite loudly because we thought Reffold was joking. Reffold repeated himself. This time the laughter was slightly subdued. For the third time, Reffold said, 'Rennie, go and get the cane.' We fell silent because we realised Reffold was not joking.

Rennie said, 'But Sir, I only said "Very funny, Sir".' Reffold shouted angrily, 'I told you that anyone who spoke out of turn would be caned. Now go and get the cane.' Rennie said, 'But Sir!' but Reffold insisted.

Rennie headed meekly for the headmaster's office for the cane. The class just sat silently. and Rennie returned after ten minutes. Reffold motioned him to the front of the class, told him to bend over and said, 'This will teach you not to break my rule.' He administered several hard strokes of the cane to Rennie's backside. Rennie returned to his seat. He didn't cry. The class was shocked into complete silence, and we didn't learn much French that day.

Reffold must have engineered the whole situation deliberately to 'establish authority', telling us the new rule and then joking around so that someone would break it.

I could not guarantee my safety just by sticking to the rules. The minute one lesson was over all I could think of was how I was going to get through the next week without being beaten. Such punishments were common then, but I consider it unforgivable to treat a child this way. I shall never forgive Mr Reffold or any of the other teachers who terrorised me this way, because they were ruling by terror.

No adult spoke out against school beatings in those days. In fact, they seemed to positively delight in these wicked assaults against children. Equally, I didn't talk with my friends about school punishments. That came years later when I put much of my history on the Friends Reunited Internet site. I received three commiserative replies from ex–

students of Orange Hill. One I remembered vaguely and two I didn't, but two letters were quite long and all were sympathetic. This is one of them.

(These e-mails were printed with the writer's permission, but their names are changed or withheld to maintain the writer's privacy.)

Hello John,

I was idly surfing the net for details of former Orange Hill colleagues and I came across your item about Mr Reffold. Oh, how it brings back grim memories. I was born in June 1947 and attended Orange Hill School from 1958–1963. Depending upon when you were born in 1950, you would have been three or four years behind me. There was unquestionably a regime of fear at the school; several teachers used physical punishment or humiliation as a means of rule. I believe that Mr Reffold was an absolute monster who should never have been allowed to be in charge of pupils, even in the 1960s, and certainly would not be permitted to be a teacher these days.

For my sins, I am now a school governor. A few years ago, the Local Education Authority issued the following definition of bullying: an unwarranted abuse of power, which may be physical, mental, emotional or psychological. I think that is Mr Reffold in a nutshell.

Our French teacher in the first year had been Mr Parker, who was deputy head and who also taught Latin. Mr Reffold replaced a young teacher, Dr Davies, who I understand was very popular with the pupils in his group.

Mr Reffold joined the staff at the beginning of my second year and the reign of terror began from day one. You will recall that he had a double speech impediment, unable to pronounce the letter 'R' and with the most marked lisp I think I have ever heard. (We gave him the sobriquet 'Wedgie Weffold' – but always out of earshot). During that first lesson – double French – I misheard or misunderstood something he said and mispronounced a word. I received a beating for insolence. It was a genuine error but maybe he thought I was taking the pith. (It is most definitely not my style to make fun of others' physical misfortunes, but I'll allow myself an exception in the case of that brute). On another occasion, he beat me hard enough to draw blood. In those days we did not have the knowledge (or the confidence) to complain. Even if we had, we would have been marked down as troublemakers as the ethos was of never telling tales.

I, too, remember the ritual of the register calling. If you remember, we were allocated to our first year classes in alphabetical order. With my surname, I was placed in class 1C – R**k, Rus***, Sa***n, Sau***, Sha****, Sher***, Sm***, [A***] S****, [G****] S****, [J***] S***, S****, Smythe.... My handwriting at that time was pretty abysmal, but I printed my name and class as neatly as I could on all my homework books. When Reffold handed out the marked work, he called out my name – 'Sardines'. He got the expected round of gratuitous laughter, but why humiliate a pupil in this way? For the rest of the year, I kept my head low, did the minimum required and avoided attracting attention, but effectively that was me and French finished.

The headmaster – 'TheDuke', K. F. Howse, MA (Oxon) – could also be *savage, as I know to my cost after playing hooky to avoid Mr Reffold. However, I cannot remember walking in absolute terror of the Duke as I did in the case of Wedgie.*

Regardless of the bullies, there were teachers there whom I held in the highest esteem. Mr Harradine, who was a former pupil of the school, Mr Shapiro (who I believe was related to the singer, Helen Shapiro), Mr Peters, Mr R. ['Chalky'] White, Mr Burkitt, Mr Parker and Mr [Jim] Farley spring to mind. I left the school after the fifth year, happy and relieved to walk through the gates for the last time. Maybe if the regime had been a little more caring, I might have been more successful, although I don't think I would have matched your close first at Oxford (for which sincere compliments).

This message is to let you know that you were not alone in your misery at Orange Hill and to express my sympathy with you. Outside of school, my childhood and adolescence were reasonably happy; not idyllic, but I had the advantage of a loving, caring family, and friends in the neighbourhood. I am not a Jew, so I cannot really comment on your unhappiness with your Jewish upbringing, except to say that my Jewish friends seemed to belong to loving, caring families; perhaps a little stricter than mine, but families to whom they were obviously devoted.

Regards and best wishes......

This is an email from another former pupil, called 'Eric'

John

Seems as though you have had a rough time lad.
I left OH in 1972, but had the pleasure of receiving a pearler of a right hand from Reffold to the left side of my head whilst in (I think it was) the first year. As I am still friendly with a few guys from my class they might even remember it. I think the ferocity of his pugilism must have got to him because he even apologised to me at the end of the lesson. The guy was a first class bully. You must be receiving hundreds of e mails to back your story up. Good luck to you.
I remember being on the right hand side of the classroom, and would have been sat next to a snivelly little runt called R____ B____.
By the way, I can still recite the register from Form 2A.

Regards, 'Eric'

These bits of correspondence on Friends Reunited made me think more seriously about taking my local education authority to task. So a few months later I wrote ...

Dear Eric,
As you probably know I am trying to make a claim for compensation against the local authority for bullying I endured in Mr Reffold's classes.

I have been told by my solicitor that my claim only has a chance if there is a Police investigation into Mr Reffold's activities. As far as I can see this will only happen if several people complain to the Police. Might I ask if you would be willing to go to the Police and make a formal complaint against Mr Reffold? It would have to be a complaint about something that actually happened to you rather than something you witnessed. I presume we would be thinking of an offence like assault or malicious wounding. Certainly receiving a pearler of a right hand from Reffold to the left side of my head would count.

(I am presuming here you were not a victim of a sexual offence perpetrated by Reffold.)

If you made a formal complaint it might help me a lot. If you do this, please would you let me know the outcome and also the location of the Police station you visited.

Thanks and best wishes,

John

The reply I got was laid out across my screen in twenty-font sized red letters:

"Get a life!
He must be 80 years old
You must be one sad person

'Eric'

This reply only confirmed to me how most survivors of abuse are treated. Nevertheless, as the correspondence continued with ex-pupils of Orange Hill High, I found out something else. I learnt that Reffold had a sexual relationship with a boy there who was probably fourteen or fifteen at the time. I was given quite a lot of detail so I think it is likely to be true. I think Reffold now lives his life completely oblivious to the trail of human suffering he left behind him.

I never trusted any teacher and even though some were not too bad, I still resented them for being so dedicated to the regime that terrorised me. At both schools I became obsessed by keeping the rules, which probably contributed to my obsessive-compulsive personality disorder, which is characterised by excessive respect for the literal interpretation of rules and regulations.

I must have received a little parenting from my teachers and tutors at Oxford, but certainly not from my parents. To me, my parents were more malicious, because my total dependence gave them more power. They would never hesitate to exploit my weak points.

There was no relationship between the teachers and my parents. My parents only cared in the sense that they wanted me to be an obedient, successful child, but they never ever listened to me. The teachers could do anything they wanted to me. If I had said, 'I'm terrified of this teacher. Please, could you do something about it?' they would never have questioned their authority. I was really terrified. I will never forgive my parents for putting me through that torture.

Activities

My father forced me to join the cubs and the scouts because he was in the scouts himself. He gave me one of his terrible lectures, so I had to, but hated it and dropped out as soon as I could. There were violin lessons at school provided by the local authority that he made me take, but honestly, getting top marks in all those O and A levels and learning the violin as well was just too much. I wanted to get into university, and playing the violin does not help you get good exam results.

To me, everybody seemed superior – and certainly happier. I didn't look down on or feel sorry for anybody, except perhaps a boy suffering the cane.

I didn't want to be in my isolated situation, but there I was. I knew what my father was doing was wrong. As I became more independent in adolescence, from about age fourteen onwards they basically ignored me. I had a school friend called Alan for a while, a victim of physical abuse, when we were around sixteen. We'd go for walks in the evening carving 'D/S', meaning 'Death Sect', on trees. Sometimes he'd paint a small graffito on walls too. I used to follow him around but was always scared of being caught by the police (and thus ruining my future escape – my career). I guess we were just expressing our anger, as we knew how, at the way we were being treated.

There was nobody I could trust to tell about my pain, but I learnt to depend on my spiritual side. After crying myself to sleep as a child I could eventually relax in bed and feel the peace of God's presence. I didn't do too badly for school friends, but boys at that time never discussed feelings or problems. When I was older I spent time with friends outside the school frequently, but very rarely at my house. Right from primary school, my parents had this amazing ability to stop me making friends. Whenever a bit of friendship or love was developing, even without formally forbidding me to bring friends home they would stop it. There was such an oppressive atmosphere, it was uncanny. Eventually, I gave up trying. You see, they hardly ever spoke to me, or offered any opinions about the other kids I knew. They maintained this kind of attitude for life. They interacted with me only when absolutely necessary, remaining detached, and expressing no affection for me whatsoever. The most overpowering feeling was of my heart being broken by those bastards.

§ Optional Questions 13, 14, 15 and 16 §

Sometimes just hating my parents was the only thing I could do, as if I couldn't control myself to do otherwise. Once when I was eleven my father went to the dentist. He had had a wisdom tooth out and it wouldn't stop bleeding. He was in bed spitting blood and saliva into a bucket, which was filling up. I hoped against hope that it would kill him.

I prayed fervently, 'God, if it's possible, please grant me this wicked man's death.' At eleven, I couldn't understand why God did not grant this. Another time when I was twelve we were on holiday in Israel and our passports got stolen. Though I couldn't say anything, I relished seeing my father upset, out of control, and in trouble.

My mother always respected my father no matter what. I am really angry that my father never listened to me, and speaking to my mother is like talking to a brick wall. I told her recently how terrified I was of Mr Reffold. She just laughed, saying, 'If you had told us, we'd have done something about it. It's your fault for not telling us.' But I don't think they would have done anything, because the school was everything for them. Sometimes I tell her my childhood was absolutely terrible; there were those devastating lectures. I told her a few days ago that I never trusted either her or my father an inch. She just refuses to believe me.

Money

I knew my parents would give me food, shelter, visits to the doctor and dentist and essential clothing, but they weren't ever generous. Whatever other things I got had to be squeezed out of them and I resented that. I don't think they squandered money, but it was a big secret and they were never straight about it. I didn't get much spent on extra-curricular activities. They were generally quite well off, but spent as little as possible on me. I never had a bicycle, for example. In my photos, I look thin and poor. Once, in a bookshop there was this book I really fancied. In the 1950s and 1960s people didn't buy books very much. I asked my father if I could have a book on archaeology, and I swear my father actually took pleasure in denying me this book. As one isolated incident among many, my father constantly looked for opportunities to hurt me. In the run-up to applying to Oxford, I was told to read a good newspaper everyday. We read the *Daily Express*, so I asked my father to get the *Times* or *Guardian* for a few months. He refused. I thought this odd for someone who claimed he wanted me to be successful. I couldn't trust either parent to give me their time, attention, or interest, to indulge me a little once in a while. I could certainly never trust them with my feelings and dreams.

§ Optional Questions 17 and 18 §

He would take the deepest pleasure in denying me fulfilment of anything I wanted to get or do, and he had plenty of money. Asking to borrow or buy things, even if it was for schoolwork was out of the question. If I so much as borrowed a screwdriver and forgot to put it back, he would fly into a rage. I learned to prepare by being pessimistic about the outcome, and only asked when I really had to. I think they spent more on my sister than on me, so I don't think they were fair. In the photos, she looks much better than me.

At Oxford I had a slightly sadistic friend who could sense I was an injured person. He once said, 'Oh, you don't want to be your *self*.' It's true that I was struggling. Between the ages of about ten and twenty, I tried to keep up, I really did, but there comes a point when you can't and realise you're not going to be able to do what other people take for granted. I have, for example, tried and tried to get jobs for most of my life, and sometimes wonder if my face is frozen in fear, because I am frightened but not aware I'm showing it. I think I'm so timid they must think I'm stupid or something. So maybe that's why I can never find work.

Things felt much worse right up until my early thirties when I was still trying to keep up with other people, yet knew I was failing. The family myth was that I was a healthy, well-adjusted, successful person, but it took a lot of pain and courage to accept that I wasn't going to be able to do much in life.

As I began to approach my 50s at last there was a chink of light from the world of psychiatry. After getting rejections after job interviews I used to reproach myself endlessly, but at last things began to fall into place. I went to a Dr Paul Bailey, a consultant psychiatrist working at the Priory hospitals, in 1998. At last I got decent treatment of an international standard rather than the NHS treatment I had got nowhere with before. Dr Bailey diagnosed social phobia, which is similar to anxious or avoidant personality disorder. Well, I paid him three hundred pounds, so he had to treat me respectfully! Good-quality professional help unexpectedly came to me again a few years later when I applied for a graduate-entry position with Shell, targeted at university leavers. I've tried to find employment for years and been repeatedly rejected, so contrived to undertake a 'project' fully expecting the same thing, but my whole purpose this time was to start proceedings under the Disability Discrimination Act. I did it out of anger and frustration, as well as curiosity about the law. In the application, I put my full medical history, my two years of professional work experience, and some years of part-time voluntary work.

Things I said in my application to Shell were like waving a red flag to a bull, e.g.:

"Unfortunately, I was unable to work for many years due to severe inflammatory bowel disease. However, following major surgery I am now well and my GP says there is no reason why I should not continue to be healthy until retirement. I suffered from very severe child abuse, which destroyed my self-confidence and made me passive and withdrawn. I have also suffered from the psychiatric disorders of depression and social phobia. However, my GP says I am now capable of work.

"I have overcome very many severe challenges in my life: maternal rejection, child abuse, childhood asthma and bronchitis, adolescent anorexia nervosa, social phobia, avoidant personality disorder, depression, homelessness. These experiences have made me strong, wise, perceptive and understanding of human frailty.

I did not expect to get an interview, however, under the Disability Discrimination Act you can sue if you are rejected due to *past* disability. I had more experience than a new graduate, and, therefore, it was likely I would be rejected due to past illness or disability. Completely out of the blue, Shell paid for extensive psychiatric consultations with a Dr Ceccherini-Nelli in 2002. I suspect they felt they could obtain an analysis that would show I was incapable of work, but after months of deliberation, Shell said they were not discriminating on grounds of past disability at all, but merely because I was too old.

Although I had to withdraw from the lawsuit because they had the right to discriminate on this ground, the psychiatric consultations were well worth having, and now I have something in writing that makes sense. Dr Ceccherini-Nelli's diagnosis included two personality disorders (avoidant, and obsessive-compulsive) with fourteen dysfunctional personality traits. He states, 'I am convinced that most organisations would do anything possible to avoid recruiting people with personality disorders.' At last, I could find a concrete reason why I could never get through interviews.

Disorders

I follow rules to the letter, no matter what. I sometimes don't understand people when they're trying to be funny, and it's almost impossible for me to be 'open' even with people I am close to, because I'm so afraid they'll mock me. I feel personally unappealing and inferior, and spend hours worrying about being criticised or rejected in social situations, so keep aloof. Sometimes, it doesn't matter to me what other people say: I'm so steadfast in my opinion that they just can't get through. At other times when I do respond to people, I find it hard to disagree with them face to face, so I step backwards and give up communicating altogether. When I try to get support from others, I volunteer to do things that are unpleasant. I may focus on details, order, and organisation, making lots of lists and schedules, and sometimes can't finish jobs because I spend so much time trying to get everything exactly right. Rather like a helpless child, I can't handle major areas of my life, including living arrangements. I live in clutter because I hoard things and what little money I have because I'm always worried I won't have enough in the future. I avoid anything that involves dealing with groups of people unless I am certain they will like me. I never make the first move, and I won't try new things to avoid embarrassment. In short, I am unable to speak the unteachable social language that everybody else speaks.

Relating as Play

As children, we all inevitably get involved in the game of relating. Even at nine or ten, I realised I couldn't play or relate normally. Later, my physical and sexual development intensified my anxiety so much, that by my early teens I gave up on that whole area of life. I tried to relate to girls, but felt so uncomfortable that I knew it simply was not possible. There were very many painful periods in adolescence and in my twenties when I realised sexual relationships would not be possible.

Repulsion

The crux of everything has always been that *I don't actually like anybody*, which may sound terrible and immoral, but that's the psychological reality. I didn't have one iota of warmth or affection for either men or women for the first thirty-five years of my life. It was at its worst in the teenage years: the word 'warmth' was unintelligible to me, and I couldn't recognise, understand, interpret, or respond to any positive feelings towards me either.

When I saw my friends going out with girls as a teenager I didn't quite know what was happening, but thought it was something I had to will myself to do, like you learn French, or history, or practise a sport. I did not have the faintest idea why people got married, and up to the age of thirty, I did not know what flirting was.

People used the word 'flirt', and I knew what it meant, but had no emotional understanding or experience of it. I remember going to the cinema with this girl, and agonising throughout the film about whether to put my arm around her or not. I thought this was an act I had to will myself to do, I was consumed with anxiety and tension. I had no idea this is the result of spontaneous feeling. I was trying to learn by copying, whilst having no feeling for the lady at all. I tried not to be rude, but at times the stress was so great there might have been a rude word or two from me, so who knows what she thought of me. So if you can see where I was starting from, 99 per cent of my life was in total darkness with regard to this.

Oxford

Oxford was the least unhappy part of my life. I had no financial worries and could breathe a bit, not being at home. I could begin to try to find out who I was and get an identity. At New College, we were well taught and looked after. People were more liberal and humane than those at school, and it was here I discovered that lower-middle-class English life has something Nazi about it. I have pleasant memories of listening to the 'Grateful Dead', when a joint would get passed round. I loved the Beatles' Abbey Road when it had just been released. I smoked dope a little, and unlike Bill Clinton I did sometimes inhale! But I was always cautious, and careful it never interfered with my work. I managed to have some friendships, and didn't find the work too difficult.

Relating

Instead of finding myself, I saw how different I was compared to most people. I'm not able to have sexual relationships, as they require trust in other people, which I don't have. In my student days I did have one or two very brief sexual relationships, but my anxiety forced me to discontinue them. Once, I was petting with this girl, but was so anxious that I ran to the bathroom to vomit; God knows what the poor girl thought of me after that! I had no girlfriends, no confidence to join clubs and societies, and was always relatively shy and withdrawn. I studied quietly, that's all. The three years at Oxford were OK, but after that I could not cope. I visited a friend the summer after graduation and was terrified of the future; there is a photo of me then in the exam uniform. I told my mother this, but she does not believe me.

Adult Life

After Oxford, I did a one-year postgraduate course in philosophy at London University, but was beginning to fall apart. I didn't have the support I was used to at Oxford. I was very depressed and my anorexia was still there, although I didn't know it then. I was tired of philosophy, so the year was a bit of a disaster. I spent much of my twenties homeless. For one year I lived in a derelict house, with only floorboards and no furniture, sleeping in a sleeping bag on the floor, without electricity or gas, just cold running water and heating from a paraffin stove. I visited my family many times that year and my father would drive me back in his Mercedes convertible.

He saw the place, came inside, but never offered me a few pounds or anything. I wasn't getting any kind of social security benefits. In the summer I was a deck chair attendant and in winter I became a cleaner. Incredibly, I worked in this situation. I certainly didn't beg or steal. Anyway, there were no young beggars on the streets back in the 1970s.

I started signing on for a bit, and I went to live in a cheap hotel in Earl's Court with some Australians for a couple of years. I was no longer alone, and appreciated the way they seemed to accept me, but this was not really for me. In 1974–75 I travelled around the USA for six or eight months and came back and ended up living on friends' floors. I developed a connection with Holland when I met Kees in London in 1975. He was Dutch, and is the only person I ever met who I thought was as damaged as I. I then went over to Holland to live for a couple of years, got jobs as a cleaner, then in autumn 1976 became ill again but didn't go to the doctor.

Work

I got a job in 1977 with British Shipbuilders for a year, then another as a librarian for a year. In 1980, after six weeks in hospital with ulcerative colitis, I went back to live in the family home, and by that time I had given up all hope of ever getting a job. Then, and throughout my thirties there were terrible conflicts between my father and me. I played music like Bob Marley's pretty loudly sometimes, which drove my father mad, although most of the time I was as quiet as a mouse. In all, I had only two years of professional employment. I could not retain jobs. British Shipbuilders moved away, there was one job left in London and somebody else got it. In the library job, I was given all the most difficult tasks in the hope I would resign. The Department of Employment just assumed I'd done something wrong by giving up and acted towards me as if I was in complete control of my chances.

I completely expect to be rejected. I am totally in awe of people who can buy a house and earn enough money for a mortgage. There is absolutely nothing I want to do, I have no confidence to do things, and do not expect anything to work out. People think being in this kind of state is like having a bad mood, or a bad day, sort of like the weather. They don't understand that I have felt like this constantly, for each and every single day of my life.

Getting Help

It may not seem that I tried to heal myself, but I did try various teachings from whatever source, if inexpensive. In the early 1980s I went to psychoanalytical groups for two or three years. One NHS psychotherapy group was absolutely useless. The lady leader was a feminist of the time. One lady member, a schoolteacher, proclaimed she wanted me dead simply because I had gone to Oxford. She went on this long, scathing speech about me, and the leader did nothing to stop it. Today, my perception is that this teacher had a career and an income, and wasn't as badly damaged as I was. At that time the whole experience left me with the feeling that wherever I go I'll just hit darkness and evil, and that nobody will ever be able to help me change my life.

Perhaps the sannyasin philosophy I have now is a withdrawal from the hatred and horror of the twentieth and twenty-first centuries, where people are labelled arbitrarily with ludicrous judgements. At Oxford, we were told to be intellectually honest and not think in clichés, and it was a positive period for the development of my intellect. It's a pity that it was too late for my development as a human being, as any promise of that had died long before then.

Spiritual Path

My Sannyasin philosophy started at around the age of thirty-three, when I came across a philosophical teacher from India who had won distinctions for his writings at university. This was Bhagwan Shree Rajneesh, now called Osho, who founded a movement in the early 1970s in Poona [now Pune], India, his country of birth. In his lectures and discourses, he talked about the importance of feelings and the value of spontaneity. When he said children are destroyed by their parents and teachers, this immediately resonated with me. He was not afraid to discuss the dark side of society. He called his disciples sannyasins and by the 1980s there were thousands throughout the world. I took sannyas when I was thirty–five, and was given the spiritual name Alok John. It made me stronger because, earlier, I had been so alienated from society that I was constantly fighting a losing battle.

'Private Eye' magazine used to call Osho's teachings 'Bagwash'! When I'd just taken sannyas I told a friend (another fan of *Private Eye)* the news. He said he thought all sannyasins were stupid, and I agreed that lots were! He has also said to me, 'You definitely have got something, John.' I never felt taking sannyas made me weak.

I joined to find myself, to decondition myself so that I could find my authenticity and my own path in life. I was loosening the bonds from the schools and institutions that did the brainwashing and it helped me enormously. It helped me deal with adversity and suffering by teaching me to trust my own feelings and learn and grow through the suffering. I grew in intelligence and compassion. Many sannyasins are highly educated, but some cannot even read. An intellectual like me would normally associate with similar types, so perhaps what many sannyasins have in common is their abusive or dysfunctional family backgrounds.

Osho's teachings of living without goals finally released me from a lot of tension, as I gave up competing with those from loving families who had had a private education. Who was going to get the jobs during the 1980s, the times of such high unemployment? I stopped measuring myself according to the outside world and adjusted to reality by going inside, learning to dispel inner pressures, while finding and facing up to myself.

Alice Miller says abuse survivors join cults to transfer themselves into dream families with glowing parental figures, only to become brainwashed and suffer abuse all over again, and get financially exploited as well. Whilst this is probably true, I was a good judge of character and I hardly had any money anyway, so I only did a few of the popular humanistic psychology groups. I could never afford a course of private therapy sessions.

Thanks to the tabloids, the sannyas movement got labelled as some kind of tantric sex cult, probably because Osho used to mock the sexual hypocrisy in society. But who knows whether sannyasins have more sexual relationships than the population at large? They may well have less. They are less secretive about sex, and because friendly hugging could be perceived as sexual, an outsider could think they are at it like rabbits! Anyway I didn't get involved because of sex. Bill Clinton said of Monica Lewinsky, 'I never had sex with that woman.' Well, I've never had sex with a sannyasin woman … but in my case, I'm not lying!

Even with Osho, I was aware I was already too damaged to have sexual relationships. Generally, I freeze if a woman touches me, and put this down to the contorted relationships I endured at the hands of my mother and sister. Sometimes, I fantasise about women, but that was – and still is – all I can manage. Nobody, from the world's best therapist to a sex goddess could help me become actively sexual, but there was one single incident in July 1986.

At a disco in Amsterdam there was this girl I really liked. Never before had I had the experience of liking anyone, male or female, but just out of the blue this was love at first sight, and it lasted about twelve hours. I think she could sense I really liked her, and she came over and we danced. We spent the night together, but without sex. By the next morning, that feeling of really liking her had completely vanished. Although I tried to keep the relationship going by writing letters, she could sense the love was not there any more and she just withdrew. That twelve hours is all I had of liking somebody, and I think it transpired because it happened at the same time I took sannyas, when I thought I could start anew.

Restriction

In the few sannyas groups I did in my late thirties, I was trying to open up and find some kind of love within. There is a lot of closeness expressed between people, but I just wanted to be on my own because all I felt was restriction and pain. Being a sannyasin didn't transform that. I've had to accept I can't change that. I'm behind a wall most of the time, and right at the bottom of the learning curve in this area of life.

Warmth and Attraction

I don't think most people feel like that, because they have the impulse to conduct relationships on an intimate level, to varying degrees. They might see someone on the tube, for example, feel attracted, but stop themselves making an acquaintance in that situation. Or they might see someone in a pub but stop themselves from having a sexual relationship because they know having two or more partners obviously makes life very complicated. That's not my experience at all, you see.

I do notice women looking interestedly at me in the park, but my heart freezes in fear and I can't respond to them. From experience, I know that if we were to speak, they'd see how my contact is somehow neurotic. It's all a mystery I don't understand. I have tried to change it. I can meditate and that has helped, but now I'm 55, I think it would take two, three or four lifetimes to change.

People have largely unconscious patterns of loyalty to our most powerful social institutions, but you can't be loyal to a guru in the same way. Osho's been dead for sixteen years and he never spoke to me in person or gave me an order. Gurus help you find God within you, and you decide whatever that means. He left video discourses, books, and many meditation techniques. I sometimes enjoy these as I feel they benefit me. I take regular exercise for similar reasons.

Gradually, things have been getting better for me, in that I go to a meditation in London once a week or so, and occasionally to social events or parties. As an eighteen-year-old, I went for politics in order to understand the world, and philosophy to understand my pain. I've studied many religions, and Osho was, I think, probably the greatest spiritual teacher ever, or since Jesus Christ. Perhaps his teachings might be accepted in a few hundred years time. But sannyas hasn't saved me, or made me feel like the spontaneous child I never was. It simply helped me live in truth, releasing me from trying to be like everybody else, and to stop trying to be what I cannot be.

179

Father's Last Years

The tension built up between my father and me so much that he moved out of the family home in early 1983 when I was still there, and then he started legal proceedings to evict me. He told the police a cock–and–bull story that I had assaulted him, perhaps to get support from the rest of the family. The bailiffs came and evicted me. But my father never moved back, not even to be with my mother.

She said, 'You poisoned the atmosphere here, that's why your father won't come back!' She blamed me for the fact that for the first time in her life, she was living on her own. My father died alone of a heart attack in one of his cheap flats at Christmas 1987. I felt greatly relieved and much safer when I heard that. I didn't go to his funeral: that would have been hypocritical when he hated me so much. I don't expect I will go to my mother's either.

I moved back home in early 1988 when I was thirty–seven, and have lived there with my mother ever since.

I had hoped the philosophy of sannyas would help heal the broken parts in me and make me free. Instead, it helped me face up to my truth.

I went to the ashram in India in 1990 when I was 40, using some money left in trust after my father's death. I met a young woman there who was with her parents. She was a heroin addict, and her parents cared enough to take her to the ashram in the hope it would cure her. The contrast struck me: I had not taken heroin, had a good degree from Oxford, and my parents never wanted to even listen to me. This young heroin addict told me I was so disadvantaged, it would be better if I died and started again. Bhagwan explained reincarnation, that after death you get reborn in a new body. I would dream of getting born into a loving family! What is said in the ashram can be confrontational, as it is often the real truth. You are taught that feelings are real and cannot be ignored, so I often think about what this woman said.

But I found one major drawback in my involvement with sannyasins: most had the New Age belief that each person is completely responsible for his situation in life. I think this is nonsense. It's obvious that life outcomes are largely determined by quality of parenting and the social class you are born into. You're never allowed to say 'I am a victim.' I haven't found that Bhagwan himself taught these fashionable New Age values. In fact, I found most sannyasins did not pay attention to what Bhagwan actually said in his discourses.

Sharing the Revelation

Before the age of 40, I never even thought such complete and utter rejection as a child could affect anybody so profoundly. As I got to middle age, I began to understand the magnitude of it, and told a couple of people I still know now about the abuse.

Their reactions were, 'Oh no, you weren't abused.' Later, they did begin to accept it, but were very guarded in their responses. Most people don't know much about child abuse. They think emotional abuse is not as bad as being raped or something. Perhaps I just have ignorant friends, but emotional abuse is at the heart of all abuse. For example, in a rape, in most cases there will not be a pregnancy or an STD. The bruises will clear up quickly. *It is the violation of the person that counts*; it is the emotional effect that is most damaging, not the physical. Please don't think that emotional abuse is minor in nature. I was left with two personality disorders: long standing depression, and an inability to trust anyone. All that created great difficulties in the world of work. Physically, the loss of my large intestine was probably a result of lifelong stress.

It's hard to tell people, as they think you're a leper or something, and are sometimes a bit hostile. I think that abuse and bullying are an integral part of society. Most people have abused or bullied someone at some time. They know it was wrong but tell themselves the person will recover. In most cases they do, but if you stand up and say, 'My life was ruined by child abuse,' you're saying sometimes people *are* destroyed. One in eight is a reasonable figure for those so damaged that they suffer the effects for the rest of their lives. Western civilisation is about exploitation, and from the workplace to the schools and everywhere else, it's all based on bullying.

Recently, I told my story to, of all people, a Catholic priest, a Father Buckley. He said most people in my position would not have survived. Perhaps most would have died through a self-inflicted car accident, or another form of suicide, perhaps drugs, or getting killed in a severely violent relationship, or spending their lives behind bars. I suppose it was through my intelligence that I was able to avoid outcomes like this.

I don't give and get what I want from my adult relationships. Today, I have one friend and ten acquaintances, and a feeling of isolation pervades all my relationships. Most people can't recognise the limits I live within. People say, 'He's not getting *on* with his life.' Or, 'He is weak, that's why he doesn't do anything.' But I had to be as strong as steel just to stay alive.

Disability

Physically disabled people can't do things everybody else takes for granted, but with me it's not physical. There's a full circle of choice in civilised behaviour, but only a small ambit that I can actually control. Some people can do things in the world, whereas I cannot, and this separates me. Because I don't abuse my body I look okay, so they think I'm moaning and acting weak. I look like a recluse who simply made a 'choice', yet I'm like a man confined to a wheelchair, and they're telling me, 'Don't just sit there. Get up!'

Reaching Out

The NHS are basically overloaded and burnt out, at least at Edgware Community Hospital things certainly seemed that way. Following Dr Bailey's diagnosis of social phobia, in 1999 I made enquiries about getting psychiatric help on the NHS. I filled in a form, saying I was a victim of severe emotional abuse as a child.

Herbert Friedman, the psychotherapist, said child abuse was very rare. He didn't seem to know that it's very common. They under-diagnose, under-treat, and then blame the victim when things go wrong. The first session with Dr Friedman degenerated into bullying when he said, 'Let's see how you got yourself into this situation,' like it was my fault. He berated me for not working and tried to push me into employment. I thought it was none of his business whether I was working or not. About my lack of career, I explained that I never had any feeling or sense about a direction in life. He said, 'That is because you are immature.'

181

Now that may well be true; I never had the love from my parents to enable me to develop maturity, but he said the words aggressively, like it was my fault. But can I choose to make myself mature? When he was criticising me for a lack of career I said, 'I went to a local authority grammar school in the middle of a council housing estate. I bet you went to a private school or a direct–grant school.' He went a bit quiet after that!

They call their treatment 'challenging your beliefs', but it bullies you into accepting their opinions and values. There was so much of this that I wrote to Friedman that I wasn't coming back. He then invited me to come for another session for closure, which was actually quite helpful. He said I was grossly emotionally deprived and was afraid of my father, never received any emotional support from my mother, and that I was extremely angry and sad. It was certainly worth hearing a professional say these things, but it was virtually useless to me, a man in his 50s. As for employment, perhaps the government had set a target to get so many 'mentally ill' people back into employment.

My GP says I am capable of work so I could sign on if I wanted income support. But working means I then have to socialise a lot, and I simply do not wish to endure the pain of that. I can't face fighting with the Department of Work and Pensions, so for most of my life I've got no kind of money at all. I am refused a disability allowance. The Social Security System only gives this to the mentally ill, or people who can do absolutely nothing. There would be a smaller slice of the cake for everybody else, so it reminds me of how cruel society is.

Pursuing the Law

I wanted to take legal action against the local authority for failing to prevent my parents abusing me. There was this scheme where you could get free legal advice from barristers, so I went to see barrister Constance Whippman. When I arrived she had already read my letter setting out my claim, saying I suffered severe emotional abuse. She said, 'Oh, I thought maybe you came from a Presbyterian Scottish family.' When I said I was Jewish, she was quite shocked and got really angry because she was Jewish too. She kept saying how terrible this was, but I could see she was really angry.

She seemed to listen, but wrote down very little. She said that probably nothing could be done – which was the legal advice I expected. But she told me to go home, write down a list setting out the abusive actions of my father and send it to her on the off–chance something could be done. Using the list, she wrote a report for the legal authorities, sending a copy to me. She chose to list the most minor things, failing to state the true pattern of abusive behaviour, thus making the point more persuasive that my case was too weak to pursue. The law does not recognise emotional abuse, and the physical abuse I endured was the norm at the time. Only one thing she said made sense; was grieving. She said, 'I've read that you can grieve for what you've lost and what you never had', and I appreciated having a professional acknowledge my grief.

Living with Mother Today

My mother's quite intelligent. She does the accounts on the computer, even though she's over 80, and the *Times* crossword every day. She's totally loyal to my father's memory, so it's quite acrimonious and rather hopeless. I end up blaming her for the abuse, even though I say almost nothing about it. People have commented that I subject myself to more abuse by living with her, but I don't see that I have any other choice. They don't understand the extent to which I don't think I can make my own way. I have a terrible CV. A third of men over 50 are unemployed, and I am obviously a prime candidate.

She doesn't respect me as a person at all and never has. She doesn't want me to die, but otherwise doesn't care. I say, 'You have contempt for me,' and she replies, 'If I have contempt for you, why do I go out shopping for you?' It is hard to know what she really thinks. She thought her duties only extended to providing for my physical needs as a child. She has no awareness about emotional well-being. I even think she believes that if I had studied physics absolutely everything would have worked out!

She tells me, 'You should make a go of it; everyone can make a go of it if they want to.' 'Making a go of it' is from the 1940s when there was a labour shortage. The only thing she loves and respects is money, e.g., she told me in an admiring tone that my sister's boyfriend had gone on a business trip to America. But I do not think she respects, say, the person who invented penicillin, and, therefore, prevented immense suffering. When she saw the bombs falling on Baghdad on TV at the beginning of the First Gulf War, she found it exciting! Like her late husband, she is a bit of a Nazi. They were quite a pair!

Since 1999, my mother has said explicitly to me that she despises me. If I said, 'You hated me even when I was a baby,' she'd reply, 'Yes, it is true: I did.' In the last few years my mother has called me a beast, brute, demon, sod, monster and a horrid man. She says she really hates me now, that she enjoyed abusing me.

Understandably, I cannot bear the sight of her, I don't make her the odd cup of tea or take care of her. The flat is large, so we keep to opposite ends. She cooks dinner for us most days, which I eat on my own. Fortunately, she is quite well so can do most things like going to the supermarket. She gets on well with her daughter and niece, and is on the phone to them most days. Some people might say I'm waiting for her to die and want her inheritance, but it's quite untrue.

§ Optional Question 19 §

Revenge

I'm aware of my desire for revenge. I think, 'I'll be damned if I'm going to contribute to the wicked society that allowed my parents and schoolteachers to torture me. I'll be damned if I'm going to make my mother happy by getting a good job and leading a respectable life.' You may think that's terrible, but feelings are real; you cannot deny them or turn them off. If you had been through what I did, you would feel the same.

I don't welcome these innermost feelings. But this is why many people become violent or turn to crime. I stop these feelings from dominating my actions, but cannot stop them erupting. Some people hit other members of their families, damage their possessions, steal from them, or torture them emotionally. Instead, I keep it all in, and carry a kind of poisonous wound around with me. From time to time when it starts to ooze, I silently dress it with a new bandage, cursing the ugliness and the chronic pain.

I'm sensitive enough to know that even if I repress these feelings, people sense them and reject me for them. It is true I have a pretty lazy, easygoing life, living in my mother's house with my two dogs, but it is a very sad life, isn't it? My father broke my heart when I was a child. I want to be alone, and grieving takes energy that is not then available for work or relationships.

Current Family

My sister is almost 50, is a part-time lecturer and lives with her boyfriend. She's reasonably healthy. A few days ago I had a conversation with her, the first in years. Because my mother is going deaf, I was talking loudly when my sister came in. In a busybody sort of way my sister said, 'Don't shout at your mother.' As I protested and we continued to talk, she said, 'I am sorry about your situation in life,' but in a harsh tone, more like she was talking to a nuisance who needed to be silenced. She was not sorry at all. She was gloating and resenting the disruption to the *Sunday Times* life that she and my mother like to lead. I kept saying, 'I am a victim of child abuse and you should treat me with compassion and respect.' She did not like that, but the message started to get through. Throughout my childhood my sister never threatened me, whereas my parents often did. But in all other respects, she has been the same. While I was growing up, all three of those I lived with enjoyed making me a scapegoat. Now, my sister doesn't want to invest any time in finding out about me.

I sometimes dream that everyone who knows me could buy a book in W. H. Smiths that tells the real truth of my life. I want to announce to my peers, 'This is why I couldn't do anything with my life; this is what I went through.' I would love to be able to buy a full page ad in the *Times* and say, 'The following people were bastards....' Most child abuse books change all the names to protect people's identities, or deal with survivors whose abusers were convicted in a court of law. But it would make me very happy to say, 'Go and get this book: it's *real*, with all the names of my abusers, including those of my parents and my worst teachers.'

There are self-help books, but they don't help much. They trivialise people's lives and make their testimonies into fairy stories. I am dubious of books that claim to teach you how to heal childhood trauma. Some of these books exploit survivors of child abuse, but my story helps far more by shining a clear light on the root causes.

The trouble with emotional abuse is that *it is subtle*. I wasn't beaten to within an inch of my life, yet I was very thin and very scared. In a way, Dr Friedman was right: it's quite rare for a child to receive not an iota of emotional support from either parent or any other adult whatsoever. As a child I promised myself that I would never forgive my parents for what they did. The scars are far too severe for me to ever heal fully, and it'll probably only end when my life ends. I sometimes wistfully long to be a happy teenager, which is the very antithesis of who I have always been. I don't visualise any future for myself, but as I go on living, I can't just sit back and do nothing.

Campaigning

Telling people has made me a bit stronger and I think I've changed a few people's thinking patterns. Sometimes I go out on my own and demonstrate against child abuse, standing in the street with a big placard giving out leaflets. Once I demonstrated outside the Jewish Board of Deputies. Another time I demonstrated outside the Conservative Party headquarters in London. I distribute a leaflet with my personal history and my name and address. I sent copies to old friends, my childhood synagogue, the Jewish Board of Deputies, the Chief Rabbi, the media, MPs, even Reffold, who is still alive! I received just about no response.

My family are very set in their minds and ways: nevertheless, I recently sent the leaflet to several of them. I sent one to my uncle in Israel who was recovering from major heart surgery. When his sister (my aunt) heard about this she was concerned that reading the leaflet might jeopardise my uncle's recovery. She phoned me in a real tizzy, so I agreed that my uncle's wife should intercept the leaflet when it arrived, but my aunt had little concern for me. When she finally read the leaflet, she said she was shocked and would destroy it.

I also sent it to my sister. These are the two e-mail replies I got.

>>> John

>>> I received your leaflet which was along the same lines as the conversation we had a month or so ago. Having sent this leaflet out, the question is, what do you want to do now?

Merle

I replied,

>> Grieve

John

>>>You've had forty odd years to grieve and it doesn't seem to have given you any comfort. Lots of people have personal problems of varying severity, they learn to deal with them and have a life of their own. Why not explore that option rather than harping on about your version of the past?

Merle

It is interesting how my sister's language reveals her attitudes. She says, 'What do you *want* to do now?' She seeks to reassure herself that I am a person fully capable of experiencing 'want' and 'choice', and then follow it through to its fulfilment. She refuses to give any thought to learn that *this is not the case.*

She has read no books on child abuse issues and refuses to, yet has the gall to lecture me on how to live my life. I find her reply quite distressing, and in future shall have as little contact with her as possible.

I do not want pity. I do want compassion and understanding, virtues in short supply. People do experience suffering, but people who were not abused have no conception of the different paradigm of suffering abuse victims endure. My sister said, 'Everyone suffers,' which is true. Then she gave the example of a girlfriend of hers who had threatened suicide because a boy would not go out with her.

How do you compare that with someone who is so damaged, just interacting with people involves little else but pain? With someone who spent a year living in a derelict house, sleeping in a sleeping bag on a dirty mattress on floorboards? Most victims of serious abuse lead their lives on the fringe, because the alternative is agonisingly painful.

Associations

One gravitates towards those similar to oneself in life, and as my understanding grew, I began to recognise the abuse in the lives of those I have known and still know today. Sometimes, I make lists of those who can't work or maintain intimate or sexual relationships.

Sakal was brought up in a council house. He got the highest marks in England in the 11-plus exam, but his parents had always been very abusive to him, and out of his anger at them has never done anything with his considerable intelligence. He was jailed in Thailand for dope and now lives in north England. He's a real doper, and coming to the end of his life now. In a photo of him in his twenties he looked really sensitive then. It's a common pattern that a sensitive child who is abused by his parents takes it out on them by failing. When I was doing my exams, I felt I was only doing them for my parents.

There was something hard and deep inside me that kept insisting, 'It's not right that I do this for you.' By dropping out I cheated my parent's happiness and caused them some suffering...not as much as *they* caused *me*, but still.... Sakal does the same by leading a life of dope smoking.

But not all of these people have survived, and one suicide case I know of was a member of a Catholic teaching class I still go to. In my ongoing search to find wholeness I recently became a Catholic. I am concerned about the atrocities carried out by certain priests, but believe only a minority abused children, and certainly abuse survivors should be well compensated by the Church. My parents were 'Jewish' only only superficially, and their devotion to the occult was what they really held sacred. This was kept secret for years, and was a major weight on my developing mind as a child. I still don't believe every word of the Catholic creed, but it has been helpful. Catholics believe evil spirits can be exorcised, and I felt drawn to have an exorcism as a kind of experiment to clear out the darkness in me. I did have the exorcism, and maintain a certain scepticism about any change. Nevertheless I do see people more often than before, and relating has become a bit easier.

Through this class I got to know Henry, who came to London from a village in Kenya to study for the priesthood. He'd spent four years studying in Africa and was like me, in that he was Mr Perfect. He was the best student at his course in London. Although he could do the intellectual part of the work quite well, you have to be quite sociable to be a priest. Henry wasn't gregarious enough, and having realised that, he decided he couldn't take on this vocation after all. I was shocked to hear that he committed suicide at the age of twenty-three. He had told me he was depressed, but I had no idea how much pain he must have been in. Looking back, he was really thin and withdrawn, just as I was when I was twenty. His family set-up was similar, with a very ambitious mother, and no support. His parents were strict, demanding, unloving, and selfish. His father beat him with a cane for years, and the result is a common pattern for a sensitive child. They wanted him to fulfil their ambitions rather than find out what his heart said. When I'd go to Henry's room he'd play music for us, and I felt he used music in the same way I used to at his age: to kill the pain in his life. Maybe Henry was another sad piece of my puzzle.

Action

It's controversial, but my opinion is that people who have endured extreme suffering through child abuse should be identified, and given large sums of money without expecting anything in return. It's outrageous I know, but it's nowhere near as outrageous as the suffering of children all around us, all the time. This is one of the ideas I want to put across. Many will not like it, but it sends a signal about how real the suffering is. Also, rich and successful people only have what they do because they were not severely abused. I told another abuse victim about this, and he said a dozen solid gold medals for courage should be thrown in as well!

Every autumn there is a survivors' march from Hyde Park to Trafalgar Square against sexual abuse of children. I once went along to one, but didn't stay because I didn't feel I belonged. 'Campaigning against child abuse' can have a wide range of meanings, so I am an independent campaigner with my own style.

I once demonstrated with a placard, 'STOP CHILD ABUSE IN THE JEWISH COMMUNITY'. I'd been standing in the street for about thirty minutes when a Jewish man came up to me and said he had not gone to his mother's funeral because she had been demonic. I was struck by his use of the word 'demonic', because my father was demonic and I didn't go to his either. A few minutes later a Jewish taxi driver waved at me and said, 'Well done! At last someone is doing something.' But most Jews do not react like this. Far more came up to me and said, 'We acknowledge there is a problem of child abuse in the Jewish community. But if you demonstrate like that you damage the reputation of the whole community.' One Jewish man phoned me and 'strongly urged me' in a threatening voice to stop my protest. When I demonstrated outside the local synagogue, about a hundred Jews from the Jewish defence turned up to 'defend' the synagogue. They even took my photo. The police came and said I would be prosecuted if I did not leave right away. All this for one middle-aged man carrying a placard and some leaflets! When my mother was on holiday I left this same placard in the front garden. The police were soon at the front door telling me to remove it, and I did. But I may demonstrate with it again in the hope that a prosecution will give me publicity. It would be a very minor offence and I would only get a small fine (if any).

Even though I was born Jewish, I cannot speak out. Religious minorities are allowed exceptions they do not deserve, and no one has the courage to point out their shortcomings. Israel is probably the only place where you can criticise the Jewish community publicly. If they bothered to listen, I would say this:

When I was a child I spent night after night crying myself to sleep, totally alone. If one Jewish abuser sees my demonstration, and just for one night does not abuse his child, and just for one night his child does not cry himself to sleep, then my

187

demonstration has been successful, and this outweighs any damage to the reputation of the Jewish community.

I would not want any child to go through a tenth of the suffering I did. I hope that telling my story will influence my family and help the public understand. I hope this will be read by parents, social workers, doctors, and many other professionals. The more knowledge there is about what child abuse does, the sooner it will be eliminated. That is why it's so important to me that my account has my name and address on it, to have the most power to change people's thinking. Perhaps my life will not have been such a complete waste after all.

Since my birth at least 3,000 infants and children have been killed in the UK by abusive parents and carers. For each one of these deaths, there are several who survive with such severe psychological injuries that they spend their whole lives on the fringes of society. I dedicate my story to Henry and all victims of child abuse here in the UK, and all across the world.

Writing the Story

Writing the story was, for me, very therapeutic, and over the one year it took, I felt good. Morven's questions were very useful, and I needed something to stimulate me and start me off. Although one or two new memories came up it didn't make me feel worse in any way whatsoever; indeed, it's made me feel a lot better simply because the truth sets you free. I will show the story to anyone who will take the time to read it, although I have been surprised to find that most of my friends and acquaintances do not care enough to take the time to read it. As a result of having written this, I feel a bit empowered. It felt fine to take part, and I really appreciate having my pain, truth, and history acknowledged.

If you want to contact John Nygate you can write to him at his email address. He would be happy to give talks to social workers or other professionals about his experience of child abuse. As he has no source of income, he is happy to receive donations. **E-mail: john_nygate@btopenworld.com**

188

Optional Questions

1. If you had a father, to some extent you will probably associate your relationship with him with your concepts about what most fathers are like.
    How far are you projecting your own ideas on to John's father?
    Open your mind, and look for clues in the text that will show you what *this* father was like, as a completely individual character.

2. How far is this a case of a son who harmlessly rebels against the older generation's beliefs, and how far is it the case that this father *actively despised* his son for being different?

3. What were John's rights within the home and family that he grew up in?

4. What power did John have to negotiate anything with his father?

    It seems quite trivial for a son to have to leave the room in the presence of adults, however, John is saying he felt alienated all the time, without fail.

5. What was it John's father felt compelled to do to his son?

6. Was he ambitious for his son, or for himself?

7. Describe what John looks like from his father's perspective.

8. He seems to have put a lot of energy into guiding and controlling John. Was this normal parental guidance?

9. If John ever felt any sadness, joy or spontaneity in his life, who could he share that with? Where could he take it?

10. Who do you think John's mother was more loyal and devoted to? Her son, or her husband?

11. To what extent did she see her son through her husband's eyes?

12. What score would you give her from 1 to 10, as a mother in her own right?

13. From whom can you see any evidence of positive bonds reaching down to John as a child?

14. How good a job did John's parents do at training him for society?

15. What elements from John's upbringing should he be grateful for?

16. If you were John, what would *you* be grateful for?

17. Might John's father have believed he was doing this to make John strong, to make him into a man who could always withstand adversity?

18. If so, how far is this just our social assumption that we have about parents and fathers in general? Can we find any evidence of how John's father expressed any love or empathy towards him in other ways?

19. How usual is it for a mother to confirm to her son that she did hate him when he was a baby, and that she still does?

Maybe it's something that could be said within a supportive relationship during a misunderstanding, a tantrum, or a burst of sarcasm, but how would we know that's what *this* is?

Reflections on John's Chapter

Because of what it can teach us, John's story could be the most enlightening one of all. When I read John's first drafts, I kept looking for the terrible abuse that I couldn't find. John could easily be a layabout and a moaner and I thought, 'God, what a sponger, fancy wanting society to *pay you* money just because you suffered as a child!' I didn't express any of these snap judgements, but I really wondered why they kept popping up in my head.

As I passed the story around for feedback, it became evident that most abuse survivors understand this story, yet most other people don't. But why? We listen whilst checking our references *from our own bank of experience*, yet we can't develop clearer perceptions unless we use every sense we have to slip into other people's experiences, and thus augment our knowledge.

This is an extract from William Bloom's book, '*Feeling Safe'*.

> "*You may be familiar with the experiments in which baby monkeys were removed from their mothers shortly after birth. They were given the best possible food and nutrients. They were kept in a perfect temperature. But they were left alone most of the time, cut off from the warmth and nurture of their mothers and families.*
>
> *These little creatures did not develop well. This traumatic beginning affected the whole of their lives. They were uncertain of themselves and easily frightened. Their big lost eyes were haunted with a need for reassuring comfort. They suffered mood swings, their behaviour moving between timid and aggressive. They had great difficulty fitting into their society.*

We assume society would never allow such experiments on human babies, but during one phase of Romanian history in the late 1970s and 1980s, hundreds of babies were brought up in orphanages in a very similar way. The children didn't develop normally, and that precious period of time they needed to do so is irretrievable. Many of those who remain are now confined to institutions.

Alice Miller talks about positive human bonds of tenderness and empathy, where, throughout at least one phase of childhood an ingredient of continual concern for the child (that is recognised by the child too) is crucial to his or her needs. The bond enables the child to go on and develop relationships as an adult. A child can live through the most devastating abuse (see the ritual abuse Story, Volume Two) and despite such violation, still be able to form relationships. A child needs *one* person, just one, where s/he can express himself in relationship and feel 'held'. Engagement follows in a regular continuity of mutual sharing. Even another child or sibling can fulfil the need to be recognised and watched over, by taking on the positive parental role.

Through long discussions with John and countless e-mails, I could find no evidence that he ever had such a person in his life. What I see is an extremely isolated child who, through not bonding, could never develop the capacity to feel that in relationship to anybody, he had any ground upon which he could actually exist.

Countless children of John's generation were caned, belted, beaten, sent to bed at six without tea and so on. So what does such rough treatment do to bonds? Despite the fact that a child's carer beats the child, how far can he also be trusted to observe him, and empathise with him as a human being, and sense some respect for justice *from the child's perspective* as well as his own? Maybe that is enough for the child to develop some right of place in relationship, and go on to get some right of place in the world. Many children who grew up to thrive despite their beatings assume that all child-carers who punish using physical and emotional pain must have some redeeming features. However temporarily a child's mind is confused and shocked by rough treatment, ultimately, they probably feel safe, and cared for within the bigger picture. If a vindictive, emotionally abusive schoolteacher hits a child, they can retreat to the safety of their positive parental bonds. Often, this works the other way, where a child with vindictive parent(s) finds faith and nurture in his bonds with an empathetic – and possibly inspiring schoolteacher. This didn't happen in John's case.

However, unless children are fully protected by law, isolated children like John can easily be the victims who suffer for life. Adults who say, 'It didn't do me any harm,' take for granted the positive elements of support they received to balance their childhood punishments. They may have had some destructive teachers or relatives who were real bullies, but they simply can't imagine any child growing up without getting some small sense of safety, reassurance and acceptance elsewhere.

Most people don't know how their instantaneous right of place and confidence to progress got there. And what possible motive could there be to look for this ground of human contact that always gets taken for granted? I believe nearly everyone has a mixture of both good and bad bonds that can be traced right back to their roots. They are there for every individual to discover, for not just the abuses from their pasts, but the positive opportunities of relationship that were more freely given. Whoever had the faith to look into the face of a child with love and respect over a period of several months or years, gave that child the grounding that s/he'll always carry whenever s/he looks into the face of another person.

John has managed to cleave something from both contemporary Eastern and traditional Catholic religion, and, from that, slowly managed to experience a sense of place in episodes of relationship with friends. The difficulties come when the sense of rejection creeps back into his life, and everything topples over. He knows his isolation, pain and anger don't rest upon an inability to forgive and forget. His point is that children, and, therefore, the people they become, are irrevocably damaged by abuse. Even if he could fully forgive his persecutors, that could never fully eliminate the remnants of damage that he, and many others, still endure.

Story Six

Events in this story remain unchanged, making this a correct and truthful account of a childhood. People and place names have been changed.

Karen

At the time Karen and I met on the net, I was living in Germany and she in England, but the last thing we both expected was for her to come and live in Germany too! We met each other about half way through the project, and agreed to meet at Hauptbahnhof; the main railway station in Munich at ten. I had her photograph, and was looking for a mother with a pram. I realise Karen's bang on time when I recognise her face through the crowded bustle; one wheel from her pram gets stuck behind the lift door, and just as the doors are closing a commuter helps pull it free. They chatter on in German as they stride towards the meeting point with sixteen-month baby Max up front. Goodbyes are exchanged, and we go off towards the café just opposite. Karen's older son Perry is at kindergarten. As I watch her chat away to Max and attend to his every need, it feels especially odd to imagine this twenty-five year old mother going through the kind of life she had growing up in the UK. Karen first met David, her German husband five years ago when he was at university in England. A year ago he found a teaching job in Germany and that's why they decided to move.

Karen sets off to get coffee, and joining the long queue she stands gazing round, her eye contact offering reassurance to whoever should meet her gaze. Max and I are deeply engaged in the soft pages of a colourful texture book all about animals. She insists on paying for the café lattés and she's right in the middle of teasing herself about the advantages of caffeine versus sleep deprivation, when I discover she's been up since four that morning, yet she hits me with a broad smile, and assures me Max could well be having his morning nap quite soon. I ask how many baby photos she's taken since he was born, and she admits she's got a few hundred pictures of three year old Perry, less of Max on his own, and loads of both boys together with their father. Evidently she's usually the one with the camera, and she jokes about the hit and miss affair of getting a really good snapshot of everyone with their heads all facing the same direction – with her included! Around the house though, she admits she has no photographs at all on display from her own childhood.

I grew up in a semi-detached house with mum, two brothers and a sister, part-time dad and numerous cats! I was born in Horncastle in Lincoln, where we lived until I was two. Then we moved to Alford, then moved again when I was six, but remained in the same town. The house was a three bed roomed semi in a nice area with a big garden, a private driveway, a garage, a garden shed, and a brick built barbecue.

Brother Gavin was the oldest. He's two years older than Colin, who was a year and a half older than me, and Liz was a year and a half younger than me. Colin had some behavioural problems and went to a special school from the age of seven to sixteen, and he came home for some weekends and holidays. Liz my younger sister was diabetic as a child and of course still is; anyway she went to the same school as Gavin and myself. At first Liz and I slept in bunk beds that my Aunt Judy bought, and Gavin was in the box room, but then it changed round. Gavin would sleep in the dining room on a sofa bed because he didn't want to share with any of us, and Colin shared the room with Liz at weekends when he was home.

§ *Optional Question 1* §

I ended up alone in the box room, which was always a terrible mess. It was usually full of my sister's stuff and storage boxes, I very rarely tidied it, and I never knew when either one of my parents would throw a fit and make me tidy it up. Our bedding was rarely washed but the house in Alford was always warm. I would never get a 'good morning' from anyone. My parents said I was a grumpy moody child and it was not worth speaking to me in the morning, a habit that caught on and stayed for years. No one could look me in the eye, unless of course I was being shouted at.

Dad worked long hours, and was away from home for long periods whenever the work took him abroad. He was chief executive and partner in an international security firm, and he had a lot of responsibilities, like providing bodyguards for VIP's, surveillance jobs, endless confidential arrangements and so on with local authorities, the police and the like. It was stressful and he travelled a lot but I don't think he was very happy. Physically he was strong and well built, with muscled arms and big hands, and he was well dressed, confident, charming and quick witted in public. I think he suffered greatly from stress and found life very hard to cope with, and didn't know how to channel his stress in positive ways, like sport or something. Drinking only gave him a beer belly, so the stress was chiefly taken out on me.

Mum suffered from depression for most of our childhood and was also an alcoholic; she did not work, in fact I don't ever remember her going out to work. She never ever kissed me or cuddled me in my whole life. Not even in front of relatives. Never. Even when I was seriously ill in hospital, or when mum knew I had been 'hurt' by my father and his 'friends' the night previously. Or even when I had her first grandchild. She always twisted everything round to being her 'drama' to gain attention for herself. For example she would say,

"It is hard to cope with a child in hospital." Or,

"Why are you putting me through this stress?" when she knew I had been abused. It was made out to be my entire fault and mum was always 'the victim'.

§ *Optional questions 2, 3 and 4* §

By the time I got to my early teens and started to learn about biology at school, at last I fully understood why I wasn't my dad's daughter. Mum had had quite a few affairs, and I was the result of one she had with a close friend of dad's. From a very early age I was aware that I did not belong, which was hard to understand when I was younger, why my siblings 'belonged' to dad, but I didn't. It was exasperating to try to be good and 'belong' but it never worked. Looking back I realise I've never once

195

cuddled my brothers or sister, or they me. Dad told me I was never his daughter and never would be; he told me hated me for being born and that they should have drowned me at birth.

Living at home was like living under a lightening storm, you never knew when you might get struck. There were no firm boundaries and I never knew where I stood. I would behave in a crazy or bizarre manner or be very naughty as a cry for help to get attention, and no one cared or listened. So therefore I'd hide away in my room but then get punished for being lazy. Dad would get in from the pub at midnight and drag me out of bed shouting and screaming, saying I was lazy for falling asleep. He would actually give me chores to do in the night. To maintain control over me, insults were screamed at me, I was neglected, deprived of food and water, or hit. Yet it seems so strange that parents administer physical punishment and mental abuse to maintain control, because it was always complete chaos in any case.

§ Optional comment and question 5 §

When I was nine, ten and over I wouldn't come home until very late at night, or I wouldn't come home at all and no one would bat an eyelid, but when I broke a plate or forgot to put the heating on, insult after insult was screamed at me. If I apologised, I would be told off for saying sorry. They'd tell me that if I was really sorry, then I wouldn't have been evil in the first place. No matter what I did within the walls of that house, whether it was good or bad, nothing made any difference.

Aunt Judy

But outside the home, there was somebody that I could trust. It was dad's aunt, my great aunt Judy that I was close to. I knew her right from the time I was a baby. She would visit our house at a weekend for a couple of hours or more about once a month, and everybody would have to act 'normal' during that time. I remember being about thirteen years old when she told dad off one time. She shouted at him, saying that I looked ill, and she was so angry that she couldn't bear to stay in the house another minute longer, so she left and went straight back home. Another time she had another go at dad for the awful way I was treated, she took me away from there all the way back to her house, because she was just so cross. I loved her; she talked to me, joked with me, fed me and so on, but I was not allowed to ring her and she lived far away, but whenever I did see her it was a happy time.

§ Optional Question 6 §

Whenever she came to pick me up, I would usually go with her for a visit to her house. I felt that these times were totally about 'escapism.' She lived in a lovely part of the country, with beautiful green rolling hills, parks and wooded areas. She was very fit and so enjoyed walking out in the country, so we would walk for miles and miles, and she would tell me the names of the plants and flowers. She would point out the birds to me and help me to name them, telling me about their different songs and calls. She was so clever, that I was in awe of her knowledge of the nature around us. We both adored animals and there would be non-stop discussions about different species. It would be lovely to see the wild rabbits running free and the birds soaring high. We would be so delighted in the rare occasions we spotted a kestrel in the sky, or a fox in the dusk. I felt free.

When things got tough at home, I would try and escape, just like I did with my Aunt Judy. Although I didn't have the countryside like she did, I would climb a tree, or sit in a field, listening to the comfort of the birds calling. In my adult life now, if things feel tough or I am feeling anxious, I suggest to my husband and kids that we should go for a walk; this helps so much. Aunt Judy taught me a valuable lesson in dealing with difficult times, probably without even knowing it. During those times together I would feel well, I would feel childlike, I would feel my mind was stimulated by something positive and I would soak up info from her like a sponge.

I wish she had been my mum. Everything about her was soft and caring, her skin was so soft, her hair was soft, her scent soft and comforting, even her soft Irish voice which chattered away, similar to the chattering of the birds to their offspring in the trees. I was happy, so happy with Aunt Judy.

Apart from when there were visitors though, I had quite a separate life from my brothers and sister. Although I don't remember punishments from before I was two, there's some evidence that it went on. When I was pregnant with my own son about five years ago, I had a lot of spinal and pelvic complications during the pregnancy, which weren't helped by the assaults I had been through as a child. One day in hospital my notes were left on my bed by an anaesthetist; I asked if I could read them and he agreed. It was all there. At four months old I was admitted to hospital on two occasions; my Aunt Judy also mentioned this to me once. She told me about when I was four months old I was naked, sopping wet, I'd stopped breathing and there was bruising to my back. On another occasion I had stopped breathing again but I know no other details, except I was placed on an apnoea alarm and sent home. The list goes on, but the most extreme entry is at the bottom, when I had the base of my spine smashed when I was fourteen. I had been pushed down the stairs and my parents said I had fallen off a new mountain bike! I had to have major surgery to fix it. The notes are all lies and cover-ups.

§ Optional Questions 7 and 8 §

When I was still quite small, for months there was a rule in our house that I was only allowed to drink water from a thimble, and strangely this rule only stood when dad was away. One time he returned from work after we had been up town shopping for the day. It was very hot and I collapsed. I was probably de-hydrated. Between four and five, I remember being held by my hair to have my teeth brushed. This happened for quite a while but then after it stopped I didn't own a toothbrush for years! I would be deprived of food and water and locked in my room, usually on a daily basis, and every day I had to either eat away from the rest of the family, or not at all. Between three and five, I have vague memories of lots of shouting and things being smashed up in anger. I often had prized possessions like comfort toys put in the loft as a punishment. My parents used to smash up toys, throw things, smash up the house and so on. Special things were broken on purpose as punishment for being 'naughty', and Colin and Liz used to copy by smashing my things up as well.

§ Optional Questions 9, 10, 11, 12 and 13 §

I never fought with my siblings; I learnt there was no point, and anyway I'd given up by the time I was eight or nine. Gavin used to hit me and I would just stand there and eventually he would get bored, but one time he attacked me with a knife and ripped my t-shirt but I ran and got away. I was told a lot that I was unbearable because I was from the devil and I deserved to be punished; so it was better for me to go round pretending I didn't exist. I felt happiest anyway if mum wasn't too drunk when I got in from school, and when she didn't want any more housework doing.

At five, six, seven and eight, they regularly put me in a cold bath a couple of times a week, for hours. Now I can't bear cold water, I have my bath or shower so hot! I would shiver so much that I thought my teeth would be permanently damaged. I had goose bumps and I was forever coughing, it would make me so ill. One time I got pneumonia. I was too scared to call downstairs, but I would often think they had forgotten about me or fallen asleep. I was petrified about getting out because I knew I was in trouble if I did. One time I was left in there for hours as a punishment for talking, afterwards I had to go to my room with no food or water and stay there till morning.

From an early age, the word 'bedtime' meant nothing to me. Bed was a pretty insecure place – it wasn't a place of rest or seclusion. I say that, yet I was sometimes not allowed out of bed for days, at the weekend for example. On the other hand, I might be kept up all night listening to dad's lectures about politics, where I'd have to reply in some way or other to what he said. Dad would often play a 'game' too. He would come in to my room at about midnight and tell me that it was time for school. I'd get up, get dressed and have to sit up till the morning, until it really was time for school. I would feel so tired and confused the next day, and go to school feeling exhausted, and get told off for yawning or even falling asleep. From time to time I felt angry for being robbed of the sleep I so desperately needed.

Dad never did this with the others. Never. He loved his children, probably more to spite me. I can count on one hand the times he even raised his voice at the other children. His main aim in life with me was to hurt me, and all of the time. That's all he cared about. It did hurt me when I could see how kind he was to my brothers and sisters. It never mattered what I did, he would never be kind to me. His games included using the other children to get at me, and it worked. They joined in because they knew no different; it was a part of life for them too. At weekends Colin my older brother would get very involved with the 'controlling' of me and sometimes carry it on when no adults were about.

§ Optional Questions 14, 15, and 16 §

The sarcastic sense of humour that ruled our house was generally aimed at the way I looked, or my behaviour. My father's wit could twist anything to make me look stupid or feel useless. It was the way he said things, sometimes he would even make me laugh; he was clever but also very evil. He would say,

"How do you do that magic trick?" and I would reply

"What magic trick?" He would say

"Where you make yourself look so fat and repulsive." Then he would howl and howl with laughter at me. I would be punished for crying, even when they'd given me good reason to cry! I very rarely cried when I was physically hurt, but the emotional abuse would make me cry at times. To be told that I was evil and from the devil only confirmed how disgusting everyone thought I was, and how much they hated me. That hurt a lot more that a punch in the face or being pushed down the stairs.

Aside from the house, there was another location where I was kept; the garden shed. Dad never used my real name, and to maintain control he would shout other names at me, pull me about or twist my arm round behind my back. He always repeated how the devil would get me if I didn't do whatever he said.

Dad always knew how much I hated the dark and the shed, and it was a good threat to use too. When he took me down there I'd be screaming through his hand, which was clamped tightly over my mouth as he dragged me down the garden in the pitch black of night. I would try to fight but to no avail. I could never actually sleep there at night and every minute seemed like an hour until I was let out. In winter I always had chilblains on my toes and sometimes my arms and legs would turn blue and go numb. There was always a horrendous smell because our cats would shit all over the floor and it was just left there. A dead cat was in there one summer, and the smell was even worse when it was hot. Sometimes I would vomit because of it. I would bang my head repeatedly, over and over on the wall; I was really afraid I'd go crazy if I had to spend one more night in that awful hellhole.

Movies

When Michael Jackson's 'Thriller' came out, I was about four or five. Since then, I can't believe I was so scared of it, but dad would become 'manic' and shout and scream, saying the zombies were coming to get me tonight in my bed, I would scream and scream and he would laugh. He made me watch horror films or anything he knew would upset me. He liked the 'Chucky' films with the possessed dolls, and I hated them. I found it hard to understand that it was only make-believe. I really thought the zombies, monsters and ghosts were going to attack me. I would say that I wanted to die and dad replied that they and the devil would get me even more when I was dead. I was petrified because there was no escape.

§ Optional Questions 17, 18, 19, and 20 §

Food

Mum would joke with other Mums about my weight and how I was the only baby ever to be put on a diet; she told everyone the doctor said I wasn't allowed sweets or cakes, and that carried on right through to my teens. At one birthday party I hid myself away whilst eating a cake because I really wanted it, but I didn't want anyone to stop me or humiliate me by telling me I was too fat to eat it. I was always reminded how fat I was. I was a fat baby, a fat toddler and a fat child. In my teens I remember constantly being called a 'fat cow'. I remember dad kicked me in the stomach when I was about fourteen saying, 'Fat cow!'

Around that time I often made myself sick so that I'd become skinny. If being fat was at the root of all my problems, surely if I were skinny the abuse would stop. Looking back now it was all so ironic, because both my parents have always been overweight.

Dad was often away for weeks or months on end. We had to fend for ourselves and mum would be so poorly we used to look after her. When dad came back home, she would transform almost beyond belief. Gavin, Liz and Colin were doted on, fed like kings and cared for properly, but when dad was away, mum would fall into a big depression and it was all up to me, and I'm afraid they were rather neglected. From the time I was around seven I tried to keep them clean and fed, but it was difficult with limited resources.

We often stole food from school friends' houses, bins out in the street and so on. On numerous occasions my sister and I were so hungry that we stood in the kitchen, eating sugar out of the sugar bowl. When dad got back home Gavin would say how I'd starved them and how they'd had to go to school with dirty clothes on, and I would be punished and dad would shout at mum, blaming her; and then she would start attacking me. It was mainly my responsibility, to look after my siblings as well as mum, which would be a huge responsibility for an adult, let alone a young child. If my brother or sisters were hurt in any way, fell over or so much as grazed a knee, my parents would punish me. Dad would say I should respect my family and not let them get hurt.

Power

Dad's power over me only ever seemed to increase the pain of my confusion, because I was so confused by his standards. He would threaten to 'get rid of me' or lock me in the shed or attic, and to the child I was, this aura of finality was terrifying. His job involved working with the police and some of them used to come and visit our house socially. When they'd gone he used to boast about how well he knew them, how they already knew I was evil and how he just had to raise his little finger and they would come and lock me up. I very rarely tried to defend myself against any punishments; there was little point. But sometimes I couldn't help reacting. I once set fire to dad's new shed, and I used to spit in his tea! And once, I put my sister's favourite doll in the bin.

Mum hit me more than dad during the toddler years. Dad was away a lot when I was between three and four and mum found it very, very hard to cope with so many young children. If she became frustrated she'd lash out at me, whether I was involved or not. One time when I was six or seven, my mum came to pick me up from school. As soon as we got through the front door, she threw me down on the floor, and I remember feeling completely baffled. I didn't know what I'd done wrong. Between the ages of six and eight, I have loads of memories of being punished by both parents.

When I was twelve I had a video that I watched a lot that had music and dancing in it. My mum smashed it up because I was 'evil'. I remember feeling very sad. I became very unattached to material items after that, they did not matter any more and they still don't. She hit me on a pretty regular basis but as I got older, dad stepped in more. He was home a bit more, and on every day that he was there, he took over.

Parties

When dad was home, they'd have lots of people to the house for dinner and parties. The house got full of drunken people, and control was thrown to the wind. They

200

came, went, stayed over if they wanted to and the entire place transformed. I didn't trust my parents let alone strangers, and I felt really anxious. I tried to hide away in my room, if at all possible. I used to wake up in my room in the early hours of the morning with people asleep on the floor of my room and on the landing. I'd never seen any of them before in my life.

One morning when I got up, an older man dressed in blue jeans and a lumberjack shirt was face down on our blue carpet on the landing, there was sick with blood in it by his head and I was petrified. I thought he was dead and that I was to blame. I rushed out the door to school and hid by the big metal bins down the road until home time. I was simply terrified the police would get me. When I got home, he'd gone, but there was still a stain on the carpet, which I scrubbed and scrubbed with a cloth and Dettol. I so wanted that stain to go.

§ Optional Questions 21 and 22 §

Sundays were always the worst. The taunts and the abuse were ten times worse, maybe because my parents would drink all day, or maybe if the house wasn't swimming with people dad would invite a couple of his 'friends' over. Now I find Sundays very hard to deal with, I just keep busy with my family and hang out with the more positive people we know.

Safety was so bizarre looking back. It just wasn't an issue, especially when my father wasn't home. Front and back doors were never locked, nor the car either. If I didn't come home till late, they'd miss the work I hadn't done. I felt unloved, abandoned even, and sometimes I wouldn't bother coming home just to see if anyone would even miss me. I would be punished because chores had not been done or because family or friends had enquired where I was. Unanswered questions made the family look bad, and that was their only concern. I remember after a very violent time when I was seven, I could not bear the thought of another weekend with them, and I ran away the next Saturday morning. I was picked up by the police about seven miles away. I had walked the whole way. The police simply took me home, and there were no questions asked.

Being hit didn't really hurt anyway; I numbed out the pain quite successfully, but found it harder to numb out the emotional side, like the fear of being locked in the dark shed all night. I always remember having a churning stomach and tightness in my chest, because so often I was trying to avoid what was going to happen next. I was a lonely child who couldn't have friends round to play, and my sisters were taught from a very young age to not play with me, and only to talk to me if they really had to. I was robbed of my childhood and had to deal with issues that other children didn't even know about, issues that most adults still know virtually nothing about, even now.

My father especially told me to respect my elders, which was a bit crazy because they were the ones who treated me so badly and let me down on such a large scale. My mum was too wrapped up in her own 'problems' to worry about me, or us, the only others I knew were the teachers at school. I remember feeling very confused. On the one hand I had to respect adults and look up to them, but I couldn't understand why they weren't actually there for me.

Telling

When I was at junior school between nine and ten, I announced to a friend in the presence of a teacher, that I'd been raped. I did not know the meaning of the word, I just had a feeling about it and I knew it was something bad. I suppose it was another cry for help but no one listened to what I was saying, and the teacher told me off for 'swearing'. In the end I isolated myself so that people couldn't pick up on what was going on. I was careful to keep most of my contact with people outside my family short and superficial, so as I got older I found it quite hard to get close to friends or people that I found attractive in some way.

Banned

Up till I was about eight or nine I was never allowed in the kitchen when dad was home because I was fat and might steal food. After that I was ordered to slave in the kitchen to produce various meals. I still wasn't allowed in the lounge for months on end unless there were visitors, and I was banned from going into certain rooms unless I had to clean them. Otherwise I was so 'disgusting and dirty' that I would pollute the atmosphere; so I had to keep away and stay upstairs. When visitors were there, we would all sometimes eat around the table, where mum sometimes cared about table manners and sometimes not, and dad always did. When dad was away of course I had to feed my brothers and sister, but then perhaps I could eat again without hoping visitors would come round so that I could eat a normal meal.

Spare Meal Ticket

Friends at senior school accepted the fact I was often hungry, and I'd turn up with no lunch and no money for the canteen and they would just help out with no questions asked! My friend Katie would share her lunch. I also had a friend called Drew, she came from a single parent family and her mother was on benefits, so Drew was entitled to a free school dinner. She was too embarrassed to get up, and walk across the room to the teacher because the other pupils would tease her! Her mum started to pack her a lunch box and she gave the ticket to me. For years the dinner ladies thought my name was Drew! I haven't eaten meat since I was very young though, as it's always repulsed me, so whenever I shared food I gave the meat away.

Filling the Gap for Mother

In the house, I worked from about eight or nine years old, onwards. On an average day I'd be the first up; then I'd get Liz up and make sure she had her diabetic medicine, and get breakfast. Often the milk was off because mum used to leave everything all over the place. I'd wash up last night's dishes and Hoover, but I couldn't ever make the beds because most of the time I wasn't allowed in the other bedrooms once everybody had got up. Lastly I'd get dressed and keep out the way until school, but I was hardly ever on time when I got there. When I arrived home the scene was never any different, but whilst walking back from school I always believed things would be transformed when I got there. I visualised arriving through the front door, smelling dinner cooking, someone rushing to greet me and hug me and ask me, 'Would you like a drink or a biscuit ... and how was your day?' I would be at my happiest walking home, and so believe that someone had waved a magic wand and at last I would be safe and loved. I put myself through this every day, and it was like being hit by a double decker bus when I turned the latchkey in the front door and the scent of alcohol and mum's vomit struck me again.

Mum was a large lady, not very tall, but big and heavy, and my job was basically making sure she was still alive. I often had to drag her to bed. Usually there was a bottle of whiskey and cans of strong lager lying around, and they had to be cleared up. I had to clear up any sick or evidence she'd been ill due to the fact it would make dad mad. She would have sick on her face and down her front, sometimes I would find it on the carpet and frantically clean in up. If she were unconscious I would panic because I had to get her up the stairs before dad got home, if he was away I would go upstairs and get mum's duvet and put it over her and just leave her lying on the sofa. I then had to get some money off my mum somehow for some bread or something from the local shops ... I used to make loads of peanut butter sandwiches for tea! I had to check my sister Liz was okay, because she really needed food and medicine; though I wasn't really old enough or qualified enough to care for her diabetes.

§ *Optional Questions 23 and 24* §

The boys usually just wanted food and I wasn't allowed to use the main cooker, only the microwave. All this was always fraught with tension and difficulty because they had no respect for me. Dad taught them that I was the 'Devil's Daughter', and I believe my brother Colin was scared of me because of stupid films and the tales dad had told him. He could build up resentment very easily because he took everything so literally. But I still loved my sister and brothers so much.

I was the one who watched over Liz in case she'd under or over eaten, or hadn't taken her medication before or after school; they didn't know how to deal with it at school. If she fainted when dad was home, he would often blame me for not taking care of her properly. I actually believed it was all my fault that she even had her illness in the first place, and this in turn made me feel very guilty and sad. I had to check all the time I could that she was okay, as I didn't really understand diabetic comas, or even what a coma was. All I knew was she was going to die. I was very scared. As mum was often drunk, it was up to me to go down to the surgery, pick up the prescription and make sure Liz had enough prescription medicine in the cupboard. Thank God it was free, I dread to think what might have happened if I'd had to get money for the prescription each time we needed some more.

I did the washing by hand as we did not have a washing machine. I used to keep the piles of washing in plastic bags and then hang it outside to dry, or hang it up in the kitchen. I tried to keep them all clean and fed but it was sometimes difficult with limited resources, and keeping the house clean and tidy was like flogging a dead horse sometimes! Usually on Saturday morning especially, there was a lot of housework. Liz, Colin and Gavin helped out sometimes, especially if mum was ill, but not on a regular basis. I did it every day without fail. When dad was there, he was due home at about nine in the evening and I did as much as I could before he arrived. Then I would hide in my room, but I knew that he would always find me if he wanted to. Hopefully, out of sight was out of mind. Sometimes I was ignored until morning, but at other times dad would come in and torture me.

School Made Pointless

In the world outside our front door, something surprisingly unexpected happened during the third year of junior school. A member from each class was chosen to win a certificate either for academic achievements or for trying hard. I remember the day I won that certificate so well. I was so pleased, especially as only one person was chosen in the class for the whole year! The certificate said 'for being a helpful member of the class'. I took it home and mum told me I didn't deserve it, as I was miserable and very moody and bad-tempered. She said every one hated me because they knew I was dirty, and she ripped the certificate up. I was told never to tell anyone else and not to come out of my room.

By the time I was ten, mum and I were clashing more and more. When dad wasn't around I'd shout at her and she'd hit me. She was usually very hung over in the morning, and on one morning she panicked, picked up the hoover and threw it at me because I simply went crazy. I spent so much time hiding, yet still looking after her, yet being shouted at, ridiculed or hit. I could not keep up with school work, I was getting into more trouble at school and at home, especially as my parents so wanted me to act 'normally' outside. They were getting so cross whenever I was in trouble at school that I just got really manic and out of control.

§ Optional Questions 25 and 26 §

Whenever they'd had enough of me, I was locked in the shed all night as punishment. I dreaded it. I felt so vulnerable, and I was so worried someone would come in, dig me out and drag me away for more abuse. In the dark I could not see what was moving around either in the shed or outside; it petrified me, and the films dad made me watch were reality to my child's mind, not fiction at all. I lived hour-by-hour hoping that I would survive the next hour, or the next day just hoping that one day I would have a family of my own, one that I could feel a part of.

Ridiculed Transformation

When I hit my teens I had a growth spurt. For years beforehand dad had taunted me with reminders that I was going to be tall, like my 'real' dad. Both my brothers and sister are quite short, and living within my changing body was an awful reminder that I was some kind of reject. My mum would say to everyone obsessively,

"She's so tall!!" I told her I hated it, so she did it all the more. I had very thick ginger hair, which mum had cropped so close to my head that everyone used to laugh, and tell me I looked like a boy!

From about fourteen, I started to get pushed down the stairs as a punishment more often, and I started to get ignored more. One time at fifteen, I was lying in bed one night staring at the ceiling and probably worrying about the GCSES which I was due to take in the summer. Dad came in as usual at about nine pm, I heard the door slam and instantly my stomach started churning. An hour or two later there was screaming and shouting coming from downstairs. I heard dad's voice, and another lady and a man whose voices I did not recognize. I tried to concentrate on the 'swirls' which patterned my ceiling, I would count them and make pictures of them in my mind, just to block out the reality of my life.

Suddenly my door swung open and a waft of whiskey entered the room. It was dad. He reached down and picked me up under one arm like a rag doll. I didn't make a sound. He dragged me across the landing and started kicking me in the stomach and face, then I was wrenched up by his crane like arms and casually tossed down the stairs. I remember remaining silent. It must have been eerily quiet, because I blacked out. I awoke in hospital, not remembering to this day how I got there. That was the time my parents told the hospital staff I had fallen off my new mountain bike. I didn't even own one. The doctor said I had injuries, typical of a child who had been involved in a road traffic accident. The base of my spine had been smashed and I needed major surgery, with lots of painful physio to follow.

I felt closer to mum, than dad. Even though she was less of a threat, the hurt went so much deeper. Neglect hurt, not protecting me hurt, insults and blame hurt. Instinctively I knew I couldn't trust her, yet became very independent at a young age. It was just as well I did not trust dad because there was only hate between us. He pretended to be normal in public, and whenever necessary just made me out to be a difficult child. I expected nothing from him, except more of the same pain and violence I'd already had before. That's all there ever was between us.

Saviour in a Friend

I had a very good friend in Katie during senior school. We are still friends today. Katie was a bubbly character who everyone liked, she had an amazing sense of humour. She is shorter than me and has short brown hair. She never pried or asked about what was happening at home, even when it was obvious something was wrong. Katie felt safe to me. I did not want her to know, because I liked her. At school I was a different person from the person I was at home; I acted one way at school and another way at home. I could joke with Katie and I felt I could just about almost be myself. I was never expected to explain my situation or myself; she was there if I wanted to talk, but she accepted me as me. She never asked me why no one could come back to my house after school, or why I never had lunch with me or anything. Sometimes I used to see Katie after school. We'd meet down town for a couple of hours and no one would notice, especially when dad was away. We started going to a local pub at quite a young age and were quite often together, whether it be bunking off school to hang about in the park, or just in town.

The very first time I went to Katie's house after school, I was taken aback at how relaxed everyone was. I was very scared of Katie's dad, but then he would joke about, offer me a sandwich and just act very normally. Katie's step mum would be pottering about in the kitchen, fixing dinner or cleaning school shoes. Whilst my mum was at home drunk on the sofa, Katie's world felt very alien to me. My punishments were probably more severe that Katie had ever known, and I know you never know what goes on behind closed doors, but she seemed happy, and her family 'normal'. She and other kids from school used to get grounded, but the idea of being 'grounded' for punishment seemed so strange and absurd to me. Life started to feel much safer outside the house than in, as I got into my teens. Occasionally I might tell Katie if I had thought I had been naughty, but Katie was my escapism. I did not want to even think about home when I was with her, let alone talk about it. I blanked it out. It was not real.

School

Going back further, I don't remember my first day at school, and I do remember that mum's friend took me in that day, but not mum. I went a year later than everybody else, and again I don't know if anybody was concerned why that was. From infants, I only have a hazy memory of being taught the time, not getting it right and being kept in at break time. At seven I remember feeling chaotic and not being in control of myself in the first year of junior school. I didn't understand anything and I felt mixed up, I can imagine my behaviour was quite bizarre as well.

In my second year at junior school, the teacher was hard faced and strict, but I liked her. She was the first teacher who seemed concerned; for example she sent me to the school doctor for limping, or stomach-ache and so on. She actually noticed me. I could not really trust anyone and I didn't understand trust, but I did like her and felt relatively safe in her presence. She probably gave me the basics I needed for all other kinds of education, and it was in her class that I got that certificate for being a helpful member of the class.

School got far more difficult after that. I often didn't do homework because I couldn't; I wasn't given the means at home to study. When people were at the house partying at the weekends, my main concern was to keep out of harm's way. Sometimes I was successful, and sometimes not. When I returned to school on Monday morning often I would have been up half the night, feeling frightened and very vulnerable.

§ Optional question 27 §

At senior school the teachers would shout at me and I totally believed their sarcasms when they told me how crap I was. I often got detention for not doing set homework. I was seen as lazy and not trying, and honestly, I would just give up! It was very hard. School reports always said the same: "Lacks confidence." This did not help with my confidence! I dreaded physical education; the showers, getting changed, and the exercise. I would often opt for cross-country running and just carry on running till I got home!

I went to one of the biggest senior schools in the country, where there were more than thirty pupils in each class. Generally I kept quiet and was ignored, but trouble would occur over homework and my falling asleep in class. My french teacher shouted this at me once,

"If you can't concentrate – don't bother coming to my class at all!" I knew I was incapable of learning French at the time. The very next day I didn't bother going to his class and a letter was sent home saying I was truanting, and I got hell for that. One teacher I did like was the English teacher, and it was the only subject I did well in GCSE. I suppose you could have called that relationship nourishing, but I trusted neither her, nor even my aunt Judy enough to tell them what exactly was going on.

§ Optional Question 28 §

Parents come to School

One time, when I was sent to the headmaster for not doing homework yet again, he repeatedly asked me why I hadn't done it, except this time he really insisted on knowing the reason. In the end I said it was because I had to look after my alcoholic mother. My parents were called in to the school and when they met, dad charmed the headmaster in his usual way, and they all came to the conclusion that I was attention seeking. Things turned bad that evening at home and I became even more bitter and angry towards the teachers, who had ganged up with my parents by branding me a liar. I longed to be cared for, but my parents only cared about being seen as 'normal'. They didn't want unwelcome attention and they were worried about being caught. They knew parents get prosecuted in criminal courts for neglect, abuse and so on. My father definitely knew that.

Today I'm extremely angry at the school for the way they dealt with me. What was I supposed to say? 'Sorry I did not learn my french verbs Sir, because I've been too busy worrying about my sister, clearing up after my alcoholic mother and fearing the next time dad and his friends have a party and rape me!' The school made a bad situation a lot worse. The warning signs were all there and adult after adult completely ignored them. I find this hard to deal with and get over now, I have been so angry at the whole of society for such a long time. I was unable to control my behaviour, I would sometimes act in a very strange way, but I was unstable because there was no stability around me. All I got was contempt, and I was seen as bad, mad and lazy. I did my GCSE exams sitting on my bed in a pelvic plaster cast. The invigilator came and sat in my room as I wrote paper after paper propped up in bed. Of course, I'd 'fallen off my new mountain bike'.

There were school open evenings that my parents attended, where they made a pretty good double act. They charmed the teachers into believing our house was a good home. I think maybe the teachers feared dad a bit because of his job, and they didn't want to contest anything he said. Dad could light up the room; he had a massive presence and a booming voice. His posture was of a powerful, confident man and at times his intelligence and wit really shone out.

Secrets About Dad

He, and on occasion his friends sexually abused me right from the time I was a toddler. I suppose it's better the devil you know, because although I was scared of dad, I was really, really terrified of his friends. I find it extremely difficult talking about the sexual side of the secret abuse. I've had nearly four years of counselling with a lady I trust completely, and she still only knows a slither of what happened to me. Perhaps that's because the force of the threats are still there, like an invisible barrier. I have memories and feelings that run right deep inside me, from simple things like the fear of nylon (because my nighties were made of it, which now I cannot bear to touch) to the fear of males of a certain age and I can't stand the smell of whiskey.

Watching me whilst I was watching horror movies weren't dad's only form of home entertainment. He had numerous porn movies that he used to show me. I constantly had the sense that both my parents were sexually frustrated, which is a weird sensation and a strange thought for a young child to go on holding. I never ever felt 'right'.

When I finally understood the facts of life, I was also beginning to understand what mental illness was, and my mum used to talk to me about her mum being admitted to mental hospitals, and getting horrendous treatment there. I honestly believed the same thing was going to happen to me, I just felt so confused and unsafe.

Dad always made it very clear that he wasn't getting sex from my mother, and it was my fault for being born, because I was not theirs. The mere fact that I was still alive put mum under stress, therefore I should not moan and just accept everything, because otherwise I could be put away in a children's home.

There was no 'love' when the abuse took place, or even any pretense of it. It was violent, cold and forceful, with no care or thought about my feelings or the pain I may go through. My dad saw me as the 'down trodden' woman of the house, I would be clearing up and he would shout at me or slap me for not fixing dinner quick enough. Maybe if my mum had not been so depressed, poorly and drunk, then she would have taken my role instead, who knows. Because my role was almost 'wife' like (but in the most negative sense) it was also my role to fulfill Dad sexually. I knew that I couldn't though.

My dad would enter my room at night, and make it clear that I was in this position due to my own fault and circumstances; I would be expected to need him sexually and meet his sexual needs, which looking back was impossible. I was a child; I was not his 'trailer-trash' wife (for want of a better expression). My dad would expect me to be able to turn him on and to be able to have sex with him just like one of the women in his numerous porn films. He used to show me, a fucking seven, eight, ten or twelve-year-old girl, porn films, and expect me to copy what those women on the screen were doing. I would fail terribly at turning him on. Maybe a scared witless child wasn't enough for him, and in his total frustration he would grab me, usually by my hair at first. He would hold me on my stomach and rape me from behind with his full weight on my back.

The strength of a grown man on a child's back, trying to force sex, is indescribable. The pain was similar to childbirth, far too much for a young child to take. I would usually faint. I would wake up covered in every possible human bodily fluid, his semen up my trembling bruised legs, my sick all over my face, my blood over my bottom and up my back, sometimes even matted in my hair, his sweat smeared in amongst it all, the stench was horrifying.

On occasions when I did pass out, I would come to and there would be masses of blood from where he had shoved his penis so hard into me and my under-developed child's body, I couldn't cope with the physical trauma. I would worry terribly about the mess and how to stop the blood flowing freely from me. I would be scared, shocked and usually sick.

But I couldn't afford to be ill or to take time to recover, I ended up frantically washing towels and rugs and bedclothes in the bath, to hide all evidence. The pain and soreness from my bottom and vagina would drive me frantic; I would try anything to stop it. I remember pouring a whole tub of baby powder on myself to stop the pain, but, of course, it made it just ten times worse, I was desperate but assumed for a long while, that all young girls went through this sort of anguish.

§ Optional Question 29 §

More from Mother

Mum didn't even begin to understand, she was very different to my dad in terms of abuse. So many strong feelings are there, yet her sexual abuse was a lot subtler. She would, when my dad was away, come in the room and stroke me, she wouldn't even talk, and she wouldn't hug or kiss. Her fat fingers with her nails bitten down to the knuckle almost; would stroke my legs and then up between my legs, this would sicken me almost more than the bloody rapes.

She was my mother, why couldn't she fuck her husband and keep him away from me, instead of playing fucking sick games with me? She knew that my dad raped me, she knew all along. She would never shed a tear or ask if I was okay. She would sometimes bathe me in dettol or washing up liquid afterwards, a strange ritual, which she almost seemed to enjoy, but she would do more. She would always make sure I felt worse than I did already, by calling me 'dirty' or a 'whore'. She would also say bizarre things like, "When you and your father live together ..." or "You two are like a married couple!" going along with the whole sick game. My mum wanted so desperately to be the child and for me to be the wife. But I had needs of a child and she had needs of a wife. I always hated her touching me and as I grew, I avoided her. She made me feel sick.

Car Parking

She would sometimes act jealous when my dad drove me to the country sometimes. He took me there for 'car parking' where couples and groups of adults would gather in a place just remote enough for them to have sex. There used to be blokes called 'doggers' who would hide in the bushes and pay to watch couples or groups having sex. The blokes who took their money watched out for any strangers some way off, and made sure the coast was clear. I was exposed to that as a child and it was the norm, but there were also men who would drive their kids to places down the road where they would be raped.

Other times my dad would just drive me out there alone, and some of his client 'friends' would just turn up. Mum would state how lucky I was, but she bloody knew, he was taking me out to the 'sticks' to be raped by him or the friends he would hire me out to, for a quick bit of cash to gamble on the horses, or treat his other 'tarts' to.

The sexual abuse was chaotic and unpredictable. Sometimes it was very quiet, and sometimes when there was plenty of alcohol and dad's 'friends'; it was like entertainment laid on at a party.

§ Optional Question 30 §

I was a different person then. It's like even though it happened, it did not happen to me. Not me. It happened to someone else. There was a different version of me living on at the same time, and a different version of reality; I used to deny one reality and live in the other one. I did not speak during the sexual assaults, but I couldn't numb everything out because that just wasn't possible. I would try to concentrate very hard on something else. I sometimes screamed or cried when I was in actual physical pain,

209

but I never ever spoke, not that I can remember. Dad would threaten that if I did not do as he said, or if I did not impress him or the other men, I would be killed, and I really accepted that without question. I was told I was so ugly I should be grateful, because no one else would be physical with me, that my body was dirty and rancid. Lots of things were said, like

"No one will believe you, and anyway no one will ever miss you when you're dead!"

"It's your way of paying me for bringing you up."

"You deserve it because the devil lives in your heart and you're evil."

On Display

I tried very hard not to think about dad when he wasn't there and I was quite successful at 'numbing' myself, but when he was there in the house, I could often hear him shouting downstairs 'brewing' for an attack. He loved to humiliate me, he was much cleverer than me and he would call me downstairs sometimes just to put me on parade and make me look awful, or look very stupid or disgusting. He would do this in front of anybody he liked, his friends, or family. Up in my room, it was always the waiting that was the worst bit. I used to visualise running away, or hiding, or beating him up, but I would be paralysed with fear.

§ Optional Question 31 §

On top of all that, I was expected to be there at family gatherings, just so it would look 'normal'. I hated it. In front of dad's friends when I was a teenager, (some of whom were involved in the sexual abuse and some not) my parents would almost boast that I was too flirty and that I would end up pregnant young. They would insinuate that I was weird, needed 'help' and was far too interested in men and boys. I hated lies being told about me to other people, and I couldn't even defend myself; I had to just take it. Of course they loved to laugh at me as if I were a fool. I suppose dad was trying to make it sound all right, that I deserved what I got and I was asking for it.

Terror

One of dad's 'friends' was a pig farmer, and dad had always told me about how he could chop me up and feed me to the pigs. You see, dad and two of his 'friends' often used to recount their plan to murder me in morbid detail, including how they would get away with it. I had always believed it, but soon after I turned eleven, this fear became the greater part of who I was.

Dad actually took me to the pig farm, locked me in there and left me there all night. Another man, a stranger, woke me up quite early the next morning. I don't remember his name or if I was even told it, but he was short, fat and reeked of whisky. He was dirty and had a horrid, scary face with harsh features. He walked around with a big stick, striking the animals. I couldn't understand why this man hated me, a small child so much, I could only guess it must have been because I was really, really vile.

He shouted to make sure I was watching. Then he walked up to the barn door, and reached over to pull a knife out of it. He came over and held it steady in front of my face, then pointed out the pig it was intended for. Then he marched behind the pig, striking it with the stick as it darted here and there, then finally he marched it all the way down into a long narrow enclosure. He shut the barrier and by the time he was tying it up by the legs and neck with rope, he was yelling at me to get into the enclosure. My body froze tight against the barrier, and the pig's incessant screaming pierced through my head, and shivered through my body like ice. Then he stabbed into the pig's throat with the knife. It flopped down in a deafening silence, and I could see splashes of wet blood all over my muddy shoes and socks. Slowly and steadily, a river of warm blood seemed to flow endlessly by the pig's feet into the hole underneath. Then suddenly he grabbed the pig's head by the ear, clenching it tight in his fist. He yanked its head up and down and roared at me that I'd better listen to my dad, or else I'd be next.

§ *Optional comment and question: 32* §

It didn't matter where I was, I was afraid to even speak to or see anyone, in case they could see into my mind. If they got just one glimpse of the real me or understood what I'd been through, I'd get killed, or everything would get far, far worse. Sometimes I think that maybe because everything about the abuse was carried out in such a violent manner and not in a loving manner, I would always have kept quiet through fear. If it had been carried out in the pretence of love, then maybe I would have told someone. Ultimately of course, I just don't know.

Silence

Aunt Judy knew what her husband (my dad's brother) had been like when he was alive. She knew I was treated badly, but I told her very little about my life, only school stuff or stuff about friends and so on. I was well trained and knew it was more than my life's worth to discuss anything with her. I was very numb whilst I was growing up and to be honest, I could not tell you how I felt, and it was almost like I was not even alive then. Even my aunt Judy, whom I adored, could not do anything about the situation I was in. I wanted to blurt out to her what was happening, but the fear of being murdered in the dark stopped me. Dad's threats, all of them, rang true in my mind. I wanted my aunt Judy to save me, I would cry and cry as she left for home, I wanted her to look after me, I was a child.

I never knew how much she knew, and to be honest I felt it was my role to protect her from the disgusting truth. I did not want her to suffer by knowing, I did not think she would be able to cope with it, she was old and I loved her.

Money

As for money, the façade must have really looked good as we were middle-class and living in a good home in a nice area, but so much was spent on alcohol or gambling that there was very little for anything else. They were often in debt and they squandered money all the time on whisky and the horses. Money was never discussed with me. I was told how grateful I should be to them for agreeing to bring me up, and they kept asking "How much money do you think you cost ... do you cost nothing ... do you?" I was not to touch or play with my sister or brother's toys or possessions, and

211

especially nothing of my parent's. I was not allowed in their rooms or to even speak to them at times. They would sometimes have money spent on them, for example if my parents could afford food type treats such as sweets. I was very rarely allowed to eat with the rest of the family anyway so I was never involved in such treats.

Holidays

From when I was six till about ten, I'm afraid we stayed with mum's parents in Suffolk for each and every school holiday, and I loathed every one. My grandmother would chain smoke and carry on with the whole 'fat' thing when I was there. She was the one who had suffered from numerous mental illnesses, and been admitted to hospital on several occasions. It was beyond me why on earth we were ever sent to stay there in the first place; she wasn't capable of looking after animals, let alone children. There was nothing for children to do, so although my brothers and sister might have had a slightly better time, I spent the whole time being put down and feeling miserable. After that we went on family type holiday parks in the UK. In the caravan there was nowhere to hide at all so for me, it was horrendous.

I loved to play instruments at school, like recorders, drums and so on but lessons were out of the question. None of us had music lessons, special sport equipment or anything like that. Mum never bought me anything when I was younger; she was too ill back then. As I got older mum would buy me silly things like deodorant or nice soap once in a while, if she felt guilty about what was happening, but that was very rare. I used to hide it for fear of it being taken away.

About Me

I hated myself as a child. I really did believe all the bad things that were said to me, that I was the devil; I was told everyday that I was evil. I did not want anyone near me. I felt so dirty and disgusting, I didn't want to exist. It did not matter how much people said they hated me – I hated myself much, much more. I absorbed the words and the voices all around me all the time, and held on to their every word. The alternative was to not even believe I existed. I played a part in some sort of sick play, where my brothers, sister and almost all the other kids from school congregated in flocks and kept their distance. They thought I was weird. I did not deserve to be alive.

I had my friend Katie. I fitted in with her. Sometimes we would not talk to each other all day at school, but we didn't need to. I felt safe with her; she would protect me against people who would bully me. That was the only time as a child that I felt I belonged. I did want to be Katie; I wanted her family and her life. She was so calm and nothing seemed to bother her, I wanted us to be sisters, and go home with her at the end of the day.

Fragile Chance of Finding Understanding

I look back now and wish I had told someone, that I had gone to the police or a social worker and then maybe I would have been fostered or put in to care, anything would have been better than the nightmare at home. I still don't think anyone would have believed me though, and it would have made the whole situation worse. Maybe I really would have been murdered, and I wouldn't have the family I have now, which I so longed for as a child.

§ Optional question and comment no: 33 §

When I was very little I did know what they were doing was wrong, but I thought it happened to everyone and it was just a part of being a child. It was only when I was about nine I realised that not everyone put up with what I had to. At junior school when I told a friend that I was raped (not even knowing what it meant) that was cast aside as my vulgar imagination I guess. I had nobody to talk it over with, so that I could even begin to understand what was happening to me. Telling the headmaster at senior school about my mum's alcoholism wasn't really anywhere near as extreme a disclosure as sexual abuse, but even that wasn't believed. I'd been shown what would happen if I went on telling. I only wish that they had thought about *why* I might appear to be weird or attention seeking, or why I said the things I did. I learnt very quickly not to trust anyone; they were the enemy. I just kept my eyes to the ground hoping that no one would notice me.

I left home, aged nineteen but the sexual abuse had stopped before then. My dad had always had women. By the time I hit my mid teens, he had no need for me and my childish attempts at sex anymore. I wish I had gone sooner and got out of that house, but my self-esteem was so low I could not bring myself to believe any one would want to live with me. I thought I'd be rejected.

Teens

Right from the start of my teens I'd be in parts of town that were quite rough and just stay out all night, but then sleeplessness was no stranger to me, after all. As a child far away from my own home, I didn't care that I was wandering around, at risk or in danger, and neither did anybody else.

I drank lots of alcohol during my teenage years. I got a false ID and went in to pubs and clubs, and sat in bus shelters or play parks with a bottle of cider. I stopped eating, as I believed if I was skinny, no one could hurt me. I couldn't bear the thought of anything in my stomach. Sometimes I think this was a sort of suicide attempt, not eating and drinking loads, because I didn't care what was going to happen to my body at all, and I sort of wanted it not to exist. I'd also been hurting myself by slashing my arms with sharp objects throughout senior school. I was clever always to go for the tops of my arms, so even if I had a T-shirt on or a short-sleeved school shirt, the cuts and scars wouldn't be seen. I banged my head a lot with my fist, or on the wall. I did this whenever I was trying to block things out and it became habit in the end. I remember my aunt Judy came to visit when I was around this age, as we had planned an outing together. She was horrified to see how much weight I had lost and flatly refused to take me out. I was very shocked; I had absolutely no idea what kind of state I was in. None whatsoever.

§ Optonal Comment and Question: 34 §

A couple of times I tried cannabis, speed, coke and so on but I wasn't very good at it! It was expensive, and I only ended up feeling sick, which was quite fortunate really. I was offered heroin, and now I thank god I didn't take it. I didn't hang around with that

213

group of people for long anyway and I couldn't imagine having a drug problem now on top of everything else. The drinking started at about fourteen and carried on until I got married at twenty–two.

Alcohol was a wonderful escape from the feelings of hatred I had towards myself. It would numb the pain, and falling asleep drunk meant no nightmares. People in the house were too drunk to notice if I took any (most of the time!). I would also go to the local pub, pull a bloke and get him to buy me drinks. Usually he'd end up taking me back to his place for the night, which was better than going home, but only just. I loved clubbing, the throb of the music with every one on a high; that was real escapism. I hated being spoken to, so I would go straight to the crowded dance floor where it was so loud you could be in a world of your own.

I enjoy alcohol now and it's an important part of my social circle. I love red wine with a curry on a Saturday night, but that's about it. I certainly I don't drink to block things out like I used to. I can escape in music or a good film or a book. But when I'm feeling low, I still feel the need to be punished in some way because I feel I'm evil. It's as if I'm trapped. I will sometimes hurt my self by punching my stomach or banging my head. I find it hard to eat and I can get quite withdrawn in company at times, but a lot of that has slowly improved with counselling, and under my David's watchful eye!

Sex

I'm still very confused about sex and find the whole subject painful. I grew up enduring sex as a necessary chore. As a child, I did not know that sex could actually be enjoyed by both sexes; I thought it was something that the man had to do to survive; that he had to find a woman to 'empty him self' in or else he would die, and the woman had to help the man with this or something terrible would happen. When I see sex on advertising posters, or in movies, or hear about it in a song, it all depends where I am and who I am with, how I feel. I do have a sensuality, and sexual desires of my own, and if I am at home and feel safe with David, then it is okay, otherwise I can feel scared, get worried and panic. Watching a sex scene with David on telly is fine, unless of course the woman is very attractive and he's enjoying looking at her too much! In the cinema with friends when there's a graphic sex scene, I get anxious but I usually cover it up by joking about it.

Sense of Self

I still feel inferior to my peers; the other students I know in adult education are cleverer, and I don't amount to much. Even though I got distinction for an IT exam and a high grade for my German 'GCSE' just before I had Max, it's hard to dispel these kinds of attitudes I still have. When I first became a mother I hated mummy–baby groups, as I felt everyone was a better mum than me and was judging me, but I'm more confident as a mum now.

Young Love

I met David about six months before I left home when I was working in a student union bar; he was a postgraduate student studying English lit. I was going out with quite a horrid and abusive man at the time. I found that David and I had a lot in common, like similar political and spiritual beliefs and we could chat for ages. My then boyfriend started to muck me about a lot and I discussed this with David, maybe I was testing the water, I'm not sure. Anyway we grew closer, I stopped seeing my boyfriend and David and I started just going out for lunch and chatting; it was very 'slowly slowly'. For periods in my life I've used books as an escape and also as a way to expand my mind, and we had a great deal to talk about and share when it came to great writers, plays and films.

Some months passed, and I was going through a particularly hard period of my life. One of my best friends was knocked down and killed in a road traffic accident when we were actually out walking together. My parents used this to get at me even more, by blaming me for my friend's death. We were both just nineteen. I was riddled with guilt and I wasn't eating, and my father had stopped me from sleeping at night, keeping me awake with his ridiculous lectures about the British National Party, or still making me watch horrific films.

One morning I was working early in the student café and David met me at the end of my road to walk me into work. I was exhausted, in every sense of the word. The night before, my father had asked me to switch the hot water off; I had forgotten and gone straight to bed. My father soon realised my silly mistake, woke me up and hit me hard right across the face. When I met David at the end of the road, I was a mess. He asked me what the matter was and I explained it was just the usual problems at home, and that I was tired.

David said, "Has your dad given you a hard time?" I half answered "Yes", then suddenly David said,

"He's hit you!"

David knew, which was strange after so many years of denials and cover-ups. I didn't answer at all, and just burst into tears, which again was weird, but sort of wonderful after 'numbing' myself for so long.

I told him just very little about the situation I was living in to begin with. Over the years he's reacted in a number of different ways. At first he seemed very upset and concerned, but later this turned into anger towards my parents, and many of the social systems that so let me down. With David, what you see is what you get. He's not a very guarded person and you can always tell what he's feeling. If he's cross or angry, sad or confused, he'll tell me; and because I know his reactions, I can help him.

Solid Ground

I didn't want him to want to be with me out of pity, especially in the early days when we were talking about moving in together. I wanted us to live together because he wanted to and because he loved me, not because he was trying to save me from an abusive home. I was scared too, because my parents always thought I was a bit of a joke. They told me anybody would find me horrid to live with, that I would never marry, never have children and end up old, lonely and weird! I always told David from the start that it wouldn't be easy living with me. Somehow I knew I had quite a long journey ahead, but this didn't put him off!! In the end we did move into our little flat but because he loved me, not cause he felt sorry for me.

215

First Disclosure

Early on I told him more about the physical abuse, but talking about the sexual abuse and the stupid mind games my parents played was especially hard. I finally managed to tell David I'd been sexually abused about a year into our relationship. After he'd heard what I had to say I felt so open, vulnerable and sensitive that I didn't want him to touch me at all. Naturally, he wanted to cuddle me, but I pushed him away. I remember saying "I feel like I have no skin". I felt disgusted with myself and I found it hard to look him in the eye. I thought he must hate me and think I'm a whore or something. I was scared, and I don't know why but I almost wanted him to be angry with me just to get it all over with. I didn't want him to be sad, which naturally he was, and I just couldn't cope when he began to cry. I felt so numb that I assumed he would be the same, and I was really quite shocked when he showed genuine sadness.

Control

At first I was very much afraid that David would then go and tell somebody else, and I still am. The thought of anybody else in my life knowing still scares me half to death! People will think I'm weird or disgusting. I hear so many sweeping judgmental statements about people that have been abused, it scares me to think that my friends may have the same views, so it's best just to deny it and carry on.

Counselling

Before David and I had kids, I asked my GP at that time about getting help, and he referred me to a clinical psychologist, but the waiting list in my area was nearly a year long so we bought a self-help book to try and help us through the issues arising because of the abuse, and David rang the victim support number listed in the back. A lady came to visit us a few times and then suggested I went to see a counsellor they recommended. When I met Pam in 2000, I knew very little about her as a person, just that she had a degree in counselling, and I knew a bit about the centre where she worked. We decided to start dealing with problems arising from abuse, and I could have sessions weekly or monthly, and sessions were subsidised to £10, although it was less when our income was lower.

Counselling began when David and I first moved in together shortly before I was twenty-one; he came with me to my first session, and he was the one who spoke first! I was absolutely petrified. It was also a traumatic time moving away from home, because I believed that no one else would put up with me, and really I felt deeply ashamed of myself; I was afraid of what I might really be like. Shortly before we started living together, my dad suddenly got really ill with a brain tumour and became dependant on others for care. I started suffering from terrible 'flashbacks' of the abuse. I was scared someone would take me back home or I would be forced to go back there. I either felt very numb or was just feeling traumatised; in fact I loathed all of my feelings and just wanted them all to stop.

Of course I felt I had to talk to this lady to get 'better' but also it was the start of a process that was the direct opposite of everything that had been enforced into me for the past twenty years; there was a very powerful battle going on inside of me. My negative mind, consisting of my family and all the demons from the past were fighting my positive mind, which consisted of my husband who I adored, and the battle for a better future which kept saying 'Keep at it! Give it a go!'

A few months after the counselling began I became pregnant and we thought strongly that I needed to sort myself out before having the baby, and try to deal with some of the issues arising. I didn't know what it was not to feel stressed, because my stomach was constantly churning and there was a constant tightness in my chest, I was so worried about how this would affect my unborn child. I thought counselling could sort everything and I would be a brilliantly calm and non-traumatised person by the time the child was born. Soon, I realised that counselling wasn't a magic wand that would make everything okay, things were going to remain hard and counselling was going to be hard, demanding work.

I found it hard to remember the goals that were set, and I doubt I could take goals seriously anyway because I was in such a mess. My counsellor reassured me constantly that she was going to be there for as long as I needed her, and she would not run away because of anything I might or might not say. She was there for me to 'offload' and talk through any hardships or things we were finding difficult in the week before the session. We worked on finding better coping strategies as a couple, and trying them out and see what worked for us.

David sat next to me throughout my sessions for many months, despite the fact that sometimes, I wouldn't even talk at all. I believe I progressed very little after the first four weeks, I am sure I still felt very scared. He knew I had been abused as a child, but he also knew it was extremely impossible to talk about, and that I needed time and space; he respected that.

Looking back now, counselling was a very long four year journey; very hard work for my counsellor, myself and my husband, who has supported me through it all. I felt every emotion possible and there have been extremely sad times and angry times and confused times, but I have also laughed myself silly through the times I've felt a bit freer and more liberated!

But by far and away the strongest feeling in the sessions is frustration, because something in my mind stops me from talking openly about experiences that are tightly locked somewhere in between my mind and my mouth. There's also frustration that I need counselling at all, that I am in this position. It's lonely too, not being able to talk to family and friends about what I have been saying and feeling, and when the session ends, there I am back in my world dealing with it all again, on my own.

Support

Counselling taught me that feelings are normal, and feelings and talking about feelings is actually a positive thing. As a child no one ever asked me, 'How are you?' or, 'You ok?' Expressing my feelings was never encouraged because I didn't matter. I learned about and developed strategies on facing and dealing with feelings as they arise, without just sweeping them under the carpet. In a small way I value myself more as a person and as a mother, but that's still rather new. It's strange for me to think that I've done well at something.

I have also learnt visualization techniques, which I had never heard of before.

Although they don't always work in the manner they are meant to, they do work! For example, Pam taught me to visualise myself in a big, safe bubble if people were being negative, or if I felt the situation was too hard to manage. All I could think of was me, like a hamster running about in one of those balls! This really made me smile and so visualizing the bubble worked on two levels, keeping me safe and making me smile!

Before we moved I used to ring my counsellor more often when things got on top of me, when feelings over-whelmed me and I couldn't cope. Five minutes talking through the strategies we made to make me feel more 'grounded', like making a cuppa, taking a bath or going for a walk, really helped. I felt like I could get back on top of it again and carry on with the day.

It's been a very gradual process, telling David about what happened when I was young. It has put massive pressure on our relationship, even now, we have days where I feel very low and I can't even manage simple things; even going to the supermarket scares me. I get sudden panics that David must have negative thoughts towards me, but the logical part of me knows it's not true. Now and then we fall out, when David finds it hard to channel his anger about the abuse, and so do I to a certain extent. We row about something silly, then look back and realise it was because we were both struggling to deal with it.

I have never felt confident enough to join a group type setting, although David did so with another counsellor who runs a group for supporters of survivors of abuse. He used to attend this in a nearby city when we lived in the UK, and he went for about a year. He actually quite enjoyed the sessions, which we didn't expect at all, but I felt safer that he could talk openly without bumping into anyone he or I knew. Sometimes it feels like David and I are living in this closed little world, because only we know about all this stuff and it can feel lonely. But in some ways it has made us stronger; we have been through so much that I don't think anything can break us! Little things seem like huge battles, but in the end we make small steps forward and we are a very good team.

Going Back to See Mum

Whilst we were in England mum was completely on her own, and I was still visiting her at least twice a week; I had to look after her so much as a child that it was hard stopping that role as her 'carer', especially since dad had gone into a nursing home. I never liked mum being near our kids and I never took them to see her often. Mum just accepts that and I suppose she would, because she still doesn't have time for anyone else.

When we moved to Germany that was the opportunity for me to move out of that role. I only visited her twice in the last year, but I still ring her to check she's okay once a week. She would never return the same favour, and never has. She still drinks heavily and I believe she is probably very ill. She attempted suicide a couple of times when I was a child, which was another big 'cover-up'. Dad said it was all my fault and if she ever killed herself it would be because of me. I still worry she will do it and the whole family will blame me; it's very hard for me to make all those thoughts vanish, or change.

§ Optional Question: 35 §

My sister takes insulin just as before, and I used to see her regularly too, to make sure she was okay. We always had a funny relationship though. She speaks to me in the exact same way as my 'dad' used to, not so much in the words she uses but in her manner and tone. She loves to make me seem stupid, but like my mum, she's sly in the way she does it. Way back when she found out I'd started counselling, she went crazy at me, saying I was selfish and had to stop it. She didn't talk to me for a while but then suddenly realised that she needed me for some baby-sitting, so rang me up! She's very fiery and thinks things should be done her way or not at all, and I lied to her (which felt bad) and told her that I'd stopped counselling. In the past, whereas I would have worried and blamed myself silly for upsetting her, I just think she's being stupid! Like mum, she never asks how I am, or about my family. Both elder brothers still treat me like a second-class citizen and I would never dream about talking about my childhood or theirs with any of my siblings; to this day it really is as if all of our childhoods never happened.

Mental Health

A year before we moved to Germany, there came a time in my 'personal growth' if you like, that was quite a big challenge, and I think I should share it here. I started going through a period where I had a lack of sleep due to flashbacks and nightmares. I knew there was more to it than the fact that I had a two-month-old new baby. I found counselling a real chore and told Pam about the nightmares I kept having. She said I should visualise beating the men up in the dreams, but that's something I found impossible. The problem could have been that despite her qualifications, she didn't specialise in counselling survivors. She suggested we should have a break, but I really didn't think she understood what I was going through and how twenty years of real hard stuff can't really be tackled with just an hour a week of talking.

Sometimes it has all felt useless; because having been through twenty years of pure hell, how can one hour a week chatting to someone about relaxation techniques, nightmares, anger, flashbacks, coping with the outside world and motherhood and so on really help? It feels like there's a heavy sphere of thick dark, concentrated pain inside of me, which nothing and nobody can reach. I simply every now and then find myself trapped right in the middle of it and I can't see any way out. Counselling is about expressing yourself mainly through language, but there are absolutely no words to describe what it was like for me as a child and young person. I feel intensely restricted when I try to describe my sadness and horror that children are out there right now, going through exactly what I went through.

My doctor had prescribed anti depressants for me well before I'd either had kids or started counselling with Pam, but I never took them. Later on when counselling began, that felt hugely distant from whatever happened with the doctor. I never took the medicine he prescribed, but about four years later I had to go back and see him. The crux was, I'd been getting panic attacks in the day, and was feeling vulnerable following flashbacks, sleepless nights and nightmares. I had such difficulties in getting out of the house in the morning that I was seriously worried about how I could respond to our kids' needs, as a mother.

219

He prescribed diazepam, I tried it once and found it wasn't the solution for me, so I went back three weeks later and tried to explain that I wasn't depressed and I felt very enthusiastic about life; I just couldn't sleep because I was scared of the nightmares and flashbacks. He suggested sleeping tablets, but because I had to listen out for Perry and the baby at night, I didn't want them, and I certainly didn't want to end up with a drug problem as well. I like to keep my wits about me!

A couple of months later I was still having counselling with Pam every week, but the flashbacks were still persisting, so I went back again to the doctor, wanting to sort it out. Perhaps he could get me a more specialised counsellor, but instead he referred me to a psychiatrist, which was really scary! I think he thought I was mad because I wouldn't agree to the medication, and I felt bad because he seemed to think I was disobedient for refusing his 'help'. I thought, 'Well, wouldn't this be funny if it wasn't so serious … *because I'm not the one who needs a psychiatrist, **my family does!*** I read on the net about how child abuse should be classed as terrorism and in fact is more of a threat than Al Quaida and Saddam Hussein! I laughed at how ludicrous this sounded, but victims of torture, war and crime suffer from posttraumatic stress syndrome, and even though I hate being categorised, the symptoms match mine very closely.

The last few days running up the to the psychiatrist appointment, I found almost impossible. I felt so vulnerable, like I had gone straight back to square one again. I didn't feel like it was worth all the hard work, and for all I knew, I was just about to lose the last remnants of control over my mental health, and possibly my life. My full assessment by the psychiatrist and the community psychiatric nurse ran over two long sessions. I was nervous, but very honest and candid. The week or so that I had to wait for my diagnosis was absolute hell, but in a nutshell, they said I was NOT suffering from depression. I was traumatised and a bit anxious but I did NOT need medication of any type! I was showing all the signs of making a full recovery.

Diagnosis

Six weeks later I had a routine follow up appointment, and my counsellor came along too. The psychiatrist reassured me again, and said she thought I showed no signs of suffering from any sort of mental health problem, which was very good news. It was a really big victory when I was discharged, because my family always made *me* out to be the crazy one! I continued with the counselling up until we moved and I'm having a break from all that now. We're keeping an eye out for a specialised counsellor in case I might need one in future.

Because of the assessment I suppose I feel less alone, and less weary of carrying this misunderstood persona that's weighed me down for so long. Yet ironically I feel a bit like I won a game of Russian roulette … as I'm a survivor of NHS luck. Purely by chance, I'm one of the few who didn't end up dulled by prescription medicine, with addiction as another problem to add to the pile.

Motherhood

I feel safer with David than anyone. It's kind of a strange destiny for me to end up married to a foreigner … but there you are! Whilst I was pregnant with Perry I hated it though. My body was out of control, I was getting fat, which I always had a big fear of anyway. I did not 'bond' with the baby during pregnancy and despite going through all the ante natal visits, I denied the reality that I was even having a baby right up to the day he was born! When they held him up so I could see him for the first time, all of that vanished and I felt that I had known him all my life. I cuddled him and never wanted to let him go. When Max came along it was totally different the second time around; anyway all the hospital staff were great. I love the relationship with my sons, even though it has been very hard work we make each other so happy, that's all that matters! There's so much love between us.

Social Life

We found a very active English speaking community in the Anglican Church in Germany. It's like a global bubble really, as half are American, with loads of other nationalities thrown in! We go as a family most Sundays, though I find some of the religious messages quite conflicting and difficult to understand at times. Despite that the community has been a great support to us all on a practical and emotional basis, what with the adjustment to what is for me, a foreign culture. They've helped me in a practical way with so many things, like transport and helpers to hospital and doctor appointments for the kids and so on. There's a good vibe from the other Mums and there's a very reliable baby–sitting circle, we live quite close by and I'm in contact with someone from that community pretty much every day.

My aunt Judy is still very much alive and I adore her. I used to see her and my old school friend Katie at least a couple of times a month and my one regret about moving abroad is losing that close contact ... but aunt Judy was so excited about the move that she's been over to stay twice already! We speak on the phone a lot, and I always visit her as much as possible. I think she's very brave, living through World War Two, and battling against cancer in more recent years, but she still manages to do loads for other people and raises money for charities. Her husband died when I was a baby, and apparently he was horrid and very similar to my father; aunt Judy seems to be able to live life much better without him.

I feel safe in the predictable rituals of the church and the lessons of looking after each other, and acceptance. We've spoken about child abuse in general, but I have never told anyone at church about the abuse in my childhood, but I may do one day. Friends we've met from there ring up just to see how we are, whereas my family only ever rang if they wanted me to come over and help with something! Having faced up to the 'demons', I can get on and live my life. I haven't got any real plans and ambitions for the future for myself, I live day by day and just do the best that I can for myself, my family and the greater community around me.

Justice

I would never in a million years ever think about prosecuting Dad or anyone. People in authority like the police, or people in any kind of uniform at all I find difficult ...I'll usually avoid them! There couldn't be a trial anyway because of Dad's illness. He's in a nursing home I never visit and I never will; he is not my Dad. I want to move on and it would hurt me greatly to see my childhood being dragged through courts, if it even got that far. It would destroy my Aunt Judy, and who knows how long she has left to live. Bringing all this up could only poison her last years, and I would never jeopardise her right to happiness. I have no energy left and want to concentrate on getting over what happened. My boys need me, and I don't trust lawyers, policemen or judges. I believe justice will be done one day, but my family would not benefit from a messy court case.

Writing the Story

I instinctively felt that doing the questionnaire would be positive, but I was quite dubious about actually contributing to a book. It started before we moved abroad and Pam (the counsellor I was with since 2000) felt the writing itself would be a big step and was very enthusiastic, book or no book. She was also delighted I was in close contact with the author, who was another survivor. I had always found it very hard to tell Pam the details; it was far easier to talk about how it affected me, even though by then I'd been with her for nearly three years.

But it was probably close to one of the weirdest things I have ever made the decision to do! The writing of the story took over a year, and I had so many mixed feelings because I was writing about the very stuff I desperately tried to hide. I never talk about this stuff. There was quite a strong force inside trying to stop me from doing this at all, because it was going against the massive loyalty I still feel to my birth family. I have felt at times that I am breaking their confidence and letting them down, that I should be ashamed of myself for talking about deep dark family secrets. Even worse, were the threats that raced through my head, violent threats of what will happen to me if I speak out. I know these threats were made years back, but the greater part of my senses still believe they're very real.

At first Pam and I thought there were so many questions, that neither of us felt it possible to answer all of them! But when I started, just the first couple of paragraphs I'd written did bring home how badly I was treated. David and I care for and love our children so much, that we'll never understand why anyone would want to be so cruel. It feels like I'm almost more upset for the poor child I've written about, but she's not really me.

Whenever I knew it *was* about me, the anger boiled up but I pushed it down, scared that if I started to get upset I wouldn't stop! I felt extremely sad a lot. The child I hardly knew wasn't even allowed to be childlike, I grieved for her, and then I remembered she was me. I worked slowly through the questionnaire, some times just looking at it and other times writing a little down, then left it for a few days and went back. It fascinated me how the mind recalls things or not, and how I had to really concentrate, or be ready with pen and a scrap of paper at the times when things came to me. Usually I try to live each day as it comes, not thinking about the future and definitely not the past! When I showed it to Pam, bits were there that I'd never been able to tell her before, so she got a better understanding. I was (surprisingly) not very upset afterwards and I felt positive that I'd gone that bit further.

There's been a lot of confusion too about mixed feelings. When describing people and events, I hit so many contradictions. I cannot say my mother was always like this …or my father was always like that … or my siblings were always like this … they were

222

constantly changing and they can't be fitted into little boxes. Its hard to get the whole picture across about how things were; I know what happened to me when I was a child and I was in a lot of pain because I was blamed for everything. I was never allowed feelings, and I still find them hard now. Perhaps that's why I still doubt my own perceptions to some extent, but I didn't exaggerate any aspect of what happened to me in what I've written.

In the end the *need* to make sense of all this stuff proved much stronger than anything. I needed to turn the situation around into something positive and if it helps just one person then all the work that I have done both on myself and on this story will be worth all the blood, sweat and tears.

Longing

It frightens me that my family may read the story and know that it's me, and then I find myself fantasising. I want my mum to pick up my story. Wouldn't it be brilliant if she suddenly realised what she was really like, what awful things I have experienced and how much pain and suffering I'll carry on enduring? Then I realise I'm forgetting one thing; she does know all about what I went through. She knows full well ... and she doesn't care.

My hubby read this all along, and although he knew most of the things already, it must have been strange for him to see it all down in black and white. He said how sad it is that the book even had to be written at all, but we're glad we were a part of this, as fewer children may suffer as a result. I won't be showing my story to anybody else though, and nobody else will know that I'm in this book. My counsellor and her supervisor read the whole thing. My counsellor feels very good about it and thinks the project will be a good thing for a lot of other survivors to work from and read in the future. We both agree it could help and inform anybody else who wants to know how child abuse affects people's lives.

~~~~~~~~~~‡~~~~~~~~~‡~~~~~~~~‡~~~~~~~~~~~~

Optional Questions

1   How far are we listening to a whining daughter who thinks gets less attention than her brother or sister?

2   How far could this be the case of a sibling who was in fact, picked out for the purpose of victimisation, and why?

3   What traces can we begin to see here of the components of Karen's emotional abuse?

4   Aunt Judy was Karen's aunt on her father's side. Perhaps that's why she was tolerated in the house, and allowed to keep visiting.

    If she had been stopped from visiting Karen, what could Karen have done?

5   What forms of abuse could have created the physical injuries that Karen had as a baby, as a little girl and as an adolescent?

6   What forms of neglect did Karen suffer from?

    Karen sustained serious injuries when she was only a few months old. If Aunt Judy had not been interested – might Karen have survived?

7   How did Karen's parents respond to her when she was crying, or when she couldn't understand what to do?

8   What can we guess about how Karen's parents perceived her, and what were their gut feelings towards her?

9   What were their parental goals for Karen, and did they have a parental goal of fairness between their children?

10 How far might such clear demonstrations of disdain for Karen have helped to instill a sense of their authority, and therefore their ability to control the other children?

11 What was their mental attitude towards her, and how did they express it?

    As you read on, you'll find more material to help you answer those questions.

12 Who was the leader whenever Karen was picked out and treated in this way?

13 What sort of doubts might stop us believing her when she says that this never happened to the other children?

14 Why would we not believe her?

15 How did Karen's Dad go about terrorising her, and how often might he have

used that as a theme to humiliate her?

16   If Karen's Dad were getting some kind of gratuitous pleasure out of treating her in this way, how would you describe that pleasure?

17   Why is there this theme about fat? Could it be because they begrudge her taking any food? If so, what might that symbolise?

18   How prevalent do you think this sort of behaviour was in the family, as a family unit?

19   Where could Karen take her anxieties, or get comfort from?

20   For example, if she mentioned any of this to Aunt Judy, what would happen, and how might those consequences affect Karen's world?

21   Colin had learning disabilities and Liz was diabetic. All the kids got to see scary, adult rated films. Why was this allowed to happen? How could that have affected the children?

22   What sort of dialogues and communication processes do you imagine going on between Karen, her two older brothers and her younger sister?

23   What do you think Karen might have been expressing at home?

24   What was she saying she needed from her family, and did she have any chance of getting it?

25   Why would Karen be feeling frightened and very vulnerable about a 'harmless' party?

Clues are to be found further on in the text.

26   What did Karen's schoolteachers know about her life?

27   Was there any professional requirement for these teachers to know anything about her well-being, her relationships, and basic things like how well she was eating and sleeping?

28   Was there anything they valued about her? If there was, did the school environment set about communicating that to her in a way that she could understand?

29   If Karen's dad was getting pornographic films, where might he have got them from? What sort of connections did this man really have? What aspects of pleasure, or gratification did Karen's dad experience from exposing this child to adult pornography?

30   What here, is the significance of dad's 'friends'? Although they were strangers to Karen, were they strangers to him? What roles in society do you think they

might they have had, and what sort of connection do you think they might have had with Karen's dad?

31 Today, how safe might Karen feel in social situations now as an adult?

She says here that some of the adults in these social gatherings were involved in her sexual abuse, and some weren't. In a normal social situation, what differences exist between how a paedophile might socialise, and how a non-paedophile might socialise?

32 Were Karen's instincts not to tell good instincts? Today, many psychologists see these instincts as primary survival skills; but they are usually talking about the survival of mental health and social functioning. Yet here, we have to push this understanding further, to life and death survival. If she *had* told, how likely or unlikely is it whether or not she would have been murdered?

33 If you had been an adult who knew Karen as a child, would you have been able to 'spot' her? What were the signs that she was an abused child? Who would you have told and what would you have done?

34 Do you think it would have been possible for a well meaning stranger to reach out to Karen and help her as a teenager? If so, what might be said to her, and what might be done?

35 There is literature about adult children of alcoholics which is well worth reading. Some survivors find it enormously helpful to see how as a child, they may have overcompensated for the adult carers they grew up with. How does Karen still overcompensate in her life? Describe the confusion she still experiences.

Reflections on Karen's Story

When I first met Karen and saw her filled in questionnaire, I had trouble believing her parents picked her out from their brood of four, victimising only her. Surely parents as crazy as this would lash out at any kid that got in their way! Karen confirmed they did, but from her answers as a whole I could see she was systematically separated from the other kids, and pushed into a very definite role. Some teachers make an example of a certain child and pick on them repeatedly; and the more powerless the child becomes, the more satisfied the teacher is they've established power over the whole class. Perhaps Karen's brothers and sister were scared by Karen's treatment, and this worked as a form of control. It also seemed odd how so much pressure was put on her to care for her older brothers and younger sister. How could she be expected to be a child carer? She was a child.

Just as public behaviour gets more violent out in the streets when the pubs close, alcoholic or drug addict child carers take their children's worlds to extremes. Clever torments of sarcasm, or sudden whacks, pinches and hits with threats of more to come bring unbearable shame and self doubt on a child. With all the justifications of how aptly deserved it all is, it cripples the child. The child will simply keep mum, with little awareness they're keeping secrets. Only the terror of exposure exceeds the terror of abuse. Battered women hide their breaks and bruises with shame and lie about them month upon year. With many aspects between the two, age is only a number.

Dialogues in films like 'Snatch' (directed by Guy Ritchie in 2001) illustrate the sort of stuff Karen suffered. Vinnie Jones brilliantly acts out displays of power and submission that get stretched to the limit. In our culture, we hesitate to admit brutality this extreme happens to children, but it does. Adult abusers pick on children to test their powers of manipulation just as they do with adult victims. Conduct this extreme towards children is rarely considered, and we look upon the world of a child through rose tinted spectacles, ignorant of how children are used. You might say Karen was like an amusement arcade, or perhaps a toilet, where adults could dump their frustrations and flush them away without a second thought.

When she got to her teens, Karen started running away by staying out, yet why did she feel such a sense of responsibility towards her family? Was it parental pressure? Did it come from her child's heart of caring and self–sacrifice? Maybe, at least partly. Or did she think that by fixing her external world, her internal world could change? Children of alcoholics often dream incessantly for change, and work hard to make a difference. Many can't expect a balanced exchange and can only give; with their efforts blinding their perception of everything.

In Peter's Story (Story 10 in Survivors' Stories Volume 2) he established a hatred towards his abusers at a young age, but this is quite rare. In Karen's case, her abusers still drain her love and attention. They still see her as an object to hurt and manipulate; Karen finds it near impossible to change or counteract the games they persist in playing. Even angry, resentful survivors who start new lives and cut themselves off completely from their roots keep on combing through their pasts, obsessively looking for what went wrong. Through the tangled memories, they dream that when they find a new way of being themselves, they'll find the invisible key that can change everything. It's hard to accept that carrying blame and responsibility on their shoulders will not transform either the suffering, or the people who generated it.

People can understand the courage of war correspondents like Jeremy Bowen, who witnessed cruel atrocities during the Bosnian conflict. Like Karen, they survive everything at the time by numbing themselves and blanking it out, but they carry the trauma and re-live it in their minds throughout future phases. Survivors of war trauma and child abuse both suffer from posttraumatic stress disorder, yet one form of destruction makes a lot more 'sense' than the other. There are many who have yet to understand why it might require courage for a survivor to revisit their pasts and talk, or why it might take courage to listen.

Karen's scenes of tortuous treatment did not happen in bombed out buildings, but in civilised suburbia. Karen never knew which moment her father might turn up with several abusers at the front door, or when she might be driven out to meet them in the family car. Unlike some other sufferers of PTSD, she didn't have the luxury of choice, about whether or not to opt for a 'courageous' career once she had grown up. She grew up in an ordinary house, in an ordinary town, and was expected to act normally each and every day through her childhood hell. It seems obvious why Karen might feel unsafe in places other people think of as ordinary.

It takes courage for society to believe how abusers act, and completely get away with it. Some won't accept that adults who otherwise act so normally, will victimise a child to such extremes.

Karen's lucky in that even though she was lonely and afraid for what must have seemed like eternity, she had aunt Judy to watch over her, and to love her. If I may say so, aunt Judy represented a future that Karen could believe in, and people like her deserve far more appreciation than they usually get. Karen's vision as a child was to arrive home from school, with dinner cooking on the stove, and hear a warm, friendly voice say, 'How was your day?' During the hours Karen was locked up in the shed, she used to imagine having a family she could care for, belong to and feel a part of.

Karen has found support from people who want to pull her through the pain from her past, and help her live in the present on her own terms. In the main, Karen has created her vision. She faces up to the joys and challenges ahead as a promising young mother within her new family, one that is deservedly her own.

The Source of Our Silence

We underestimate our capacity to do anything about the horror of child abuse, and help one another. Depreciating ourselves, we hold lawyers, social workers, the police force, judges, psychiatrists, psychologists, health care workers, teachers, policy makers and parents in either high regard or frustrated contempt, as we allow them to define the very boundaries that we have imposed on ourselves. When we were small, we either took on certain attitudes in order to emulate and impress the taller ones, or we rebelled. We're no longer children, yet we still bow to experts, believe automatically what they tell us, and resist thinking and acting for ourselves whilst children continue to suffer.

The assumptions and limitations we've absorbed have very real origins but these are, as yet, unexamined and misunderstood. By looking into these origins more closely, we can gently give ourselves back the human capacity that is rightly ours – the capacity to care for one another. This final section is the last part of our pilgrimage. It's where we reflect upon the power that makes us powerless, and assess our own ability to properly respond to children and to survivors.

If you were to ask yourself which profession, in terms of matters pertaining to child abuse,

1. Has the clearest perception about how men and women behave.

2. Has the most authority to define the condition of someone's mental health irrefutably, in public.

3. Most understands what it means to be a living, thinking, and feeling human being.

The answer to all three would probably be the consultant psychiatrist or psychologist. Most of us, though outside these professions, still borrow snippets of their conventional wisdom and insight. But why? That hardly equips us to understand what happens to so many of our children. Moreover, the status of psychiatrists, in itself, calls many of our social perceptions into question; especially our perceptions of ourselves.

Greater scientific understanding of our physical health and our environment has liberated most of us further than we might ever know, and we now live with advantages of which our forefathers could only dream. But should we necessarily accept what psychologists tell us because of the 'scientific' way they appear to present their knowledge?

Psychology, psychoanalysis and psychiatry are not only tools for understanding people and how they behave. Professionals from these fields play a decisive role in our legal processes, with deep-seated consequences upon either a plaintiff's or a defendant's life, and with consequences that filter down to society as a whole. Thankfully, not all of us are faced in our lives with an actual court case, but when we encounter the legal system, for example in jury service, we witness how consultant psychiatrists may have the last word over someone's state of mental health. We are all vulnerable to this authority. In the field of child abuse even today, it is perfectly acceptable for a psychiatrist who, following Freudian fundamentals, stands as an expert witness, to state that a victim of abuse is not telling the truth but is either suffering from false memory syndrome, or delusions, or both.

The professions of psychological expertise rarely require themselves to focus on how destructive, and unjust aspects of the abusive mind operate in families and in wider society, nor do we expect them to. Much work still needs to be done on how a skilled child abuser controls their victims, and what it is that both allows and compels them to do it. Culprits who have tortured children all their lives manipulate and abuse the legal process itself, and often their rank in society will ensure that they get no custodial sentence, especially if they plead guilty. Still, the psychological professions neither require of themselves, nor are they required by others to switch focus. In the public arena, the court focuses upon the the victim's psychiatric needs, while the perpetrator hides and asserts their 'sanity' in total silence. It's only when the thoughts, feelings and behaviour of the abuser are given at least as much attention as the abused, can there be any kind of justice.

Sigmund Freud (1856 – 1939) is the big daddy of psychology and psychoanalysis, but many remain unaware how far we still labour under the power structure he instigated. Because of his unfamiliar language, and the alienating, strange concepts he chose to describe human experience we often accept Freud's reasoning without really trying to understand it. Freud professed to be scientific, but even in his time his techniques were (strictly speaking) unscientific and publicly criticized as such. Those criticisms were ignored, and even today quite a few eminent psychologists refuse to discredit Freud's theories, or the way they are put into practice. Although his work is no longer even taught in most universities, something strange happens when Freud is extracted from our culture. We lose our most fundamental concepts about what sanity and mental illness is. We lose our attitude towards those who need help, the way we approach them and also the whole sequence of events they go through when they start to receive whatever expertise they are told they need.

Criticism

Freud and his thinking obstructed any possibility of understanding child abuse, and there are papers by the most studious psychiatrists, physicists, mathematicians, philosophers and psychologists that criticize many other aspects of Freud's legacy. In each case the fundamental veracity of that legacy is usually upheld, and the critics are criticised for misinterpreting the 'true' rationale within Freud's original thinking. As the ball bounces back and forth, where does such a 'tennis game' take us, if anywhere at all? Criticism provokes little more than a re–assertion of the original position, whereas it should serve as part of a rigorous process of scientifically based enquiry. There are many who would not risk disrespecting these worthy professionals and their towering standards, yet their allegiance stands upon a mechanical respect that's extraordinarily shy of its own rationale. Instead of looking for where they could improve right in the face of child suffering, all they do is refine their individual opinions further and insist on being better respected and understood. This response in itself is close to barbaric. Customarily, fine examples of similar masquerades of genuine concern can also be found echoing from the echelons of major political and religious institutions. Such utterances are all wearing rather thin.

Genius Interrupted

Freud's genius emanated a power, as do still his basic insights. His legacy cannot be discarded since it gave us the foundational concepts of the psyche, the conscious and unconscious mind and insights into group dynamics individually and in society. Critically, it gave us permission to start considering whether adult sexuality might after all be a healthy reality of life. So what follows is not just another intellectual, scholarly criticism of the work and thought of Sigmund Freud and its power over children, society, and ourselves. My concern is for the abused children, a tiny number of which have found voice in the attached stories. My concern is to reveal how psychologists and other so-called experts stole the ability from us all to talk to each other and to face up to child abuse; whether it be from the past, present daily living or in the future. Until ordinary people allow themselves to talk, think and listen, nothing will be done, and more children will suffer. We need a fresh approach, one based on our basic humanity, and our common love for our children. So instead of arguing against Freudianism in a Freudian way, I will bring you a refreshing alternative via Sándor Ferenczi (1873–1933), Freud's contemporary whose views were not based upon dogmatic monologue, but upon diverse and finely-tuned listening and self-searching response.

Sándor Ferenczi (pronounced **FERENTS**) had a remarkable sensitivity that still shines out from his somewhat intrepid body of psychoanalytical work. He obtained the title of psychiatrist at the Royal Court of Vienna, having graduated in medicine with a further specialism in neurology beforehand. Whilst practising as a psychiatrist in his native Budapest, he met Freud in 1908 and quickly became one of the hierarchs of Freud's psychoanalytical circle. He joined in with the pioneering work, often being allocated the most challenging cases. Whilst Sigmund Freud was a genius, Sándor Ferenczi was a great human being.

Whether Freud believed he was God or not, no one knows but Freud's key discoveries prompted an unshakable faith from those who knew him. Many of those who eventually broke away from his inner circle, like Jung, Adler, and others, retained that unshakable faith. They shared his desire for the tidal wave of prestige, success, and money that was on offer from the upper classes of Europe and America. Freud and Ferenczi shared a closeness in the first ten years of their relationship, whereby Freud even confided a wish to have had Ferenczi for his son-in-law. Freud saw Ferenczi as successor to his leadership position, but after those years as Freud's 'favourite son', Ferenczi gradually broke away from Freud's inner circle.

At the height of Freud's fame (shortly after his 75th birthday in 1932) Ferenczi clearly expressed his diametrically opposite views. The original title of his paper as announced was,

"The [Sexual] Passions of Adults and their Influence on the Character Development and Sexual Development of Children."
(also known as the "Confusion of Tongues Between Adults and the Child.")

Ferenczi read it in September 1932 to the entire psychoanalytical community of the time, in Wiesbaden, Austria. He said the perpetration of child abuse was not only real,

231

but that a child could be just as well abused psychologically as abused sexually and physically. Freud denied all of this. Ferenczi also said psychoanalysis was overly intellectualised, and presented his ideas about how the psychiatrist could have a more open and equal approach towards their patient. This was not based upon the analyst's self-indulgence, but an essential element of being a humanly authentic psychoanalyst.

Ferenczi discovered that when a child is being abused, he or she identifies with their perpetrator, and will try to alleviate the perpetrator's suffering by taking on that suffering as their own. He believed that to urge the patient to reproduce his childhood trauma in a cold analytic setting does no more than replicate the abusive situation. He said that a negative, unconscious dynamic takes control which becomes unbearable for the patient.

Freud saw no merit in this, and did more than reject Ferenczi and his findings. Ferenczi died of pernicious anaemia in 1933, and Ernest Jones, Freud's official biographer stated that it was Ferenczi's 'mental illness', which created his radical ideas, and further, it was this 'mental illness' that caused his death. Ferenczi's diaries and papers more than contradict this notion. His friends who saw him during his last year firmly denied he was mentally ill. Jones reneged on his promise to translate Ferenczi's work into English, which happened over fifty years later in the latter part of the 1980's. Henceforth Ferenczi's work was derogated, and largely ignored. If nothing else, Ferenczi's efforts made one thing abundantly clear. Freud not only established an acceptable attitude of denial about child abuse, Freud's success was utterly dependant upon the total denial of its existence.

We will return to Ferenczi later. However, to understand the fate of abused children in the modern world, you must begin with Freud in order to understand and benefit from the astonishing insights of Sándor Ferenczi. This means that we must work our way over a fair amount of 'Freudian' terrain before we arrive at the borders of where we are going. This is an opportunity to understand the power behind our imposed silence, and we'll see that to tackle child abuse you don't have to be an expert at all; you only have to be human. Please be patient.

Origins

Few people can claim to be a genius in isolation, and just as we were born into the Freud's body of knowledge, the Austro German society of the late nineteenth century was steeped in Greek ideas. These ideas strongly correlated to Freud's findings about the ego; findings which reinforced the harshness of attitude towards children that he himself had inherited. Although Freud and his circle ventured into the unconscious world of a patient, not one questioned the hostility of the real world that might encompass a child. Their 'science' was focused entirely upon the rule of a well-developed ego, which was (and still is) something thought to be the socially desirable goal, over and above all else. The implicit insight threaded through his theories was that no maturity is achievable for the adult unless any acknowledgement of a child as a person within is erased. For Freud, childhood was a disease. As we shall see, Ferenczi came to disagree strongly with these ideas.

Freud used his theories to justify his power, and understanding the fundamentals of his theories shines some light upon the workings within our silence. In Freud's three-part explanation of the mind, the central part was the 'ego', or the self. The supreme part was the superego, which had the role of checking through the choice of actions of the ego. It was like a mixture of philosophy, principles and values with a bit of conscience and guilt thrown in. The term for self (the German 'ich', in English 'I') that was ego, was the ordinarily conscious mind of a person. A primitive 'id', which means 'it' in Latin, inhabited this conscious ego, and was not much more than a primitive life force. What many therapists now call the inner child (the perception and acceptance of which developed from the mid eighties onwards, and which is now being confirmed by scientific neurological studies) Freud didn't recognize. For him, the essence of childhood was problematic to the adult self; it was a 'thing', or object ruled by a pleasure principle, that ensured nothing more than physical survival.

Der Fuhrer

Freud used to write sympathetically on the theme of the 'Fuhrer Principle', which could translate as a law of leadership. This 'leader' is the superego, and it is the superego's image that the ego always tries to achieve. A child's growth and development is all about adjusting the 'id' to family standards and cultural values. The superego guides the ego as it gets on with the job of subduing and mastering the 'id'. This 'super person' who, if we use the clichés of his day, would equate to a superman, a natural leader (in the German, a 'Fuhrer') of the self generated inside the person under psychoanalysis. If the person is not sufficiently ruthless in imposing the dictates of the super–ego upon his inner 'id', or if his inner 'id' turns out to be uncooperative with egocentric demands, mental disease follows. Freud thought his main hypothesis was scientific, because it correlated to how the mind (realm of ideas from the super-ego) affects the body (matter, or the primitive 'id'). Where there is conflict, the forces of either repression, or positive channelling of sexual energy (possibly in other creative ways) must come into play, because an inner 'id' will create unrest and insanity if it is not channelled and controlled.

The world soaked up this judgment of what it is to be a human being, like a sponge. These Freudian theories can still reveal our most basic attitudes in how we behave and interact. We can carry this model of control into the internal relationship we have with the self, the relationship between two individuals, relationships between adult and child in the family or group of origin, and the relationships between whole sections of society and whoever and whatever represents them, one to another. It may be a puzzling parallel between the inner world of one individual and then again their connection with another individual or larger group, but it's the power pattern in these relationships that's easy to detect. It's within aspects of this unspoken power our assumptions lie about what is wrong and right, and it guides our perceptions of what goes on within the closer and wider relationships around us. Freud probably wasn't the originator of these attitudes and assumptions, but he toughened certain dominant social constructs that we still see around us today.

Beginnings

The society of Freud's time was feudalistic, and drunk with adoration for everything Greek. In Plato's Greece, man mirrored the soul and was meant to embody it, and control, shape and govern the world. Man was the 'Philosopher–king' that fully comes into being under the guidance of Reason. Through Reason, the Realm of Eternal Ideas is born into the world, the most supreme, being the Idea of the Good. For Freud, the 'ego' is the Philosopher–king of man, and the super ego is Reason, and the Realm of Eternal Ideas. Freud's primitive 'id' is very close to Plato's view of both woman and child as being essentially formless. Whatever was merely material or born of it was chaos, with an intrinsic tendency towards the sort of evil described by the Greek, 'anarche' (anarchy), which was without ruler, principle, or reason. The function of the male was to control, shape, and govern, and the formation of society depended upon men to guide women, children, slaves and working classes, all under the guidance of the aristocrats.

Freud's picture of the interaction of the ego, super ego and id parallel's that of most modern nations, whose structure rests on a prior sacrifice of person–hood. This sacrifice can be from 'successful' people who cow tow, but whose personal integrity suffers either fractionally or entirely. Apart from two–faced displays of allegiance to conventional power, there are a myriad of situations wherein either adult or child is openly or privately bullied. Groups like homosexuals, transsexuals, the handicapped, the disabled, immigrants, adult prostitutes (that may not sit well here, but think about it), are all shamed into thinking they are a nuisance. If these oppressed groups or individuals persist in thinking that they are something in and for themselves, the use of force or violence against them, and possibly some sort of psychoanalytical intervention becomes appropriate. Today, both the self and the government still function best alongside the abuse of certain groups and individuals. Despite laws and citizen's rights declaring equality for all, within the small ways that we behave towards one another, we succumb to and perpetrate power structures that we think are set in stone.

Of course there are many nits to pick over about the origins of Freud's thinking, but what comes across most of all is how Freud and his system of practices, attitudes, and beliefs made no effort to liberate children, or change the social relationships wherein they were virtually kept as slaves to a somewhat appalling range of adult wishes. The female liberation movement began to expose Freud's dogma as oppressive years ago, and we will discover why soon, all the same we would be fifty years behind in our perceptions about how children live today, without it.

Just like bound copies of legal precedents superseded long ago, Freud's volumes sit in various libraries all over the world, gathering dust. Their self–proclaimed idealism is as seductive as it ever was, and all kinds of mental health workers still labour under various modifications of the same old distorted perceptions. Why does the profession still perpetuate the view that being a singularly stable, subdued individual in society is all that is required, when that alone cannot possibly counter the perpetration of abuse upon children? Sándor Ferenczi was asking that question well before his audience was ready to listen.

Potent Theories

Freud's findings derived from his analytical practice and at various times Freud used different theories to explain the causes of depression, flashbacks, bad dreams, relationship struggles, or whatever else troubled his patients. But the most important theory is the one that hid child abuse away from society; and below, we shall look into the workings of how this concealment actually happened.

Seduction Theory

It was the openness and cooperation of Freud's earliest patients from 1895 onwards that enabled him to compose his 'Studies in Hysteria'. His 'Seduction Theory' (1895) started out from thirteen cases who as children, had a sexual relationship with nursemaids, governesses, domestic servants, teachers, or brothers slightly older than them. These were never referred to as child abuse survivors but, nevertheless, that is precisely what they were. Six from this sample also took part in active pleasurable sexual experience at around the age of eight or ten, and had been subjected to sexual molestation in infancy too. A year later by 1896 Freud went into more detail, increasing his first study group to eighteen; but here, the perpetrators now included adult strangers and close relatives in addition to those previously listed. By 1897 he believed abusers were generally fathers, but by 1906 there was a change, and his interest in the perpetrators virtually vanished.

As Freud's patient, you would lie on the couch on average three or four times a week with your symptoms of hysteria and obsessional neurosis. He would use his regressive techniques to help you connect with your unconscious. Before 1900, if any repressed memories of your sexually abusive experiences from childhood came up, he thought you were an (either unwilling or willing) child participant of sexual activity with an adult from your home and family circle. Your obsessional neurosis was there because of pre-pubescent, unwanted, overwhelming sexual stimulation, and your dis-ease was the consequence of pre-pubescent sexual shock. But a few years later on, things changed. He would re-interpret what you told him, effectively altering your original testimony. You then had to work through your feelings about being raped, forced or seduced into sexual acts as a child, and however often you were violated, your hysterical delusions were perceived as being based upon your repressed sexual urges and fantasies. In other words, your suffering was no longer something imposed on you, but something that appeared inside yourself because you were creating it.

It Doesn't Exist

Why was there this change of mind? Freud's colleagues either couldn't accept that adults would treat children like that, or they could not accept that such an approach to therapy could be valid. When Freud's core interest intensified into his patient's unconscious 'phantasies', and made the victim the cause of his own pain, he regained popularity. From 1906 onwards, he relayed how the whole experience of abuse was created in the patient's mind during puberty, to cover up their repressed memories of infantile masturbation. When Freud's patients told him their parent(s) or another adult or older child had seduced them, involved them in sexual activity during childhood, or confessed a parent's brutality, he discarded their words as symptoms of delusion. Contradicting his earliest case studies from 1896, his patient's testimony now became symptoms of a greater mental illness. In the end, he and the widening circle of professionals around him used his theories to counter any accounts of child abuse, as a matter of course.

Digging for 'Truth'

Although Freud's genius cottoned on to something truly important when he discovered the basic concepts of child development and the unconscious mind, he does not appear to have had much reverence for them, that is, whenever they were beyond his powers of manipulation. Freud placed his hand on the patient's forehead and encouraged him or her to report any images or ideas that came to mind, but when still nothing came through, Freud termed that 'resistance' and kept on pressing on the forehead, adamant that a picture or an idea should emerge. He would then piece everything together, rather like editing a roughly shot film based on a storyboard that was already fully sketched out in his own imagination.

Freud once confessed,

"The work keeps coming to a stop and they keep maintaining that this time nothing has occurred to them. We must not believe what they say, we must always assume, and tell them too, that they have kept something back. We must insist on this, we must repeat the pressure and represent ourselves as infallible, till at last we are really told something ... There are cases, too, in which the patient tries to disown [the memory] even after its return. [They can easily say,] 'Something has occurred to me now, but you obviously put it into my head' . . . In all such cases, I remain unshakeably firm. I . . . explain to the patient that [these distinctions] are only forms of [the patient's] resistance ..."

(Quote from 'Burying Freud' by Professor R.C. Tallis ©The Lancet.)

Under what we could call a hypnotic power, psychiatrists can even ignore physical pain. They can disregard symptoms of genuine biological physical illnesses and call them manifestations of hysteria, or resistance. In stark contrast, Ferenczi takes the root cause of resistance and lays it right at the feet of the therapist themselves, as you will see further on.

Talking About Theories

Crucially, Freud believed the penis was the human symbol of power, knowledge, wealth and status. This rather odd concept turns out to be crucial when we get to Freud's Oedipus complex (which is quite different for men, as opposed to women). His ideas about women seem alien to our modern understanding of what a woman is and can be, but they were very acceptable in 1925. Freud took his inspiration from the tragic Greek myth 'Oedipus the King' when he conceived the theory that attempts to explain how the id, the ego and the super-ego become formed. It became the backbone upon which all understanding of mental disease depended.

Oedipus Complex for Men

As a newly born male baby, your mother was your whole sensual world, and the object of your love and attention. Your first sexual urges and the fulfilment of your needs for food, shelter and care, were one and the same. Gradually you also experience pleasurable sensations in your penis, and your phallic or masturbatory stage begins. By the time you are two, you realise your mother is sexually attracted to your father and you start to experience feelings of envy and hatred towards him. Your father (who symbolises your super–ego) gets angry. Because your penis symbolises your desire for your mother, you fear he will castrate you, and thus rob you of your power and your will.

Castration Complex

This stage fills you with shame and tension. You want to maintain your phallus and all that it symbolises, so you submit to your father's power. Your desire for your mother wanes as your super ego shifts your father's presence into a central dominance within you. You identify with him, but these fears and feelings of shame as a baby and toddler enable you to fit in, and behave in a balanced moral way when you grow up.

As a man, this development of your super–ego shows that you are biologically and psychologically capable of making and maintaining moral relationships. You understand power, and capable of social interactions in the outside world with a healthy respect for rules and procedures.

Oedipus for Women

As a woman, your early stages as a baby and toddler were the same, but your ego development was entirely different. Just like a male baby, you enjoyed having your mother as your world of nurture, and when you were playing with and discovering your genitals, you remained sexually attached to her. But when you reach four, five and six you realize that you don't have a penis and you start to feel envious of boys. You feel of no value. This is what Freud called the first stage of the Female Castration Complex, which he also said was probably the cause of female sexual repression.

When you discover your mother doesn't have a penis, you realise that no other woman has one either. But you only originally loved your mother because you thought she had the power, knowledge and wealth a penis represents, so you feel betrayed. You then turn to your father for the penis your mother denied you. If you can just have a baby by your father; that would be tantamount to having your own penis, which you crave. The love you once had for your mother switches to your father, yet you see your mother as a rival for your father's affections. It's only when you actually have a baby of your own (especially if it's a son) that your longing for a penis is at last fulfilled.

For the female incest survivor, how damaging might Freud's Oedipal theories have been?

Freud really believed that women had a lot of envy in their thought patterns. This meant the concept of justice that is so evident in the formation of the male ego was missing in the female. Freud thought since motherhood does not guarantee complete fulfilment, for a female, perhaps happiness is never truly possible. In society, a woman can find completion only if she surrender to a man, and accept his treatment of her, whatever that may be. Preferring the comfort of her home as her retreat and sanctum, a female is just not capable of moving through society in a fair and just way, like men. Freud sometimes admitted these studies of women seemed incomplete, but he still felt

237

females were incapable of forming the Super-ego necessary for moral behaviour.

Death Instinct

There was a third body of theory, called the 'Libidinal Instinctive Drives'. On one side this meant sexual energy, the force behind every creative action or thought that produced or affirmed life. Naturally, there had to be an opposite force, which he called the 'Death Instinct'. This denoted a longing for a state of stillness and non-existence, and would manifest as a desire to cease to struggle and go home to the grave. Freud ascribed periods of extreme melancholia, depression and suicidal tendencies to this drive, which he considered a biological drive. Any form of self-destructiveness could be ascribed to it, as well as obsessions, compulsions, some traumas, and repetitive behaviour. He also thought that people projected this instinct outwards whenever they expressed sadomasochistic behaviour or went to war. But it is the aspect of negative therapeutic reaction that is the most worrying. If his therapies led towards more suffering and suicidal tendencies in his patients, he could quite easily ascribe this development to the 'Death Instinct'.

Insignificance of the External World

Freud's inner circle of therapists probably had as many English speaking clientèle as they had German, and the upper classes of Europe and America had no trouble in buying their attentions. Freud and Freudianism had no experience with, understanding of, or sympathy with democratic ideals, and he showed no interest in female liberation movements. In 1911 the first International Women's Day took place in Austria, Germany, Denmark and Switzerland, where more than one million women and men attended rallies. Neither was there interest in the achievement of the women's right to vote in Germany, Austria and Britain in 1918. Perhaps he thought the whole Suffragette movement was founded on female jealousies!

Social constraint and the oppression of children never entered Freud's discourse. His Oedipus complex theory dominated his understanding of how men, women and children actually lived, with society as a natural consequence of the way that men and women were. He would never look, for example, for outside causes of female jealousies. It may be inaccurate to say that Freud thought the feudal, monarchical, elitist society in which he formulated his theories was perfect, but this society had a profound effect on his thinking.

Mindboggling Ambition

Many who listen to these theories and try to understand them seem to glaze over with dulled confusion. People happy to study the intricacies of Freud enjoy the respect of those who are confused and lessened by it. But these theories are not confusing just because our minds wander, or because our attention spans are too short, it's because there is nothing in them that's worth more than a fraction of our understanding. We feel we must respect the 'solid' ground of countless hours spent in writing, recording and analysis. I submit that the ambitious eye that plots its course through the bewilderment of this maze is after nothing more remarkable than power over their fellow man.

Since Freud, all sorts of differing brands of analysis and therapy have developed.

Freud's gateway to the unconscious via the interpretation of dreams, hypnosis, or physical and verbal stimulation is still practised today. Whether they are religious or not, various new age movements and cults see their adherents' lack of spiritual or ideological 'progress' as some kind of 'resistance'. The pathway to the Holy Grail of the purest form of liberated consciousness is nothing new, but Freud packaged his version up and sold it as respectable, 'scientific' thinking. It's Freud's notion of 'resistance' that makes psychoanalysis both exceptional and untouchable. As a treatment of mental illness, psychiatry is not so much a service to patients, but more like the ultimate in human consciousness within our own culture, in which it sees its own arrogance as virtue. Any disagreement with the profession is perceived by it as a sign of resistance; and so it shakes off decisive criticism, every time. It's rather like the world is divided between mature therapists and disobedience.

Therapists are supposedly trained not to be susceptible to the very human practice of projection i.e. seeing people as we think they are through our subjective experience, rather than as they actually are. The focus on analysis, self-analysis and logic is meant to overcome this. Whilst there is obvious merit in cultivating objectivity, the question remains as to what extent are the patient's (as well as the therapist's) common sense and normal human instincts manipulated, devalued and at times destroyed. It was this question that was the centre of Sandór Ferenczi's whole life.

From Sandór Ferenczi's address (as titled below) in 1932, we can see that a true spirit of openness and willingness to expose child abuse and those affected by it was more than incidental. It was diligently and respectfully presented to the intellectuals of the time, but nullified by Freud's 'superior' ideas. Every single person at the Weisbaden Congress where this was read, believed as a matter of near religious faith that both adult and child patient reports of abuse were fantasies growing out of infantile sexual perversion. Ferenczi knew full well he was going up against a particularly totalitarian and fascist body of belief, of which he himself had once been one of the hierarchs.

This address was not meant for the published page, but meant to be delivered out loud in an animated and dynamic fashion. One by one, each elementary component part of child abuse finds its place right here in Ferenczi's clear cut understanding; which is offered here as a foundational framework for 'Survivors' Stories'. As you read and reflect, layer upon layer of essential knowledge about these issues is revealed within an astonishingly small space. Every sentence is a book, and whenever you return to a favourite paragraph, you always find something new. Here, I have roughly cut and pasted parts of his address and put Ferenczi's writing in italics. The entire document can be found in the excellent work, 'The Assault on Truth' by Jeffrey M Masson.

"Confusion of Tongues Between Adults and the Child"
(The Language of Tenderness and the Language of [Sexual] Passion)

The original title of the paper as announced was "The [Sexual] Passions of Adults and Their Influence on the Character Development and Sexual Development of Children." Below are excepts from the translation by Jeffrey M Masson and Marianne Loring.

Resistance

Ferenczi begins his address by getting to the bare bones of the communication process between therapist and patient. He's concerned that this communication in itself can be a harmful misuse of power. He says the patient's '**resistance**' can be sourced right back to the analyst, whose attitude is rather similar to that of a strict teacher towards their pupil. He says the patient becomes too subservient, and afraid of displeasing the analyst. Within the psychoanalytic community it was common to coin the phrase *"professional hypocrisy"* because it was accepted that it was impossible to like all patients, so analysts at times admitted to adopting a two faced approach. Analysts would see a patient three, four, even five times a week, and the power of the dynamics in such a relationship was bound to cloud analytical judgement.

He said,

"… In reality, however, we might find certain external or internal characteristics of the patient difficult to bear. Or perhaps we feel the analytic hour was an unwelcome interruption of a professional; or personal, private matter which was more important to us. Here too I see no solution other than to seek the cause of the interruption in ourselves and to discuss it with the patient, to recognize it not only as a possibility but also as a fact. It is remarkable that giving up the "professional hypocrisy," which until now was thought to be unavoidable, gives the patient a noticeable sense of relief instead of hurting his feelings. The traumatic–hysterical attack, if it came on at all, turned out to be much milder; past tragic events all of a sudden could be reproduced in thought without leading once again to the loss of emotional equilibrium; in fact the level of the patient's personality seemed to be considerably raised.

For the first time Ferenczi touches lightly upon his unique concept, 'the confusion of tongues'

"What brought about this state of affairs? In the doctor–patient relationship there was something unspoken, insincere, and discussing it loosened, so to speak, the tongue of the patient.

At that time an analyst's training was short, and Ferenczi perceived a serious need for the analyst's further development, so that analysts could better adjust themselves to the client's needs.

" … Let us not forget that the in–depth analysis of a neurosis generally takes many years, whereas the usual training analysis frequently lasts only a few months or at the most a year or a year and a half. This may lead to the impossible situation in which

little by little our patients become better analysed than we ourselves. That is, they show signs of such superiority, but are incapable of giving expression to it; in fact they often become extremely subservient, clearly because they are incapable or afraid of displeasing us with their criticism. A good part of the repressed criticism of our patients concerns what might be called "professional hypocrisy."

"The analytic situation, with its reserve and coldness, professional hypocrisy and masked dislike of the patient ... was essentially just as bad as what had led to the illness in the patient's childhood."

"Above all, we must be more than well analysed, right down to "rock bottom."

He says that for an analyst to discuss, openly recognise and subsequently avoid any professional errors can enhance the patient's trust. He cited an analytical situation whereby after listening to *'a most intelligent woman patient'* complaining about him, he soon afterwards acquired *'access to previously hidden or little noticed material.'*

He states quite bluntly ...

"... we must also, more than we have done until now, look for the existence of repressed or suppressed criticism of us'

"We are much too inclined to insist on certain theoretical constructs and frequently ignore facts that would weaken our self-assurance and authority'.

He says here that patients do not respond to theatrical phrases expressing compassion, but only genuine sympathy.

"I do not know whether they can tell difference by the sound of our voice, by the choice of our words or in some other way. They display a strange, almost clairvoyant knowledge of the thoughts and emotions of the analyst. In this situation it seems hardly possible to deceive the patient and if such deceit is attempted, it can only lead to bad consequences.'

Moving over to the subject of child sexual abuse, in the following uninterrupted quote of three consecutive paragraphs, Ferenczi states his findings quite clearly.

"Even children from respected, high-minded puritanical families fall victim to rape much more frequently than one had dared to suspect. Either the Parents themselves seek substitution for their lack of [sexual] satisfaction in this pathological manner, or else trusted persons such as relatives (uncles, aunts, grandparents), tutors, servants, abuse the ignorance and innocence of children. The obvious objection that we are dealing with sexual fantasies of the child himself, that is, with hysterical lies, unfortunately is weakened by the multitude of confessions of this kind, on the part of patients in analysis, to assaults on children. Thus I was not surprised when a short time ago an educator known for his high-minded philanthropy came to see me in a state of veritable despair to tell me that thus far he had been unfortunate enough to discover five families of good society in which the governesses lived in a regular conjugal state with nine- to eleven-year-old boys.

"The following is a typical manner in which incestuous seductions come about: An adult and a child love each other; the child has the playful fantasy that he will

241

assume the role of the mother to the adult. This game may also take on erotic forms, but always remains on the level of tenderness. This is not true of adults with a pathological predisposition, particularly when their equilibrium and their self–control have been upset by some misfortune or by the consumption of intoxicating substances. They confuse the playfulness of the child with the wishes of a sexually mature person or let themselves be carried away to engage in sexual acts without consideration of the consequences. Actual rape of girls barely beyond infancy, similar sexual acts of grown women with boys, even sexual acts of a homosexual character by force are commonplace.

"It is difficult to fathom the behaviour and the feelings of children following such acts of violence. Their first impulse would be: rejection, hatred, disgust, and forceful resistance. "No, no, I don't want this, it is too strong for me, that hurts me. Leave me be." This or something like it would be the immediate reaction, were it not paralyzed by tremendous fear. The children feel physically and morally helpless, their personality is still too insufficiently consolidated for them to be able to protest, even if only in thought.
The overwhelming power and authority of the adults renders them silent; often they are deprived of their senses. Yet that very fear, when it reaches its zenith, forces them automatically to surrender to the will of the aggressor, to anticipate each of his wishes and to submit to them; forgetting themselves entirely, to identify totally with the aggressor.

Identification

In most dictionaries, just above the word 'identify' is the word 'identical'. Indeed, 'identify' has a second meaning, where two or more things are considered as being entirely or essentially the same. Between adult and child, neither body nor mind could be described as identical, so the child's identification with the abuser develops between two separate worlds of constantly shifting thought, feeling and emotion, between that of the adult and that of the child.

"As a result of the identification with the aggressor, let us call it introjection, the aggressor disappears as external reality and becomes intrapsychic [internalised] instead of extrapsychic [externalised];…

"… In any event, the assault ceases to exist as an inflexible external reality, and the child, in his traumatic trance, succeeds in maintaining the former situation of tenderness.

"Yet the most important transformation in the emotional life of the child, which his identification with the adult partner, an identification based on fear, calls forth, is the introjection of the guilt feeling of the adult, which gives hitherto innocent play the appearance of a punishable act.

To continue with this theme of identification, you wonder how far an abused child's feelings are truly theirs. For the child, this mechanism of identification becomes an all–absorbing world of dread and anticipation. The child soaks up the adult's cravings to inflict pain on the child, and to shame and blame them, and takes on each and every consequence for every aspect of the abuse.

"When the child recovers after such an attack, he feels extremely confused, in fact already split, innocent and guilty at the same time; indeed his confidence in the testimony of his own senses has been destroyed. In addition to this, the behaviour of the adult partner has become harsh, for he is now more than ever plagued and angered by remorse, which makes the child feel even deeper guilt and shame. Almost always the perpetrator acts as though nothing had happened, comforting himself with the thought: "After all, this is only a child, who still knows nothing, and will soon forget everything again." Not infrequently the seducer becomes overly moralistic or religious after such an event and seeks to save the soul of the child by means of such severity as well.

In Ferenczi's explanatory Appendix, he talks about the basic emotional capacity in an adult for a split within an intimate relationship between love and hate. A child does not have this capacity.

"This train of thought calls attention to the [distinction between] tenderness in the erotic life of the child and passionate [sexuality] in the erotic life of the adult from a purely descriptive point of view, but leaves open the question of the real nature of the difference between the two. Psychoanalysis can approve the Cartesian idea that passion [Leidenschaft] is caused by suffering [Leiden]. But perhaps it will at the same time discover an answer to the question of what it is in the playful satisfaction of tenderness that introduces the element of suffering and thereby of sadomasochism. The above considerations allow us to surmise that, among other things, it is the sense of guilt, which in the erotic life of the adult turns the love object into the recipient of ambivalent feelings of both love and hate, whereas this split is still foreign to the tenderness of children. It is the hate [the adult feels for the child] that traumatically surprises and terrifies the child who is seduced by an adult, and transforms him from a spontaneous and innocently playing being into a guilt-ridden love-automaton, anxiously and, so to speak, self-effacingly imitating the adult.

"The adult's own guilt feelings and the hatred toward the seductive [child] partner shape the sexual intercourse of the adult into a battle (primal scene) that terrifies the child. For the adult this terminates with the moment of orgasm, whereas the erotic life of the child, in the absence of the "struggle of the sexes," remains at the level of foreplay, or knows satisfaction only in the sense of "satiety" but not the feelings of annihilation that accompany an orgasm ...

Telling

Ferenczi then speaks immediately about what happens when the child tells, and the resultant outburst of feeling that s/he cannot understand. This is irrespective of whether the feelings are outwardly expressed, or inflict themselves inwardly.

"Usually the relationship to a second person of trust, in the chosen example the mother, is not intimate enough either to provide help. Timid attempts of this kind on the part of the child are rejected by the mother as nonsense. The abused child turns into a

mechanically obedient being or becomes defiant, but can no longer account for the
reason for the defiance, even to himself ...

The child then loses his or her 'self', and the fear that consumes them pushes them
into a defenceless accommodation of the aggressor's demands.

"... The scientific importance of this observation is the assumption that the still not
well–developed personality of the child responds to sudden displeasure, not with
defence, but with identification and introjection of the menacing person or aggressor, an
identification based on fear.

Sacrifice

As Ferenczi says "at its core" the child can no longer live from its 'self' but goes
through the motions of living. Displaying or expressing despair is too unbearable when
there's no one there who can understand a confounded child.

"Only now do I understand why patients so stubbornly refused to follow my
suggestion to react to misfortunes they suffered with unpleasure, perhaps with hatred
and defence, as I would have expected. A part of their personality, indeed its core, at
some point got stuck on a level where one is still unable to react in an alloplastic
manner: one does so auto plastically, as it were with a kind of mimicry. Thus we reach
a form of personality consisting only of id and superego, which therefore lacks the
ability to maintain itself even in unpleasure. This parallels the fact that for the not fully
developed child, being alone, without motherly or other care, and without a
considerable measure of tenderness, is unbearable.

Identification, but between Unequals

Ferenczi here embraces Freud's theory of identification preceding object love, but
then goes further. He doubts Freud's assumption that identification is just the same
between adult and child. 'Identification' from the adult world is quite different from that
of the child's world of play and tenderness. Ferenczi's term 'confusion of tongues',
more than explains this. The child's world sparkles with insistent desire for interactive
play and discovery; its utter vulnerability encircled with what are meant to be strong,
safe and loving bonds. As beings who feel, adult and child both experience happiness,
love, joy, fun, play, sadness, despair, envy, anger and frustration, but from two
completely different contexts. For an adult, whenever rejection or lovelessness leaves
them in a perilous position, they still have a large degree of control and choice. They
can negotiate between safely and danger, and scan lists of possible consequence with
their sovereignty of will enabling their decisions. In comparison, a child can't even
fantasise about what an adult's sexual desire is about.

"Here we must revert to ideas long ago developed by Freud, who even then pointed
out that the capacity for object–love is preceded by a stage of identification. I would
like to call this the stage of passive object–love or tenderness. Traces of object–love
already surface here, but only in fantasy, in a playful manner. Thus children also, a
most without exception, play with the idea of taking the part of the parent of the same
sex, to become the spouse of the parent of the opposite sex. But, it must be stressed,

244

only in fantasy; in reality they do not wish, nor are they able, to do without tenderness, especially the mother's tenderness. If during this phase of tenderness more love is forced on a child or love of a kind other than what the child desired, this will lead to the same pathogenic consequences as lack of love, in which heretofore the cause [of illness] has almost always been sought.

Transference

At this point, Ferenczi has plainly abandoned Freud's Oedipus theory and has declared that a child abuse survivor's plight is being misinterpreted because the analytic community treat two entirely different stages in life as if they were one and the same. Ferenczi continues here by talking about transference, a concept that is much used in the world of professional care, and originated in psychoanalytic practice. Those who identify with the parent, the abuser or aggressor, or even the analyst, can be set free.

"It would take us too far a field to point here to all the neuroses and all the characterological consequences brought about by premature grafting of forms of passionate sexual love riddled with guilt onto a still immature, innocent being. The consequence can only be that confusion of tongues to which I allude in the title of this lecture. Parents and adults, as much as we analysts during analysis, must learn to accept that the desperate wish to free oneself from an all too oppressive love lies behind the submissiveness, indeed adoration, as well as behind the transference love of our children, patients, and students. If we can help the child, patient, or student to give up the reaction of identification and to ward off the burdensome transferences we can say that we succeeded in lifting his personality to a higher level.

At this next point in his address, he briefly talks about the nature of punishment upon a child, and the consequences of depression and guilt. Really, he's sourcing the guilt back to the events that created it.

"Only briefly do I wish to point to a few additional insights to which this series of observations promises access. We have known for the longest time that not only forced love but also unbearable punishments can have a fixating effect. Perhaps the preceding observations will facilitate understanding of this seemingly senseless reaction. The child's playful offences are lifted to the level of reality only upon administration of passionate, often enraged punitive sanctions, with all their depressive consequences for the child, who had, until then, felt free of guilt.

Resurrection and Wisdom

Now he mentions a degree of personality split, but also states that a brutalised, or sexually violated child often experience a sort of 'illumination' that bursts out from within, to re-balance and heal the defenceless, violated child. The person the child grows up to be can go through the motions of adult life ... if not in spirit, in all outward appearances lead a successful, or normal life.

"The more detailed examination of these processes during the analytic trance also

teaches us that there can be no shock, no fright, without traces of a personality split. It will not surprise any psychoanalyst that one part of the person regresses to pre-traumatic bliss and seeks to undo the trauma. It is more surprising that in the course of identification one sees a second mechanism at work. I, at any rate, knew little of it.

"I am referring to the sudden, surprising blossoming, as if by magic, of new faculties following violent shock. One is almost reminded of the magic skills of the fakirs who, it is said, can cause stems and flowers to grow from a seed before our very eyes. Extreme adversity, especially fear of death, seems to have the power suddenly to awaken latent, still uncathected predispositions, which awaited their ripening in deepest tranquillity, and stimulate them to action. The sexually violated child can suddenly bring to fruition under the pressure of traumatic exigency all future faculties which are virtually preformed in him and are necessary for marriage, motherhood and fatherhood, as well as all feelings of a mature person. Here one can confidently speak of traumatic (pathologic) progression or precocity in contrast to the familiar concept of 'regression. It is only natural to think of fruit that ripens or becomes sweet prematurely when injured by the beak of a bird, or of the premature ripening of wormy fruit. Shock can cause a part of the person to mature suddenly, not only emotionally, but intellectually as well.

He now sends us on a mission through our imagination and inner wisdom, with his concepts about the wise child.

"I remind you of the typical 'dream of the wise baby" singled out by me so many years ago, in which a newborn child or infant in its cradle suddenly begins to talk, indeed teaches wisdom to all the family. Fear of the uninhibited and therefore as good as crazy adult turns the child into a psychiatrist, as it were. In order to do so and to protect himself from the dangers coming from people without self-control, he must first know how to identify himself completely with them. It is unbelievable how much we can learn in reality from our wise children, the neurotics.

Now he brings us to the basic concept of personality disorder that involves the splitting-off and seemingly almost independent development of either one or more sub personalities. Experts have a variety of different terms for this, but it's a concept most people can easily relate to.

"If traumatic events accumulate during the life of the growing Person, the number and variety of personality splits increase, and soon it will be rather difficult to maintain contact without confusion with all the fragments, which all act as separate personalities but mostly do not know each other. In the end one might reach a state, which one need not hesitate to call atomization, to continue the metaphor of fragmentation. It takes much optimism not to lose one's courage in the face of this condition either and yet I hope that even here connecting paths can be found.

Now Ferenczi touches upon emotional abuse, calling it the 'terrorism of suffering'. He also talks about the child's self sacrifice that quietens the hostile adult world.

"In addition to passionate love and passionate punishments there is a third way of binding the child to oneself and that is the terrorism of suffering. Children have the

*compulsion to smooth over all kinds of disorders in the family, say, to take onto their
tender shoulders the burdens of all others; naturally, in the final analysis, not out of
pure unselfishness but to regain the lost peace and the tenderness that is part of it. A
mother can make a lifelong nurse, in fact a substitute mother, out of the child by
bewailing her suffering, totally disregarding the interests of the child.*

Here, I've taken out the beginning of Ferenczi's final paragraph because it is
somewhat complicated. It takes us in the opposite direction of Freud's work, and talks
about the environment. It touches upon his admitted failure up to that point, to
recognise an important question about how far sadomasochistic abuse could be derived
from the very culture we find ourselves living in.

*"[The] distinction between the phase of tenderness [of a child] and that of passion
[of an adult]. How much sadomasochism in the sexuality of our time is determined by
culture (that is, derived exclusively from introjected feelings of guilt), and how much
develops autochthonously and spontaneously as an independent phase of organization,
is reserved for further investigations. It would please me if you would take the trouble
to examine, in practice and in theory, what I have communicated here, and especially if
you would follow my advice to pay closer attention than you have in the past to the
strange, much veiled, yet critical manner of thinking and speaking of your children,
patients, and students, and, so to speak, loosen their tongues. You will hear much that
is instructive.*

Ferenczi reverses everything in the psychology of his time. The expert is not the
expert, but a student. The child is the teacher. What then of the nigh godlike expertise
of Freud and his circle? What then of parents who believe that a little one is nothing but
a white page for them to write their choice of wisdom upon? What then when people of
power and authority fall under the influence of the abusers, don't listen to the victims,
and refuse to humble themselves and learn? 'Survivors' Stories' demonstrates and
validates SF's thesis that it is the child, this mangled, crippled little being, who is,
marvel of marvels, the expert. For him, the one sacrificed has the right to speak. Only
s/he has authority. The implications of SF's observation are vast and far reaching, not
just for any effort to alleviate the suffering of children, but for the human sciences
themselves. They force us to consider again our capacities and capabilities which we
have been trained to undervalue. It is now time for us to sit down at the feet of the wise
child, and begin our education again.

Ferenczi is now far more frequently studied than ever before. Psychology and
psychoanalytical professionals often comment that Ferenczi's concentration,
receptiveness and empathic capability were (certainly back in 1932) particularly
uncommon.
He disentangled two entirely different worlds, and shows us the vulnerable,

subservient world of the child, a world that gets lost and confused in translation. Abuse survivors live with their pasts and perceive the world just like any adult, but they carry their inner child's suffering of violation and indignity. It lies waiting, only to be experienced again along with the deeper, more painful adult perceptions that embitter it even further. Authorities that rarely recognise crimes against children suppose everyone's respect. For the most part survivors will respond with respectful behaviour, whilst their inner child feels itself in peril. For violated children of two or three score years or more, the world is still a dangerous place, especially when nobody speaks your language, and shuns you when you do. As Freud says, what is an 'id' if it cannot be schooled and controlled? A mere animal, an abomination. From the stories you may already have read, you can see that for survivors of abuse, talking about their true childhoods is like speaking to a dictator about their misuse of power. Such conversations tend to be brief.

Ferenczi Sentenced

The elitist, competitive behaviour that Freud encouraged between psychiatrists silenced Ferenczi, and sentenced him to death. Upon his death one year later, it was virtually official that it was his 'mental illness' that created his radical ideas, and also led to his death. Likewise, therapists with dissimilar views still privately or publicly 'therapise' one another, articulating their views with infinite and elaborate intricacy, while accusing one another of suffering from unconscious complexes and reactions. Amidst the peer and sibling rivalry that still takes place under Freud's distant shadow, the fight for glory still goes on. One cannot help but wonder whether in such an environment, true self-questioning is even possible. Therapists often claim to contain their self-gratifying power through self-analysis, but this process itself can so easily become contrived, manipulative, and dishonest. They openly discuss the dilemmas caused by their power, but the allure of that power still leads to little more than the obligatory appearance of addressing them. Wherever their patients originated from abusive, oppressive environments, one is still left wondering. On one hand therapists need to be unyielding in their authority as the select holders of truth; on the other there is a need for access to vulnerable people with whom they can experiment, and inflict their views.

We might think that those who steer clear of psychoanalysis will not be affected, but Freud's attitudes have spread far further than the psychoanalytic consulting room. Freud is still quoted today by those from all kinds of traditional and contemporary therapies, thought and religion. People hope to claim credibility and respectability by doing so, but they rarely think about the problematical use of power his legacy left us.

Dressing Up

Generations of analysts all over the world have been a privileged and exclusive audience to their patients' testimonies about what really happened in their childhoods. Like priests of a surreptitious religion, they dressed up the truth into neat, orderly interpretations, so when it was time for them to tell the world what they were doing, nobody but the elite few really knew what on earth they were talking about. Denial then was so much deeper than it is now, that who can say whether they even touched upon the reality they refused to describe? Clearly, their elaborate interpretations quickly transformed their client's original testimony to dust; to be swept aside by the dazzling brilliance of the analyst, and his intricately structured insight.

Early on in his career, Freud himself had conducted autopsies upon children who had been raped and then murdered; yet for him, this side of children's lives was wholly exceptional. Despite his written responses to studies of the time, of domestic households where a child would suffer years of ongoing inflicted abuse, these children didn't exist as a matter of prime importance. The clarity of pathologist's evidence got silenced with the dead, whilst the living went floating around in a sea of hypocrisy. The heavy burdens of lies, deceit and silence reinforced themselves further as psychiatrists and psychoanalysts became part and parcel of the whole scientific world community of doctors, hospitals and medicine. The most obvious example of Freud's time moving into the present day can be found in several aspects relating to the practice of ritual child abuse. * Much of this abuse has been prevented from becoming public knowledge by both governments and the judiciary. Typically, these crimes begin when the victims are children, but often continue through adulthood. They are rarely investigated, and in most cases the victims are expected to live on with neither police protection from their abusers' ongoing attacks, nor any publicly supported credibility of their testimonies. Historically, when it comes to abuse against children, the interfaces between criminal evidence, psychology and the public have never been straightforward, nor even logical. In the wider society in which we live, the sham of Freud's fundamental scientific hypothesis about the ego and how it had to correlate to how the mind (realm of ideas from the super-ego) ruled the body (matter, or the primitive 'id') still wields control over our ideas about what is and what is not real.

Freud's fundamental foundation was dispersed, grown, reaped and re-sown again and again among hundreds of thousands of believers all over the globe. Today there are still lawyers, social workers, police officers, judges, psychiatrists, psychologists, health care workers, teachers, policy makers and parents who have no idea how influenced they are by these perceptions. What's of particular enormity is how Freud's legacy has controlled and influenced the assumptions we make about the inter-personal relationships we see operating in our own environment. In the last five years, child rape has begun to appear in our news headlines. Our capacity to communicate about this has improved, but has still not broken free from Freud's restricted outlook. When it comes to integrated understanding, an experienced social worker is light years ahead of the average doctor in a modern general practice.

Black is White

Thanks to Freud's methods of access to the unconscious, any therapist with a patient who has no recollection of sexual abuse can be persuaded otherwise, and vice versa. With an arbitrary patching together of recovered memory, therapists can damage those who have not been sexually abused, just as much as those who have, and anybody's true, heartfelt testimony can be discredited. Freudian therapists today tend towards a denial of real sexual abuse, and other therapists from different genres often

See the ritual abuse story from 'Survivors' Stories' Volume 2

249

employ adaptations based upon Freudian recovered memory technique, yet claim their methods are different. Predictably, current arguments in society emanate from, on the one side, denial; and on the other, the conviction that child abuse is endemic. Both sides are sold down the river by attitudes and techniques that are Freudian in origin, but make both views perfectly valid. We are, and remain in a situation where ordinary men and women are no longer able to trust their own minds.

Freud's Oedipus complex rests on the belief that a child's inner world is full of its own repressed, developing sexuality. To my mind, this is, broadly speaking, a massive misinterpretation of the role of a growing child's playful imagination and senses, where the giving and receiving of benevolent touch is crucial for the child to thrive. A child's body is play in perpetual motion within interactive relationships. Whilst a healthy adult sexuality relies upon a grounding of good childhood bonds that included a kind, accommodating world of touch and movement, a child's need for physical expression of tenderness within relationship is nothing to do with 'sexual desires' and 'fantasies'.

The Gap Years

With Ferenczi's work rejected, psychiatry took about fifty more years to even recognise the importance of the main carer's response to an infant's emotional and feeling needs. This was partly due to Mary Ainsworth's ground breaking work on attachment theory ('Strange Situation' from the early 1960's). Ainsworth was one of the first to work with human infants, as up to that time understanding human behaviour had developed through the 'scientific' observation of rats. Medical and scientific opinion believed that to become a healthy adult, a human organism needed only food, light and air. Normal human instincts were belittled by experts who said the one difference between a plant or animal grown in a laboratory and a human, was the need for a basic education. For a growing child, consistently beneficial relationships were not seen as a need worthy of respect. Patients were ongoingly studied via psychoanalysis, and further research was derived via psychiatrists' case histories, which were often built upon the use of prescribed drugs or EST (also known as electro-convulsive therapy).

Ainsworth's attachment theories were finally recognised by the mid 1980's, and it took longer still for that influence to permeate through to the practice of social work and social policy. Ferenczi's work has similarities with Carl Roger's person-centred work, which brought in the idea of equality, and a more 'human' communication between patient and therapist. R D Laing, as well as other influences fueled the spirit of the humanistic psychology movement, which broke away from the dictates of analytical theories that seemed sure to create a contrived form of aliveness and individual freedom. In therapy, there appeared to be no limits to the client's right to expression, yet strangely, child abuse was still not fully constituted for what it actually was. It was conceivable that child abuse was unfortunate, but not that it was an injustice. The goals of the movement towered over it, weakening its significance, and making any mention of its realities, or its damage, effectively taboo. Whilst Roger's work with new models of parenting shunned the traditions of of child punishment, it did not face up to the other secret abuses that happen to children. This left children unprotected, and disowned the damage that remained locked up, within the adult.

Diagnosing and curing mental illness is a complex business yet Freud's passion for the concept of the singular, well developed ego as the prime measurement of physical and mental health still reigns supreme. I say this, because all survivors from Survivor's Stories who sought professional help and attention were primarily received as the originator of their own problems. Whatever a human being's vulnerabilities were during their upbringing and within their present circumstances are of negligible importance in a doctor's or mental health worker's approach. If professionals do offer something to those who have to heal their childhood wounds, their intimidating and unaccommodating social presence lets them down. For example when out patients don't take their prescribed medication or 'get better', these professionals can proclaim the patient is simply being uncooperative. Taking prescribed drugs can offer a helping hand for survivors through certain phases, but for many it's too big a risk. They fear that they may worsen during treatment and end up sectioned, which can easily equate to losing their children, their houses, their jobs and whatever liberty they have left. Significant numbers of people hide their true problems from doctors because when they are disbelieved or misunderstood, they are made to feel that it is their fault. So long as victims of child abuse are badly received, they will actively avoid doctors, therapists, psychoanalysts and psychiatrists because they are afraid. They go on suffering for years, being physically and emotionally abusive to others around them, or using food disorders, self-harm and other forms of self-abuse as coping mechanisms.

Stunted Judgement

To a greater or lesser extent we have all probably colluded with these authoritarian views and practices, and unknowingly and unquestioningly perpetuated their influence. Subjective portrayals of children's suffering still get converted into Orwellian double speak, where the same old objective views that make the victim both the primary and the ultimate point of focus, often win. The abuse of children attracts far less severe custodial sentencing than the same crimes when committed upon an adult, because children are still seen as both dubious victims and unreliable witnesses. Amongst the members of an average jury (through no fault of the jurors) knowledge of these matters is still likely to be minimal. Thus the possibilities of any child abuse case being properly discussed and realistically considered, are remote.

As we glance across at those we have looked to to guide us, we might wonder about bringing them to task. This rejection of truth had such authority, that many patients who believed their analysis deteriorated into suicides, or were committed to mental institutions as irretrievably delusional. Upon thinking about the unknown statistics who died in these places, morally, one cannot help but question further. Talk of mental institutions may seem melodramatic when the majority of survivors who seek help visit doctors or hospitals as outpatients. Having been on medication day in, day out for decades, most haven't even been heard, never mind identified for what they really are. Mental health workers still fail to examine their own discrepancies of both confirmation and denial about child abuse. Whilst balancing their interests of professional status and self-preservation, they misrepresent and malign the vulnerable people they should be serving.

It's difficult to see to what extent their authority comfortably rests upon our collective ignorance. Those with more than average knowledge have given up waiting for them to

251

openly discard their errors. There is little obligation to stick a neck out and reveal what destructive professional behaviour towards survivors of abuse actually looks like, and what the consequences might be.

Breakthroughs

In the last fifteen years, largely, the USA seems to have led the way. Scientifically authentic neurological studies have bourne out the reality of childhood trauma, and its treatment is becoming more and more successful with techniques like EFT (Emotional Freedom Technique), EMDR (Eye Movement Desensitisation and Reprocessing), and Sensorimotor psychotherapy. As usual, only a lucky few and those who can afford a specialist's attentions might benefit from this welcome change. As a whole however the profession still remains split, and out of its habit of working with individuals and small groups, will probably remain that way.

Whilst these neurological breakthroughs have validated what survivors have been trying to say for years, the allure of the singular liberated ego can easily remain the Achilles heel. Improved therapies may shine in their glory, yet accept and condone child abuse through the practice of working in a virtual closet. Exactly as in Freud's era, the 'unclean' survivor must go get better whilst their families and original groups remain utterly uninvolved and unaffected. Only a fraction from the mental health professions will communicate about how the perpetration of child abuse goes on wherever there's a double standard of behaviour towards children, both in the family group and in the community at large. Each person from a child's circle is a notable part of the cause, whether they are aware of the abuse or not. Very few therapists emphasise the obvious importance of defining abusive behaviour, and will show the courage to progress towards working directly with abusers, and co-abusers. Fresh support for a different future based on the honest exposure of cause and effect within family bonds and relationships cannot thrive where Freud's notion of the singular liberated ego is still worshipped in our understanding. Where professionals think their practices are wanting, they could collaborate with other groups outside their own professional branch more often. A more equal and open partnership may add skillful expertise in relation to the broader picture.

Now is the Time

As humans, we mostly express ourselves according to whatever we think is required, yet we could well allow our capacities for concentration, receptiveness and empathic capability to flower when we break free from the manifold traditions that still hold us. We have thought ourselves incapable of taking these matters on ourselves, but compassion has the patience to understand complexity, as well as the courage to face up to frightening, but simple truths.

As we attend to the Wise Children like those ones who have spoken to us here in Survivors' Stories, we stand stronger in the reality that surrounds us. As our own understanding increases, we can become a gentle revolution on behalf of childhood. We can be the humanly authentic people who can face up to these matters, using our gifts and aptitudes to help in any small, or any large way that we can.

Conclusion

The stories teach us how child abuse has been hidden, so therefore each one of us can consider the effects. As that recognition ripples through our understanding in a time line of past and present, we'll find manifestations of abuse appearing in some of the children and adults who, for however long, enter our lives. As our knowledge matures, we can gently take part in the challenge of including them in our lives, so it won't pass from generation to generation in that old familiar cycle of abuse and abandonment.

It is my impassioned hope that this book has been far more of a human journey than any other kind of experience. In 'Who is this book for?' I reached out to people right across society, and outlined how and why their being smart to the realities of child abuse is so important. The Introduction described the way the project 'survivors' stories' came together, and underpinned the importance of the stories themselves. This was followed by 'Why should I need to know?' whereby studies and statistics were exposed not as a solution, but as a starting point to respond to both children and adult survivors in our homes and communities. This section led in to 'Barriers', whereby we explored what barriers we tend to put up either as individuals, or in partnership with others within our own families, and in institutional groups. We looked into how they stop us seeing and addressing abused children and survivors for what they really are. The Questionnaire was included partially as an explanation for the stories' content, but it's a handy communication tool that can be used in many different ways. 'How to Talk about Abuse' we learned to tackle communication issues, and looked at the building blocks and requirements that enable active conversation with the people around us. From 'Source of our Silence', we've seen how Ferenczi's honest witnessing, and brilliantly clear insights were rejected in favour of power driven preferences that actively hid child abuse, and abandoned the adults abused children grew up to become. Society was only respectable because of the sacrifice survivors felt compelled to give, yet through journeying through 'Survivors' Stories', something new and different comes to the fore. The truth that was once regarded as a shameful weakness reveals its power and its worth, and the false sense of honour that society once clung to recedes into the past. There is a saying that goes,

"Whatever you concentrate on in life, the bigger and more powerful it becomes."

If this is true, we could hardly abandon these issues fast enough, especially if they leave us feeling hurt and powerless. It's as if the very discontent that results from knowing about child abuse grows its own arm, and sweeps all this aside. Yet child abuse is the one and only exception to this saying, whereby the very opposite is true,

"Whatever you concentrate on in life, the smaller and less powerful it becomes."

Gladly, we learn through our links with survivors. For the most part, society's growing awareness about good parenting and child protection is indebted to survivors' courage in speaking out. Through their efforts, the most common forms of child abuse are believed to be lessening. (continued at top of page 255)

'Declaration'

Whatever you suffered at the hands of your abuser(s)
should never have happened, and it was wrong.
I know I wasn't there at the time personally,
but the truth is we all failed to protect you.

There are no excuses.
Even a profession of ignorance from the time,
the context and all that rubbish is wrong.
There are no excuses.

I am more than sorry.
And you are right.
And we are wrong.
You are right to be angry
because we all failed to see the reality
of your life as a child.
That should make us even more resolved
not to fail you now.

You are a beautiful person, who is continuing
to create your own beautiful life.
You must never think for a minute
that you are unworthy of anything but the best.

You deserve to have your days free from care.

I know it's not possible, but
I would wish to take all this away from you
for ever.

Maybe you won't ever be entirely free,
yet you still deserve to be free from the wrongs,
the lies and the pain that were once a part of you.

It is our wish that some day you will heal.
We hope that you are able to, and at your own pace.
Take from us until you can take no more.

We wish you well.

Being typical of our age, as individuals we tend to seek out yet more knowledge before we feel ready to take action, but abuse has happened to people that we probably already know. More authentic relationships with children and survivors cannot really be tackled without the active contribution each one of us has to make. So are we up to the challenge? Can we bring some aspects of this subject into a chat in the kitchen, over the coffee table, out on a walk with close friends and relatives? Are we able to raise the subject with a teacher in a local school classroom? One survivor I spoke to burst out laughing when she read this text and said...

"... well ... may as well invite the vicar round, and bring it up over tea and cucumber sandwiches!!" It doesn't really matter whatever the emotion is that goes along with our communication, as long as it isn't squashed down by fear.

This is about what our sensibilities are telling us now, and each one of us has a right to find their own voice. With heart, mind and intuition, we need to think about what building blocks we can put down in order to bring survivors' experience and wisdom into our family groups and communities. Perhaps the best start would be some sort of expression of regret at having been born into a society that has historically failed survivors for so long.

'Declaration' is that expression of regret, and Survivors need to hear words like these that come from the heart. They need to hear words like these from their loved ones, from their friends and from anybody who can recognise a survivor's need to come back more fully into their skin, and to take up their place amongst the people and places they originated from. For each survivor the length of time will vary, and it will take time, until they can truly feel a sense of belonging again. From that belonging, they will be able to share, give more of themselves and make the original contribution that they were born to bring.

When talking doesn't feel appropriate, listening, feeling and journeying with respectful recognition is an equally powerful healing force. It provides the truth with a place, and a steady ground upon which we can all share the road towards the future.

'Declaration' is the foundation of that road, it's a new journey based upon acknowledgment, where we can surrender to the lessons from the past and grow towards a future free from pretence. What is left, are simple values of the heart that shine out in the lessons of relationship between adult and child, and between child and their original group throughout all the years lived towards adulthood. It is my wish that readers of 'Survivors Stories' have been able to grow through the simple lessons I have been able to pass on through the survivors I've met. I hope this journey has enabled new feelings and insights, which will find a lasting place in your life and relationships.

More Stories ...

In Survivors' Stories Volume 1, we covered some ground to enable us to concentrate on what child abuse is, and how we react to the realities. Volume 2 of Survivors' Stories is due out in 2008. It will simply contain six stories, and relay some of the feedback and public response from Survivors' Stories Volume 1.

Until then, responses and feedback can be shared on the website, survivors-stories.co.uk.

Correspondence can also be sent by email to survivors-stories@hotmail.co.uk.

At these last stages of writing it is hard to second guess the response to this project, however the author will endeavour to reply to all correspondence.

There are other survivors whose life's experience can teach us still more, so Survivors' Stories will not stop as long as there still interest. Future volumes will be written and published over the next few years. From volume 3 onwards, separate stories will be in groups that share one theme in common.

The Author

Born in Glasgow in the 1950's, Morven believed she'd come from a loving family. Although that was true, it wasn't until she got to her forties that she began to see the consequences of her abuse as a child. Throughout her twenties, she searched for healing through the study and experience of humanistic psychology, alternative therapy and spiritual development. In the field of psychotherapy and counselling, she worked with some of the biggest pioneers of their day. She went to America and trained as a bodywork therapist, and learned a great deal through her seven years of practice. Still, even with the innovations of new and alternative therapies, she felt that some strong element of human experience was missing. She switched to the 'ordinary world', working in legal offices and then moving on as a teacher in adult education. Through her conversations with more and more survivors of abuse, 'Survivors' Stories' slowly and steadily emerged. Morven works voluntarily with child abuse survivors, and is developing adult education programmes as an alternative, or welcome addition to therapy and counselling. This will enable survivors and their friends to actively contribute, and interact upon a safe platform that invites social change. Her 'Regeneration Bodywork' practice is now running in south east England, UK.

Printed in the United Kingdom
by Lightning Source UK Ltd.
123294UK00002B/55-300/A